WITHDRAWN

Waugh

Women and
Culture Series

The Women and Culture Series is dedicated to books that illuminate the lives, roles, achievements, and status of women, past or present.

Fran Leeper Buss
  Dignity: Lower Income Women Tell of Their Lives and Struggles
  La Partera: Story of a Midwife

Valerie Kossew Pichanick
  Harriet Martineau: The Woman and Her Work, 1802–76

Sandra Baxter and Marjorie Lansing
  Women and Politics: The Visible Majority

Estelle B. Freedman
  Their Sisters' Keepers: Women's Prison Reform in America, 1830–1930

Susan C. Bourque and Kay Barbara Warren
  Women of the Andes: Patriarchy and Social Change in Two Peruvian Towns

Marion S. Goldman
  Gold Diggers and Silver Miners: Prostitution and Social Life on the Comstock Lode

Page duBois
  Centaurs and Amazons: Women and the Pre-History of the Great Chain of Being

Mary Kinnear
  Daughters of Time: Women in the Western Tradition

Lynda K. Bundtzen
  Plath's Incarnations: Woman and the Creative Process

Violet B. Haas and Carolyn C. Perrucci, editors
  Women in Scientific and Engineering Professions

Sally Price
  Co-wives and Calabashes

Patricia R. Hill
  The World Their Household: The American Woman's Foreign Mission Movement and Cultural Transformation, 1870–1920

Diane Wood Middlebrook and Marilyn Yalom, editors
  Coming to Light: American Women Poets in the Twentieth Century

LYNDA K. BUNDTZEN is winner in the Hamilton Prize competition for 1980. The Alice and Edith Hamilton Prize is named for two outstanding women scholars: Alice Hamilton (educated at the University of Michigan Medical School), a pioneer in environmental medicine; and her sister Edith Hamilton, the renowned classicist. The Hamilton Prize competition is supported by the University of Michigan and by private donors.

Plath's Incarnations

Plath's Incarnations

WOMAN AND THE CREATIVE PROCESS

Lynda K. Bundtzen

The University of Michigan Press   *Ann Arbor*

Published in the United States of America by

The University of Michigan Press and simultaneously

in Rexdale, Canada, by John Wiley & Sons Canada, Limited

Manufactured in the United States of America

1988   1987   1986   1985   5   4   3   2

LIBRARY OF CONGRESS CATALOGING IN PUBLICATION DATA

Bundtzen, Lynda K., 1947–

  Plath's incarnations.

  (Women and culture series)

  Bibliography: p.

  1. Plath, Sylvia.   2. Poets, American—20th century—
Biography.   I. Title.   II. Title: Woman and the creative
process.   III. Series.

PS3566.L27Z588   1983   811'.54   83-6829

  ISBN 0-472-10033-5

For Kim and Jacob

Acknowledgments

Grateful acknowledgment is made to the following for permission to quote copyrighted materials:

Basic Books, Inc., for excerpts from *Collected Papers,* vols. 4 and 5, by Sigmund Freud. Copyright © 1959 by Basic Books, Inc., Publishers. Reprinted by permission of the publisher.

Harper and Row for: excerpts from *The Mermaid and the Minotaur: Sexual Arrangements and Human Malaise,* by Dorothy Dinnerstein, copyright © 1976 by Dorothy Dinnerstein; excerpts from *Naked and Fiery Forms,* by Suzanne Juhasz, copyright © 1976 by Suzanne Juhasz; excerpts from *Chapters in a Mythology: The Poetry of Sylvia Plath,* by Judith Kroll, copyright © 1976 by Judith Kroll; lines from *Ariel,* by Sylvia Plath, copyright © 1963 by Ted Hughes; excerpts from *The Bell Jar,* by Sylvia Plath, copyright © 1971 by Harper and Row; lines from *The Collected Poems,* by Sylvia Plath, edited by Ted Hughes, copyright © 1960, 1965, 1971, 1981 by the Estate of Sylvia Plath; excerpts from *Johnny Panic and the Bible of Dreams,* by Sylvia Plath, copyright © 1952, 1953, 1954, 1955, 1956, 1957, 1960, 1961, 1962 by Sylvia Plath, copyright © 1977, 1979 by Ted Hughes; and excerpts from *Letters Home by Sylvia Plath,* edited with an Introduction by Aurelia Schober Plath, copyright © 1975 by Aurelia Schober Plath.

Alfred A. Knopf, Inc., for: excerpts from *The Second Sex,* by Simone de Beauvoir, translated and edited by H. M. Parshley. Copyright © 1952 by Alfred A. Knopf, Inc., Vintage Books edition, August, 1974, published by Random House, Inc.; and lines from *The Colossus and Other Poems,* by Sylvia Plath, copyright © 1957, 1958, 1959, 1960, 1962, published by Alfred A. Knopf, Inc.

W. W. Norton and Company, Inc., for: excerpts from *Of Woman Born: Motherhood as Experience and Institution* by Adrienne Rich, copyright © 1976 by W. W. Norton and Company; and excerpts from *On Lies, Secrets, and Silence: Selected Prose 1966–1978,* by Adrienne Rich, copyright © 1979 by W. W. Norton and Company.

Pantheon Books, a division of Random House, Inc., for excerpts from *Psychoanalysis and Feminism: Freud, Reich, Laing, and Women,* by Juliet Mitchell, copyright © 1974 by Pantheon Books.

Sigmund Freud Copyrights, Ltd., The Institute of Psycho-Analysis, and the Hogarth Press, publishers, for excerpts from *The Standard Edition of the Complete Psychological Works of Freud,* translated and edited by James Strachey.

The Estate of Sylvia Plath, Olwyn Hughes, Executrix, for permission to reprint material written by Sylvia Plath.

I am also grateful to the Lilly Library, Indiana University Libraries, for providing access to and permission to publish from their Plath manuscript collection; to Edward Cohen and J. Melvin Woody for permission to quote from their letters to Sylvia Plath; and to the Yale Alumni Office for its assistance in my search for J. Melvin Woody and Richard Norton.

I am especially grateful to Lawrence Graver and Lawrence Raab and to the judges of the Alice and Edith Hamilton Prize for providing valuable criticism in the revision of my manuscript.

Every attempt has been made to find and secure permission to reprint material from copyright holders.

Preface

*W*HEN I began thinking about Sylvia Plath in 1973, I had no
idea that I might eventually write this book. I felt only that I
understood her poems and *The Bell Jar* and sympathized with the
wit and courage of the voice I heard. I found myself frequently
annoyed with what I regarded then (and still do) as premature attempts to assign Plath a "place" in literary history as a "confessional" or "suicidal" poet or, at times, simply a "hysterical woman."
Nor did I define my work in 1973 as feminist in impulse, although I
sensed that Plath's voice, in addition to the subject matter in much
of her work, was distinctly feminine.

Reviewing now what I have done, and its place and time, I
believe that my portrait of Plath is shaped and conditioned (not
necessarily determined) by a current feminist awareness of the difficulties peculiar to being a woman and an artist. Sensitivity to gender
as an important consideration in a poet's development was not,
regrettably, part of my graduate education. The growth in my understanding of Plath's life and work since 1973 reflects, I believe, a
larger change in perception of what knowledge is most worth having about a woman artist. Inevitably, I worry that my portrait of
Plath depends on a critical perspective that may be viewed skepti-
cally as feminist ideology of the eighties applied to a woman not of
my generation. (I have been warned by one of Plath's former boyfriends that because I came of age "since the advent of the pill," I
"may therefore have difficulty thinking [my] way into the sexual
experience of an ambitious young woman at Smith in the days when
Smith careers were all too often cut short by pregnancy.") I hope
not, though, since this critical spirit is re-visionary in a sense which
demands a sharing of women's experience that crosses without eras-
ing differences in time, class, race.

I am less troubled about the chapters of my book devoted to
interpretation of Plath's novel and poems, even though it is clear
that they are informed by the same feminist impulse. Like many

critics, perhaps, I feel more secure in the presence of a text, more confident in dealing with "the words on the page," than with the shadowy lives, presences, which emerge from letters, journals, diaries. I have tried in my interpretive work to present a generous view of Plath's achievement as an artist, one that I hope will make her accessible to readers on grounds other than morbid interest in a suicidal poetess-priestess of the sixties. By generous I do not mean agreeable, and by accessible I do not mean easy. "Black statements" are habitual to Plath and her view of the world and human relationships; but it is time for us to measure ourselves and our own perceptions against their truth-value, a truth-value that extends well beyond the provisional, confessional circumstances of Plath's personal life. Similarly, gaining access to many of Plath's poems is difficult, but the rewards are an enriched understanding of what it feels like to live in a woman's body, with her view, in Plath's words, of "the hurt and wonder of love; making in all its forms—children, loaves of bread, paintings, buildings." Like the poets she admired, Plath's finest poems "seem born all-of-a-piece, not put together by hand" and to get inside a poem such as "Lady Lazarus" or "Ariel" is to be "possessed" as "by the rhythms of [her] own breathing."

Contents

One. Lady Lazarus and Divine Activity

*T*HE single most important critical issue in dealing with Sylvia Plath's life and work is her suicide in February of 1963. To a degree unmet with in discussions of other contemporary writers who have taken their lives, the perceived significance and value of Plath's art depend on the attitude of critics toward her death. Unlike John Berryman or Ernest Hemingway, for example, Plath is fixed in our minds as a suicidal artist, as a woman who played with death as other writers play with images, metaphors, and symbols. But then, these other artists do not say things like "Dying / Is an art," or "I / Am the arrow, / The dew that flies / Suicidal."[1] These are lines that have been taken to express Plath's "pathological" sensibility. For most critics, she is the poet in love with death, the woman who perversely made suicide a metaphor for her creativity. When the posthumous volume *Ariel* appeared, reviewers were so stunned by her suicide that they saw Plath fondling death in every line. For Robert Boyers, "*Ariel* is a poetry of surrender . . . to an imagination that destroys life instead of enhancing it"[2]; Charles Newman claims that she was "courting . . . experience that kills"[3]; and Robert Lowell compares the final poems to a game of Russian roulette with all cartridges loaded.[4] Even pieces on Plath's earlier volume, *The Colossus*, were rewritten to account for the final act of self-destruction, and her poetic development was then explained as one long rehearsal and preparation for death.

Despite the lavish attention Plath initially received after her death, there was very little actual interpretation. The rubric "confessional poetry" often substituted for detailed examination of the poems. One might expect from this dearth of explanation that *Ariel* is a straightforward self-revelation where the outlines of Plath's life are exposed with bold clarity. In fact, it is an extremely difficult volume, and many critics' statements about its overall meaning turn out to be based on a handful of poems and on lines and phrases quoted out of context. As Mary Kinzie explains this phenomenon in a review of early Plath criticism, it was unnecessary to deal extensively with the poems because "the feeling is that her aesthetic, after all, is nothing more than the chronicle of a nervous breakdown." Her admirers praise the "coincidentally successful phrases of a 'disturbed consciousness' " and her detractors, reacting to these mere "accidents" of pathology, "have felt justified in setting their lives against hers, and judging her, not by her poems, but against the measure of their own decorum."[5]

Little has been done to qualify or complicate this initial assessment of Plath. She is still popularly known as the end-game poet. The only difference, it seems, is that now critics feel compelled to judge the celebrity they created for her and whether or not her charisma as death goddess is a symptom for the sickness of the times. David Holbrook, for example, describes Plath and her poetry as "dangerously schizoid": "We must defend ourselves against her falsifications, especially when they are the object of cults, in an atmosphere in which we are being urged to cultivate our psychoses and endorse decadence and moral inversion."[6] For Holbrook, the enemy is feminism. He makes Plath's poetry the occasion for several swipes at women's liberationists.

At a National Poetry Festival Germaine Greer claimed that Sylvia Plath was the most "arrogantly feminine" poetess who ever wrote. A phenomenological analysis suggests that, while knowing well outwardly that she was a woman, Sylvia Plath could scarcely find within herself anything that was feminine at all. . . . She is sadly pseudo-male, like many of her cultists.[7]

She has unusual insights into the special state of the mother. But, in her awareness, these insights are so disturbed by her schizoid perspectives that what she largely conveys is a fear and hatred of female creativity. This is why women's liberationists applaud her, because what they want to be liberated from is being female and being human.[8]

From critical eminences such as Irving Howe and Elizabeth Hardwick, the judgment is more severe because it is more skillfully argued. Plath's popularity violates their sense of both poetic and human decorum. In his dissent from what he witheringly terms the

"Plath celebration," Howe invokes the old Eliot orthodoxy against the confessional poem: " 'Daddy' persuades one again, through the force of negative example, of how accurate T.S. Eliot was in saying, 'The more perfect the artist, the more completely separate in him will be the man who suffers and the mind which creates'."[9] Howe's indictment of Plath's technique is hard to answer because he alternately accuses her of the most calculated, self-aggrandizing manipulation of her audience's feelings and of being completely out of control. Poems such as "Cut" and "Lady Lazarus," admired by others for their brutal and self-directed irony, offend Howe because they yield to the confessional "temptation to reveal all while one eye measures the effect of the revelation." While others see Plath's voice as having a remarkable authenticity and directness, Howe detects a "willed hysteric tone" and a phony posturing that ends in "sentimental violence."[10] In Howe's view, Plath's attempts to widen the scope of her concerns, from personal anguish to the suffering of the Jews in the Nazi holocaust, are self-serving and poetically illegitimate. Although he says that he cannot judge Plath's final value to human society, Howe concludes his essay with a series of rhetorical questions that add up to a total denunciation. He asks, "What is the relation between a sensibility so deeply captive to the idea of suicide and the claims and possibilities of human existence in general?" Implicitly, a negative one. And he challenges her admirers by noting that none of them have "offered a coherent statement as to the nature, let alone the value, of her vision."[11]

At the moment, one must agree with Howe that this is so. Despite occasional efforts to reconstruct her as a vital figure, Plath emerges from critical commentary as a morbid and depressing woman whose art offers, in Howe's words, only "ease at the gate of dying."[12] More moderate in tone, but equally broad in her dismissal, Elizabeth Hardwick is "disinclined to hope for general principles, sure origins, applications, or lessons" in the work or life of a woman whose "elements of pathology are so deeply rooted and so little resisted."[13] Neither Howe nor Hardwick can see any social, moral, or communal values in art (they seem, in fact, reluctant to call it art) as personal and sick as Plath's. The terrible, swift sword of critical judgment would seem to have consigned Plath to the comparative oblivion of interesting, but minor poet.[14]

Have there been any answers to Howe's challenge or any de-

fenses of Plath against the sweeping dismissal of Hardwick? Yes . . .
and no. Certainly these harsh judgments have not stopped the flow
of criticism on Plath and she now receives more thorough interpretation of her poems. The question, though, is whether this new attention provides a coherent statement of the nature and value of her
vision or significantly broadens the appeals of her poetry beyond a
confessional pathology.

Critical Fictions: Plath as "Bitch Goddess" and "White Goddess"

Two lengthy studies are representative of later criticism on Plath:
Sylvia Plath: Method and Madness and *Chapters in a Mythology: The
Poetry of Sylvia Plath.* Edward Butscher's biography, *Method and
Madness,* illustrates the critical tendency to deflect Plath's artistic
intentions toward private obsessions, and, if anything, confirms
the image of her projected by Howe and Hardwick. His portrait of
Plath is extremely unattractive. From interviews with friends and
acquaintances, Butscher creates a Sylvia who is an awful "bitch
goddess." Butscher defines a bitch as a "discontented, tense, frequently brilliant woman goaded into fury by her repressed or distorted status in male society" and a "bitch goddess" as simply a
"more creative" bitch.[15] Plath's life appears as one long effort to
disguise this megalomaniacal bitch within from public view until
she has enough power to go on a rampage. Even Plath's self-
destructive impulses are interpreted in this light. On her first suicide attempt, for example, Butscher speculates on why she sur-
vived: "The hidden bitch goddess would not take kindly to the
idea of being murdered by an alternative self—that it would, in
fact, fight back fiercely to remain alive to manipulate the world and
its puny inhabitants" (p. 118). As an account of the slow reestab-
lishment of self-esteem after a suicide attempt, this is distressingly
single-minded and unsympathetic.

When Butscher engages in literary interpretation, he often col-
lapses art into life and creates multiple confusions. About one of the
characters in *The Bell Jar*, for example, he explains,

Doreen could thus absorb Sylvia's own guilt feelings and act as a screen for negative projections of the hidden bitch self. How real "Doreen" was is impossible to say since Sylvia had reached that juncture in her breakdown where only fiction could maintain her equilibrium. The girl is based on an actual person, as are the other nine guest editors portrayed in *The Bell Jar*, but her behavior has obviously been heightened and distorted somewhat to fit what was required—an evil second self: "Everything she said was like a secret voice speaking straight out of my bones." Another guest editor has characterized the original as a "pre-Bunny, platinum blond." (P. 104)

It is impossible to sort out the real and fictional Doreens in Butscher's discussion, and there also seems to be a basic confusion of Sylvia Plath at the age of nineteen, going through a mental breakdown, with Sylvia Plath, ten years later, reshaping her experience into a novel. As for the description of Doreen offered by "another guest editor," it oddly tends to confirm the realism rather than the neurotic distortion Plath supposedly indulged in for her portrayal of Doreen as a vamp.

Butscher does manage, through the force of negative example, to illustrate the major faults with pigeonholing Plath as a confessional poet who can best be understood by hunting down private references in her poems. Often he turns away from a thoroughly accessible public meaning of a poem toward some event from her life as an explanation. Hence, his reading of "Kindness" depends on knowledge of Ted Hughes.

In "Kindness" Sylvia poses the situation of Ted's act of treachery to her and the children. Here she utilized his radio play about the man who ran over a rabbit and then sold the carcass to buy his wife two roses as a central motif. Roses were perfect symbols, not only for the beauty and innocence of the children, but as Dantesque emblems of art leading to paradise. The basic narrative frame, however, is a return to the double image. "Dame Kindness" is the bitch goddess's *good* double, the cheerful surface Sylvia who speaks out of her mother's mouth: "Sug-

ar can cure everything, so Kindness says." And it was this
Sylvia who went about "Sweetly picking up pieces" after the
separation from Ted. In the final stanza, which is addressed to
Ted, the depressing change in Sylvia's mental state becomes
pathetically blatant. (P. 361)

The biographical information is interesting, but unnecessary for ex-
plaining the poem. Why should we assume that the last stanza is
addressed to Hughes? Everything in the poem indicates that the
"you" of the final stanza is the speaker's antagonist throughout—
Dame Kindness.

> And here you come, with a cup of tea
> Wreathed in steam.
> The blood jet is poetry,
> There is no stopping it.
> You hand me two children, two roses.
>
> (*Ariel*, p. 82)

Dame Kindness is, as Butscher argues, the female stereotype for the
good little housewife—sugar and spice and everything nice. She
smoothes over domestic problems with her sweet disposition.

But Butscher ignores the threatening qualities of Dame Kindness: "My Japanese silks, desperate butterflies, / May be pinned any
minute, anaesthetized" (*Ariel*, p. 82). Like female finery in other
poems (e.g., the veil over the mouth of the woman in "Purdah"),
the silks suggest a proverbially servile femininity—the Japanese
woman who walks a few steps behind her husband. In this light,
Dame Kindness represents an inner self-reproach. She is an allegori-
cal figure reminding the poet of the claims of motherhood: "What is
so real as the cry of a child?" When Kindness hands her "two
children, two roses," an insoluble choice is offered: Your children or
your poetry. For the mother, "Sugar is a necessary fluid / Its crystals
a little poultice"; but for the woman as artist, "The blood-jet is
poetry" (*Ariel*, p. 82). As with the comparison of children to roses,
one could hardly find a more vital metaphor for the compulsion to
write: Poetry is like the heart pumping her life's blood. But a contradictory meaning is there as well: Poetry is like slashing your wrist

and watching the blood jet from an open artery. This contradiction is crucial to the meaning of the poem; it dramatizes the difficulty of choosing between the role of saccharine-sweet matron with its threat of numbness and anesthetization, and the role of poet, with its risk of violence. Both alternatives have an equal emotional pull on the speaker.

Butscher ignores this final tension in the poem and provides his own answer to the woman's problem. He resolves the ambiguity and the speaker's ambivalence by tacking on the final stanza from another poem. Without telling us what he is up to, he ends his analysis with the last three lines from "Contusion," giving the impression that they belong to "Kindness."

> Poetry has ceased to be a weapon for attack or defense and has deteriorated into a wound. The last stanza summarizes what has happened—the narcissistic retreat into an obsessive concern with the ego's wound that has resulted in the end of poetry and life: "The heart shuts, / The sea slides back, / The mirrors are sheeted." The body is dead, the womb is open, and the dances of the doubles forever put into storage. (P. 361)

The rewriting of one poem by ending it with lines from another is, I suppose, legitimate if one sees the poetry as one long confession and chronicle of a nervous breakdown. But if the poems are separate entities, distinct attempts to render experience in artful form, then this kind of criticism is simply inadequate. There should be no confusion between "Contusion" and "Kindness" and their final lines. "The heart shuts" is a very different statement from "The blood-jet is poetry." "Contusion" is, indeed, about the end of a struggle, about surrender. There are no more choices to be made.

> The size of a fly,
> The doom mark
> Crawls down the wall.
>
> *(Ariel,* p. 83)

"Kindness," however, is an ambivalent poem about an ongoing conflict between equally compelling forces in a woman artist's life.

There is one other characteristic to Butscher's study that is quite common in Plath criticism—his facile use of psychoanalytic lingo. Plath invites a psychoanalytic approach to her work when she describes "Daddy," for instance, as about a "girl with an Electra complex" or when she delves into her psychiatric experience in *The Bell Jar*. There is a big difference, though, between the scalpel-like precision of Freud's terms and the psychologese in *Method and Madness* and many other essays on Plath: "narcissistic retreat," "obsessive concern," "ego's wound," "neurotic distortion." This language is seldom refined or defined; it creates the impression of penetrating analysis while in fact it is a blunt instrument for hammering home the message that Plath and her poetry are sick.

One of the few critics to depart from the confessional thesis and the inordinate concern with Plath's "pathology" is Judith Kroll. She begins *Chapters in a Mythology* by declaring herself interested only in the meaning of the poetry, because "as literature, her poems would mean what they do even if she had not attempted suicide."[16] Kroll argues that Plath is not a confessional poet because, unlike Robert Lowell or Anne Sexton, she subordinates autobiography and the mundane details of everyday life to an impersonal and mythic system in which "the future is foreclosed." In contrast, "much of the vitality" in Lowell's and Sexton's work arises "from a sense that there exist possibilities of discovery and change" and from "observing the self in encounters whose outcome is not foreclosed" (p. 3). Kroll is not concerned with the sensational "confessional surface" of Plath's poetry (she admits that there is one for the reader unfamiliar with Plath's myth), nor with "themes and imagery as illustrations of pathological symptoms." Instead, she will investigate the poems' "deeper meanings" (p. 1).

As Kroll explains the design of Plath's myth, it depends on three crucial themes: (1) a male god or devil who dominates her in the roles of father, husband, lover, and bridegroom; (2) a division of personality into false and true selves as a result of this domination; and (3) the struggle to kill the false self, who represents a death-in-life, and to be reborn as the hidden true self. Self-murder in this scheme is only a ritual for achieving wholeness (pp. 12–13). There is some confusion in Kroll's elaboration of this myth. She seems to start in one place and end in another. In chapter 1, Kroll tells us that the true self (the positive, whole reborn self) is associated with artistic creativity, and with the autonomy possible only if one is not defined primarily in relation . . . to a man. . . . When wife-hood, daughterhood, and motherhood appear primarily as male-defined roles . . . then these roles are negative and may be considered forms of the false self. Lady Lazarus, the lioness, and the queen bee are not male-dependent, and they represent triumph over the negative, male-defined aspects of these typical female roles. (P. 10)

This is a very convincing (but not terribly mythic) statement of what Plath is trying to do in many of her final poems. It also sounds familiar—the subject of many recent essays and books: A woman striving to free herself from a social and psychological oppression that threatens to reduce her to female stereotypes. There is an added dimension of the woman being an artist, and therefore the struggle is defined in terms of her creativity—the youthful poet seeking a new and authentic voice.

Kroll's argument might provide an answer to Howe's and Hard-wick's charges that Plath has little social or moral significance, ex-cept that Kroll heads in a different direction. She turns primarily to Robert Graves's White Goddess myth to explain the action and imag-ery of the final poems. In this scheme, Plath is the "Triple Moon-goddess" who manifests herself in a variety of forms that encode "some phase in the life, death, and rebirth cycle of which the God-dess is the cumulative concrete symbol" (p. 50). Plath's father, Otto, and her husband, Ted Hughes, are the Demons of the Waning and Waxing Year and the White Goddess's consorts, murder victims, and objects of mourning at sundry points in the mythic cycle (p. 65). This pattern seems to contradict Kroll's initial argument that Plath strives to create a self who is not defined primarily in relation to a man, and the myth is not even her own, but derived from a male author, Robert Graves.

Although Kroll hopes to universalize Plath's poetry into an all-embracing vision—"The central motifs of Sylvia Plath's myth are closely parallel to motifs that occur universally in the history of myth, religion, and literature," she says (p. 13)—the ultimate effect of her scholarly research into Plath's reading is to reduce considera-

bly the dramatic impact and immediacy of many poems. An instance
of this is her reading of these lines from "Ariel":

> White
> Godiva, I unpeel—
> Dead hands, dead stringencies.
>
> (*Ariel*, p. 26)

Kroll explains that "the Godiva legend derives from a disguised
form of a White Goddess procession—Godiva actually being a White
Goddess of Love and Death, specially associated with the death of
the sacred king. (In this connection, it is worth noting that an earlier
draft of the poem referred to shedding 'dead men')" (p. 182). She
does not mention the more common legend of Godiva as the woman
who defies her husband by riding through town in the nude, even
though a protest against domination is implied both in the line as it
stands, "Dead hands, dead stringencies" and the earlier draft's
"dead men." Either way, the speaker breaks free from psychological
fetters. Kroll reads against the rebellious tone of the poem in order
to make it a humble expression of "selflessness" and "the (conventional) longing of the soul for union with God" (p. 184). She is also
at great pains to show that "Ariel" represents neither a sexual sublimation nor a suicidal death wish—more common readings of the
poem. The consummation implied in the fusion of the stallion with
rider and in

> The dew that flies
> Suicidal, at one with the drive
> Into the red
> Eye, the cauldron of morning.
>
> (*Ariel*, p. 27)

only sounds sexual, "because of the conventions of mystical religious
language" (p. 184). As for the dew, it is called "suicidal" "because,
true to its nature, it flies or evaporates into the sun. But this image
expresses mystical union or transcendence, 'sui-cide' in that it represents the death of the (personal) self—the little 'I' " (p. 184). While it
may be uncharitable to call this pedantry, it certainly expresses an

impulse toward mystification. One would like the surface meanings, however ordinary, sexual, or sensational, touched upon before turning to the more serious "deeper meanings."

There can be little doubt after reading Kroll that Plath was influenced by Graves and that the source for many of her eeriest images may well be his White Goddess mythology. Kroll is also very convincing on the poet's susceptibility to a whole range of superstitions—astrology, the tarot pack, witchcraft, the Ouija board. Not so convincing, though, are Kroll's efforts to systematize everything into a preconceived myth. She discovers, for instance, in Plath's outline for a novel that "she refers to the principals as 'heroine,' 'rival,' 'husband,' and 'rival's husband' " and interprets this as evidence for a "mythic view of these roles" (p. 66). Why a commonplace plot line like this should indicate a "mythic view" is unclear. In an unpublished letter to Olive Higgins Prouty (November 20, 1962), Plath simply describes her second novel as "semiautobiographical about a wife whose husband turns out to be a deserter and philanderer although she had thought he was wonderful and perfect."[17] There is also a BBC interview where Plath says that she was beginning to prefer novel writing over poetry for the opportunities it provided to talk about the trivia in her daily life—not myths, but "toothbrushes." Likewise, whenever Kroll transforms a strong female figure in Plath's poetry into a manifestation of Graves's White Goddess, I think of Plath's final description of Lady Lazarus as "just a good, plain, resourceful woman."[18]

While Kroll's tone is primarily one of cool, scholarly detachment, she is certainly more sympathetic to her subject than Butscher. Yet ironically, there is a strong resemblance between Kroll's White Goddess and Butscher's bitch goddess. Both are unappealing females—whimsically cruel and power-hungry. This may be why, in the concluding chapters of her book, Kroll deemphasizes the White Goddess material and turns increasingly toward a religious conversion theory for Plath's final poems. Instead of a White Goddess, Kroll ends with a view of Plath as a mystic, "beyond drama," and removed from the passions of ordinary mortals.[19]

What I am suggesting is that despite Kroll's earnest efforts to enlarge Plath's world, we end up with an image of her vision as depersonalized, obscure, and more than a little eccentric. She may no longer be quite so morbid and depressing as other critics have made her, but she also has little to say about experience except on a mythic and religiously exalted plane. Nor does Kroll's Plath seem to fit very well into literary tradition. She looks like a throwback to the system building of William Blake, but next to his prophetic breadth and grandeur, Plath's lyrics appear slight. As for Kroll's insistence that she is examining Plath's poetry apart from her life, the footnotes to *Chapters in a Mythology* are filled with useful biographical information in support of her argument, and Ted Hughes is regularly appealed to as an authority on what Plath read and how she worked. Kroll's unstated assumption is that by referring her interpretations to Plath's library, she engages in a more intrinsic, therefore more legitimate form of inquiry than the critics who use the events of her life. Both methods, it seems to me, are equally dependent on information outside the texts of the poems, and, more importantly, on the discrimination of the critic who uses that information.

While this is by no means an exhaustive review of the criticism on Plath, it illustrates a widespread tendency to see her as an oddity. She is an outsider who travels next to, but not with, the main line of literary tradition; or, as Marjorie Perloff cautions, we will understand and place her accurately only if we eschew large claims for her significance and acknowledge her dementia: "Sylvia Plath was the Christopher Smart rather than the Yeats of the early sixties."[20] Whether she is presented as a bitch goddess, a schizoid personality, or, more commonly, as a suicidal poet, we are being warned that her poems are novelties and her biography belongs to the investigator of abnormal psychology rather than the cultural or literary historian. To repeat Elizabeth Hardwick's pronouncement, we cannot "hope for general principles, sure origins, applications, or lessons" in the work or life of a woman whose "elements of pathology are so deeply rooted and so little resisted."

A Feminist Perspective: The "Bitch Goddess" and Bloomian Poetics

I do not wish to suggest a conspiracy against Plath, but this insistence on her aberrant qualities looks to me and to other feminist critics like an evasion of what is typical and representative about her life and art. For Suzanne Juhasz, the issue is not whether Plath was the Christopher Smart or Yeats of the early sixties, but her exemplary qualities as a woman poet: "She is the woman of our century who sees the problem, the situation of trying to be a woman poet with the coldest and most unredeemed clarity."[21] The "problem" is a predominantly male lyric tradition, which puts the woman poet in a double bind.

> Since poets in Western society are traditionally white and male, a person who is black, or brown, or female, of necessity brings qualities different from the norm to the poetry that she or he makes. How, then, to succeed as a "good" poet? If the woman poet "writes like a man," she denies her own experience; if she writes as a woman, her subject matter is trivial.[22]

In *The Madwoman in the Attic: The Woman Writer and the Nineteenth-Century Literary Imagination*, Sandra M. Gilbert and Susan Gubar state this problem with even greater simplicity: "For a woman-artist is, after all, a woman—that is her 'problem'—and if she denies her own gender, she inevitably confronts an identity crisis as severe as the anxiety of authorship she is trying to surmount."[23]

Gilbert and Gubar offer the "anxiety of authorship" as a female analogue to Harold Bloom's "anxiety of influence" for male authors. In a series of critical books, Bloom transfers Freud's "family romance" to literary tradition, propounding the thesis that each great poet struggles with and overpowers a literary father (e.g., Blake vs. Milton, Yeats vs. Shelley, Stevens vs. all the Romantics), in order to overcome the "anxiety of influence" from the past and make a place for his own art. The great poet becomes autonomous, self-propagating, father to himself. The mantle of the great poet is not passed on in an unbroken line of benevolent fathers and dutiful sons. Instead, the patriarchal tradition in lyric poetry is a history of Oedipal strife, and there is a willful "misreading" of the father's work—a "killing" of the poet-fathers by their sons.

As one might expect from this brief outline of Bloomian poetics, the relation of the woman poet to a tradition defined by masculine conflict is very different from that of her male counterparts.

The woman author experiences an "anxiety of authorship," according to Gilbert and Gubar, that is more crippling than the "anxiety of influence," both as it is primary (dare a woman pick up the pen at all?) and as it threatens her with madness, loss of her feminine identity, and various forms of punishment: imprisonment, death, social ostracism, loss of love. These terrifying consequences are dramatized, I believe, in the critical fictions of White Goddess and bitch goddess applied to Plath, which closely resemble a stereotypical figure in literary history, described by Gilbert and Gubar. When Plath departs from her role as the cloying, sweet matron Dame Kindness, a figure Butscher describes as the "good double" for the bitch goddess and Gilbert and Gubar would describe as the stereotype of genteel femininity, "the angel in the house," she supposedly transforms herself, not into a poet, but a destructive "monster-woman"—the bitchy Lady Lazarus or the parricidal daughter of "Daddy." As Gilbert and Gubar describe this "monster-woman" in male art, she threatens

> to replace her angelic sister, embodies intransigent female autonomy and thus represents both the author's power to allay "his" anxieties by calling their source bad names (witch, bitch, fiend, monster) and, simultaneously, the mysterious power of the character who refuses to stay in her textually ordained "place" and thus generates a story that "gets away" from its author. (P. 28)

While we are considering critical rather than literary fictions, the name-calling may well serve the same purpose—to allay the anxieties Plath's poems arouse. Juhasz implies as much in her assessment of critical reaction to Plath: "Her last poems were then and are now frightening, and very good; they ought to hurt and are meant to hurt. Yet the fact of her death has enabled readers and critics to handle them in an anaesthetized way. Because she is dead, no one need feel the blame or the responsibility that these poems engender."[24] Plath's story is that of a woman who succumbed to madness, unhealthy creative energies that presumably deformed her as a woman and a poet, and for this reason we can dismiss her poetry—and its effects—as abnormal.

Holbrook's description of Plath as "sadly pseudo-male" in many ways sums up this critical attitude and conforms with the cautionary tales cited by Gilbert and Gubar, where the reader is persuaded to condemn a cunningly inventive and active villainess (an artist figure) and approve a passive or silent, suffering heroine: the stepmother-queen vs. Snow White; Duessa vs. Una; Goneril and Regan vs. Cordelia; Becky Sharp vs. Amelia Sedley. These villainesses are invariably "pseudo-male" in their ambitions or portrayed as sexual grotesques—women who have denied their femininity in some monstrous way. They are usually far more interesting characters than the heroines, because they are actors where the angelic heroines are more often acted upon—but they are also invariably punished for their illicit activities. Such fictions give rise to the "anxiety of authorship" in women who choose to be writers. A woman like Plath, who chooses lyric poetry, may suffer the most anxiety, because she is "working in a genre that has been traditionally the most Satanically assertive, daring, and therefore precarious literary mode for women" (p. 582), and while "shaking a Promethean male fist 'against God' is one perfectly reasonable aesthetic strategy . . . , stamping a 'tiny' feminine foot is quite another" (p. 542). Even worse is the frightening defiance of the monster-woman—of a Lady Lazarus, who does not stamp a tiny foot, but threatens to "eat men like air."

Gilbert and Gubar argue that "a woman writer must examine, assimilate, and transcend these extreme images of 'angel' and 'monster' which male authors have generated for her" or they will find themselves "killed" into "male art," their choices limited to those of "angel in the house" and "madwoman in the attic" (p. 17). The women writers Gilbert and Gubar examine do not appear to transcend these choices, but ambivalently adopt both identities in their work, identifying femininity with self-abnegating "angels" and artistic impulse with madwomen-monsters.[25] With Lilith as a mother-precursor, women artists have themselves helped to perpetuate a mythic history of insanity, defiance of divine authority (Eve tempted by the serpent), and an illicit, "unwomanly" usurpation of the mighty authorial pen, which, as Gilbert and Gubar show, is frequently identified with a penis (pp. 3–4). Where the male poet assumes his rightful place by challenging the authority of his father-precursors, for the woman poet (who more often escapes or circumvents than actively combats Daddy), the powerful male Other may be internalized as a figure of guilt: a sadistic father-master, silent and unforgiving, a censorious patriarch to the presumptuous woman artist. Hence, their reading of Emily Dickinson's Master as a disapproving father-muse to a fearful little girl.

> . . .—the Pinching fear
> That Something—it did do—or dare
> Offend the Vision—and it flee—
> And They no more remember me—
> Nor ever turn to tell me why—
> O Master, This is Misery—[26]

Like Lilith cast out of Eden by God for refusing to lie beneath Adam, and doomed to child-murder and the company of demons, so Gilbert and Gubar imply, the woman poet like Dickinson or Plath suffers the most extreme anxiety, a mental world of demons, for "Something—it did do—or dare— / Offend the Vision" of her Master-father. "It" (she) "flees" (escapes) from his authority, but inevitably returns to abase herself, a fawning puppy before the master, expressing her need for his love.

> What shall I do—it whimpers so—
> This little hound within the Heart—[27]

> O pardon the one who knocks for pardon at
> Your gate, father—your hound-bitch, daughter, friend.
> It was my love that did us both to death.[28]

For Gilbert and Gubar, this anguish over daring to take the father's place—confronting his vision with her own—cripples the woman artist's sense of imaginative autonomy in a different way than the male artist's "anxiety of influence" restrains his genius. To a large degree, the difference seems to be a result of "our culture's historical confusion of literary authorship with patriarchal authority" (p. 11). Our literary history affirms and celebrates bold egotism on the part of a male poet like Whitman ("I celebrate myself and sing myself") as a natural masculine norm for the lyric tradition, while Dickinson's humility ("I am Nobody! Who are you?") reflects a self-acknowledged minor status.[29] She lives as the "slightest" in her father's house and plays the anonymous role of "mad child," while Whitman takes poetic fame as his right. Despite Dickinson's eventual fame, she is the isolated feminine eccentric, while Whitman is the American epic genius.[30] As Suzanne Juhasz illustrates in her brief examination of Plath criticism, the same double standard is applied to comparisons of Plath with Robert Lowell. His work is the "confessional" norm, the standard against which critics measure Plath's slighter work.[31]

Gilbert and Gubar's description of women writers' "anxiety of authorship" is at once a feminist critique of "Bloomian poetics," and an invaluable reformulation of his thesis to encompass the work of women writers. One consequence of their reformulation is assuredly a more generous understanding of the extreme measures women artists adopt to challenge their male precursors. They read Dickinson's self-imposed isolation and rejection of an adult feminine identity (as defined by nineteenth-century mores), for example, as a conscious choice rather than a sign of her abnormality. Only by adopting the mask of angel in her father's house could she continue to write her poems—a madwoman in the attic—unencumbered by the responsibilities of being a wife and mother. In this context, too, Plath's development of a bitch goddess or White Goddess persona may be explained as making a virtue of necessity. She plays the role of "monster woman," since it at least provides her as an artist with an identity commensurate to her powers of invention—however perverse or mad they might be.

On the negative side, Gilbert and Gubar's critique also suggests that Plath—like women writers before her—does not transcend the literary and critical categories imposed on her by male tradition. She remains in her "textually ordained 'place' "—as another madwoman—but one who refused, unlike her precursor Dickinson, to renounce her adult sexuality and femininity, or to confine her "intransigent female autonomy" to writing anonymous poems in the attic of her father's house. In Gilbert's essay on Plath in *Shakespeare's Sisters*, she implies that Plath creates a story that "gets away" from

her in the final poems and that she ends by literally killing herself
into her own art.

> Then one day a friend who worked at *The New Yorker* called to
> say "Imagine, Sylvia Plath is dead." And three days later "Pop-
> pies in July," "Edge," "Contusion," and "Kindness" appeared
> in *TLS*. Astonishingly undocile poems. Poems of despair and
> death. Poems with their heads in ovens (although the rumor
> was at first that Plath had died of the flu or pneumonia). Finally
> the violence seeped in, as if leaking from the poems into the
> life, or, rather, the death. She had been killed, had killed her-
> self, had murdered her children, a modern Medea. And at last it
> was really told, the story everyone knows already, and the out-
> lines of history began to thicken to myth. All of us who had
> read her traced our own journey in hers: from the flashy
> Women's House of *Mademoiselle* to the dull oven of Madame,
> from college to villanelles to babies to the scary skeletons of
> poems we began to study, now, as if they were sacred writ. The
> Plath Myth, whatever it meant or means, had been launched
> like a queen bee on its dangerous flight through everybody's
> psyche.[32]

> Being enclosed—in plaster, in a bell jar, a cellar, or a wax
> house—and then being liberated from an enclosure by a mad-
> dened or suicidal or "hairy and ugly" avatar of the self is, I
> would contend, at the heart of the myth that we piece together
> from Plath's poetry, fiction, and life, just as it is at the heart of
> much other important writing by nineteenth- and twentieth-
> century women. The story told is invariably a story of being
> trapped, by society or by the self as an agent of society, and
> then somehow escaping or trying to escape.[33]

Gilbert's version of the Plath myth is a frightening one. Like other
women writers, she is torn between two identities, one angelic and
saintly—"Plaster, the outer shell, fastidious defence, checks and
courtesies, docility"[34]—and the other, free, but "hairy and ugly"
and, like her other predecessors, dangerously mad and finally self-
destructive. The fact that Plath dies by her own hand in this version
of the myth, rather than by the sword of Western literary patriarchy,

does not make her any less an instrument of the male authorial will—any less the victim of "Milton's bogey," his vision of Eve, Sin, and Chaos as incarnations of the perversity of female creativity when set against a "solitary Father God as the . . . sole legitimate model for all earthly authors."[35] Although Gilbert wants "to honor the achievement of her poems" and "to stress the positive significance of her art and its optimistically feminine redefinition of traditions that have so far been primarily masculine," she still sees Plath imposing the punishment that tradition has always exacted from the woman who attempts her escape.

> But just as the fertile poet's re-vision of daddy is killing, so the suicidal cauldron of morning is both an image of rebirth and a place where one is cooked; and the red solar eye [in "Ariel"], certainly in Freudian terms, is the eye of the father, the patriarchal superego which destroys and devours with a single glance.[36]

The argument of this book, while dependent on Gilbert and Gubar's reformulation of Bloomian poetics, takes a somewhat different stance toward Plath's madwoman persona and toward her dilemma as a woman writer—a stance that I believe comes closer to Plath's own awareness of the tension between her desires to be a "normal" woman and also a writer. The angel in the house and madwoman in the attic are replaced by the earth mother and Lady Lazarus in this analysis—Plath's early and late archetypes for feminine creativity. In the following brief introduction, I will argue that Plath often breaks free of the critical categories imposed by a Bloomian poetics by a re-vision of the myths on which they are based.

Plath's Poetic Personality: From Earth Mother to Lady Lazarus

The woman writer's anxiety of authorship is evident everywhere in *Letters Home* (*LH*) , the voluminous correspondence between Plath and her mother Aurelia. One of the repeated themes in *Letters Home* is Plath's search for an artistic identity compatible with her femininity. This quest comes to a tentative resolution shortly before Plath's marriage to Ted Hughes and then reappears with a new urgency when the marriage falls apart. This is not to imply a simple cause-effect relationship between Plath's marriage and her poetic identity, but there is also nothing subtle about Plath's attempts to define herself first in relationship to her poet husband and later as an independent voice.

At Cambridge on a Fulbright, she writes to her mother that she fears becoming identified as an old maid scholar.

> I see in Cambridge, particularly among the women dons, a series of such grotesques. . . . They are all very brilliant or learned (quite a different thing) in their specialized ways, but I feel that all their experience is *secondary* [second-hand?].[37]

> I know there are, no doubt, brilliant dons here at Cambridge, and many men who are mature and integrated emotionally and intellectually, but I just haven't met them. The best ones we get on the lecture platform, but our women supervisors in Newnham are, as I have so often said, bluestocking grotesques, who know more about life second-hand. As a woman, my position is probably more difficult, for it seems the Victorian age of emancipation is yet dominant here: there isn't a woman professor I have that I admire personally! (*LH*, p. 219; February 25, 1956)

Revulsed by Victorian feminists, these "bluestocking grotesques" as she calls them, Plath goes to the other extreme, rejecting all definitions of herself as an intellectual.

> Again, I have decided that I would like to combine writing . . . simple short stories about people I know and problems I have met in life with a home & children. I love cooking and "homemaking" a great deal, and am neither destined to be a scholar (only vividly interested in books, not research, as they stimulate my thoughts about people and life) nor a career girl, and I really begin to think I might grow to be quite a good mother, and that I would learn such an enormous lot by extending my experience of life this way! (*LH*, p. 201; to Olive Higgins Prouty, December 13, 1955)

While she enjoyed the flattery and romantic fatality of comparisons sometimes made between her and major women writers like
Virginia Woolf, she did not like their implications. She feared cutting herself off from what she saw as the "normal" experiences of
womanhood—marriage, home, and, most important, children (*LH*,
p. 230; March 18, 1956). In her art, she aspires to be no more than "a
competent small-time writer (which will make me happy enough)"
(*LH*, p. 213; January 29, 1956). As she tells her mother, "Don't worry
that I am a 'career woman,' either. I sometimes think that I might
get married just to have children if I don't meet someone in these
two years" (*LH*, p. 208; January 17, 1956). At Cambridge, she is
preoccupied with these two tasks: finding a husband who will give
her a home and family and "making a self, in great pain, often, as
for a birth" (*LH*, p. 223; March 9, 1956). Her sense of self clearly
depends on finding a husband rather than fulfilling her writing ambitions. In all these musings, she seems apologetic about her "small-
time" writing abilities and when she includes writing among her list
of ambitions, it frequently comes last. "But I am definitely *meant* to
be married and have children and a home and write like these
women I admire: Mrs. Moore [Sarah-Elizabeth Rodgers], Jean Staf-
ford, Hortense Calisher, Phyllis McGinley" (*LH*, p. 208; January 17,
1956).

After she falls in love with Hughes, her desires become more
flamboyant. She tells her mother that she is creating her "self" as
yielding, eternal woman, absorbing pain and triumphing over it
with her fertility and innate joy in life. Pardon the overripe prose—
but it corresponds with the tone and substance of Plath's letters at
the time. A few months before her marriage, she tells her mother,

> I believe it is destructive to try to be an abstractionist man-
> imitator, or a bitter, sarcastic Dorothy Parker or Teasdale. I
> shall be one of the few women poets in the world who is fully
> a rejoicing woman, not a bitter or frustrated or warped man-
> imitator, which ruins most of them in the end. I am a woman
> and glad of it, and my songs will be of fertility of the earth
> and the people in it through waste, sorrow and death. I shall
> be a woman singer, and Ted and I shall make a fine life to-
> gether. (*LH*, p. 277; October 8, 1956)

I am true to the essence of myself, and I know who that self is, . . . and will live with her through sorrow and pain, singing all the way, even in anguish and grief, the triumphs of life over death and sickness and war and all the flaws of my dear world. . . .

I know this with a sure strong knowing to the tips of my toes, and having been on the other side of life like Lazarus, I know that my whole being shall be one song of affirmation and love all my life long. (*LH*, p. 243; April 26, 1956)

This first Lady Lazarus is a bit naive—an earth mother who blithely faces the Four Horsemen of the Apocalypse with a song of affirmation and love.

Despite the assertiveness of the letters, it is important to note that the earth mother persona is born out of contradiction. Plath continually says, "I am not like this, but that": "My voice is taking shape, coming strong. Ted says he never read poems by a woman like mine; they are strong and full and rich—not quailing and whining like Teasdale or simple lyrics like Millay" (*LH*, p. 244; April 29, 1956). These contradictions and denials will be examined more fully later, but for now it is sufficient to see that very early Plath saw conflicts between her poetic ambitions and her desire to be "fully a rejoicing woman"—between her art and her life. Her resolution of this supposed incompatibility is the earth mother woman singer persona, and in this she saw herself as the exception rather than the rule. The gushing idealization of womanhood is highly suspect for just this reason; it is matched by a persistent assault on "whiney" and "intellectual" women writers—as if to exercise one's critical intelligence is to be unfeminine. While such statements show that Plath intuits the dangers of a madwoman persona, she also appears to embrace a culturally glorified and male-approved version of what a woman should be and not to have found an autonomous poetic voice at all.

The emergence of the earth mother singer also seems completely dependent on her relationship to Hughes. He is, she says, teaching her "how best I can be for a woman" and "will work with me to make me a woman poet like the world will gape at; even as he sees into my character and will tolerate no fallings away from my best right self" (*LH*, p. 248; May 3, 1956). He is "always just that many steps ahead of me intellectually and creatively so that I feel very feminine and admiring" (*LH*, p. 270; September 11, 1956). She is fond of describing herself as "this adam's woman" (*LH*, p. 328; from "Ode for Ted," April 21, 1956).

> I can appreciate the legend of Eve coming from Adam's rib as I never did before; the damn story's true! That's where I belong. Away from Ted, I feel as if I were living with one eyelash of myself only. . . . Everything I do with and for Ted has a celestial radiance, be it only ironing and cooking. (*LH*, p. 276; October 8, 1956)

He is also a father figure and muse, "very strictly disciplining about my study and work" (*LH*, p. 290; January 9, 1957), "educating me daily, setting me exercises of concentration and observation" (*LH*, p. 267; August 2, 1956), and ultimately he "fills somehow that huge, sad hole I felt in having no father" (*LH*, p. 289; November 29, 1956). In turn, Plath's "whole thought is for him, how to please him, to make a comfortable place for him" (*LH*, p. 263; July 14, 1956), and "to find such a man, to make him into the best man the world has seen: such a life work!" (*LH*, p. 252; May 6, 1956).

If Plath's correspondence accurately reflects the division of responsibility in her marriage, then it was a marriage where she played, with great enthusiasm and conviction, the roles of housewife, secretary, and literary agent for a "genius of a husband." Hughes broke into the American poetry magazines after Plath began to type and systematically send his manuscripts off; and while Hughes is always portrayed as generous with assistance in caring for their first child, Frieda, and considerate of Plath's need for time and space with her own writing, it is also clear that they were in agreement about his career coming first.

> Ted is starting to work regularly over in Merwin's study, which is a great relief for both of us. It is impossible for him to work in this little place with me cleaning and caring for the baby, and when he is out, I have the living room and desk to myself and can get my work done. . . . I find my first concern is that Ted

has peace and quiet. I am happy then and don't mind that my own taking up of writing comes a few weeks later. (*LH*, p. 381; May 11, 1960)

Even a modest fame brings flocks of letters, requests. . . . If Ted didn't have his study, he'd be distracted by the phone, the mail, and odd callers so he'd get no work done at all. And as his secretary and my own, I have a personal reason for being strict. So please help us by not steering anyone our way. (*LH*, p. 384; May 30, 1960)

Even though she complains,

I really hunger for a study of my own out of hearing of the nursery where I could be alone with my thoughts for a few hours a day. I really believe I could do some good stories if I had a stretch of time without distractions. (*LH*, p. 392; August 27, 1960)

her "one aim is to keep Ted writing full-time" (*LH*, p. 389; July 9, 1960).[38]

Because they feel cramped in a London flat, Plath and Hughes eventually buy a thatched-roof manor house in Devon. As Aurelia Plath describes the move in the summer of 1961, it "delighted Sylvia and aroused all her homemaking instincts" (*LH*, p. 427). Although Plath develops a darker vision of motherhood in her poetry after a miscarriage and the birth of her second child, Nicholas, her letters in this period persist in projecting an image of matronly contentment.

Today came a big Christmas parcel from you with the two *Ladies' Home Journal* magazines, which I fell upon with joy—that magazine has so much Americana, I love it. Look forward to a good read by the wood fire tonight and to trying the luscious recipes. . . . I remember before Frieda came, I was like this; quite cowlike and interested suddenly in soppy women's magazines and cooking and sewing. (*LH*, pp. 438–39; December 7, 1961)

> I think having babies is really the happiest experience of my life.
> I would just like to go on and on. (*LH*, p. 450; March 12, 1962)

Even as her marriage begins to fall apart in the spring of 1962, Plath can still speak gushingly of her womanly fulfillment. According to her mother, she claims total happiness: "I have everything in life I've ever wanted: a wonderful husband, two adorable children, a lovely home, and my writing" (*LH*, p. 458); and she unswervingly associates herself with the blooming nature outside her home, with her beekeeping and gardening.

> I weeded all our onions and spinach and lettuce—out in the garden from sunrise to sunset, immensely happy, with Frieda digging in a little space, "helping," and Nicholas in the pram sunbathing. This is the richest and happiest time of my life. The babies are so beautiful. (*LH*, p. 455, June 7, 1962)

When Hughes leaves her in August of 1962, Plath's tone and self-image change radically. In contrast to her initial dependence on Hughes and her effusiveness over being a new lyrical woman, Plath's succinct statement of who she is, four months before her death, sounds almost subdued: "I am a writer . . . I am a genius of a writer; I have it in me. I am writing the best poems of my life; they will make my name" (*LH*, p. 468; October 16, 1962). And a few days later, she writes to her mother in a voice like the Lady Lazarus with whom we are more familiar.

> Don't talk to me about the world needing cheerful stuff! What the person out of Belsen—physical or psychological—wants is nobody saying the birdies still go tweet-tweet, but the full knowledge that somebody else has been there and knows the *worst*, just what it is like. It is much more help for me, for example, to know that people are divorced and go through hell, than to hear about happy marriages. Let the *Ladies' Home Journal* blither about those. I know just what I want and want to do. (*LH*, p. 473; October 21, 1962)

Plath formerly "slaved" and "slaved" to "break into" "slicks" like the *Ladies' Home Journal* with her short stories (*LH*, p. 290; January 9, 1957), and she read them avidly for their recipes and "Americana." Now they come under special attack for their insubstantial optimism and for their associations with her mother Aurelia, whom she sees as a purveyor of their homely wisdom and a coward in face of the world's ills.

> Now stop trying to get me to write about "decent courageous people"—read the *Ladies' Home Journal* for those! It's too bad my poems frighten you—but you've always been afraid of reading or seeing the world's hardest things—like Hiroshima, the Inquisition, or Belsen. I believe in going through & facing the worst, not hiding from it. (Box 6, MSS II; October 25, 1962)

Plath's final antagonists are not the Sara Teasdales and Dorothy Parkers—the neurotic lady writers and "poetesses"—but the bluebirds of happiness promised to American girls in women's magazines.

Her letters are filled with bitterness for the roles of devoted wife and mother that she formerly played with so much ardor. The "celestial radiance" of cooking and cleaning is now gone. She feels "stuck down here [Devon] as into a sack, I fight for air and freedom and the culture and the libraries of a city" (*LH*, p. 465; October 9, 1962). She despises her country life: "I miss brains, hate this cow life, am dying to surround myself with intelligent, good people. I'll have a salon in London. I am a famous poetess here" (*LH*, p. 466; October 12, 1962). To her brother Warren and his new wife Maggie, she writes of the years she spent helping Hughes achieve fame: "I feel I did discover him and worked to free him for writing for six years" (Box 6, MSS II; October 12, 1962); and to her mother, she describes the feelings of being old and used up: "The foulness I have lived, his wanting to kill all I have lived for six years by saying he was just waiting for a chance to get out, that he was bored & stifled by me, a hag in a world of beautiful women just waiting for him" (Box 6, MSS II; October 9, 1962).

Despite this disillusionment with her self-image as an ideal wife and mother, Plath's new voice is by no means a repudiation of her femininity. As if to confirm her early declaration of strength when she found Hughes—"And the woman I am stretching to be is one whom no man can send crying out of life" (Box 5, MSS II; April 29, 1956)—Plath insistently casts Hughes as jealous of her artistic powers and contrasts her fertility to the sterility of her rival, Assia Gutman.

> It is as if, out of revenge for my brain and creative power, he wanted to stick me where I would have no chance to use it. I think now my creating babies and a novel frightened him—for he wants barren women like his sister and this woman. (Box 6, MSS II; October 21, 1962)

> Now I've got rid of Ted, to whom I've dedicated such time and energy and for such reward, I feel my life and career can really begin. He's taken with him the barren bitches who bare [sic] me only envy and now everyone I know is good and loving. (Box 6, MSS II; December 14, 1962)

Instead of succumbing to depression, she begins "writing like mad—have managed a poem a day before breakfast. All book poems. Terrific stuff, as if domesticity had choked me" (*LH*, p. 466; October 12, 1962). Many of these poems reflect the fury of a woman scorned: "a wife whose husband turns out to be a deserter and philanderer although she had thought he was wonderful and perfect" (Box 6, MSS II; November 20, 1962). But Plath manages to distance herself from an unbearable situation with humor, irony, and satire, so that poems like "Lesbos" stand quite independently in their criticism of domestic bliss.

> The fluorescent light wincing on and off like a migraine,
> Coy paper strips for doors—
> Stage curtains, a widow's frizz.
>
> (*Ariel*, p. 30)

The housewife of "Lesbos" is stuck in the kitchen with a "stink of fat and baby crap." The vine-covered cottage of Hollywood "happily-ever-afters" has proved a jerry-built sham. The substance of the poem

is like the letters. The woman has been sold a bill of domestic goods
when her real destiny was to be a femme fatale—a mermaid, a vamp,
a sex goddess.

> I should sit on a rock off Cornwall and comb my hair,
> I should wear tiger pants, I should have an affair,
>
> Once you were beautiful,
> In New York, in Hollywood, the men said: "Through?
> Gee baby, you are rare."
>
> (*Ariel*, pp. 30–31)

In a parody of Hollywood plots, Plath as "mad housewife" fantasizes that she was once a beautiful woman who sacrificed a promising career for marriage. The career, though, is as a Marilyn Monroe
figure with a multitude of male worshipers. The Hollywood sex
goddess is no less a type than the little homemaker of *Ladies' Home
Journal,* so that "Lesbos" can hardly be said to offer a valid alternative identity. It is only a satiric exposure of the connubial bliss cele-
brated in the media.

Elsewhere Plath does create a reborn woman: Lady Lazarus.
Her appearance, however, is, as we have seen, commonly read as a
negative phenomenon. Here is the "bitch goddess," the "ugly and
hairy" monster woman, celebrating her escape and vengeance on
men. This poem is where the Lady who "knows the worst" claims,
"Dying is an art," a phrase repeated many times in critical commentary as evidence for Plath's sickness and suicidal tendencies. As a
partial test of these censorious pronouncements about Plath's overall
significance and her development of a "madwoman" persona, let us
take a look at that line in context. It comes from the middle of "Lady
Lazarus."

> I do it so it feels like hell.
> I do it so it feels real.
> I guess you could say I've a call.
>
> It's easy enough to do it in a cell.
> It's easy enough to do it and stay put.
> It's the theatrical

Comeback in broad day
To the same place, the same face, the same brute
Amused shout:

"A miracle!"
That knocks me out.
There is a charge

For the eyeing of my scars, there is a charge
For the hearing of my heart—
It really goes.

And there is a charge, a very large charge
For a word or a touch
Or a bit of blood

Or a piece of my hair or my clothes.
                              (*Ariel*, pp. 7–8)

These are boasting lines. Lady Lazarus tells us twice that the easy part is dying. It's the "comeback" before a "peanut-crunching crowd" that demands special skills—that really knocks her out.

Throughout the poem, Christian symbolism is yoked with three other actions: the sideshow striptease; the suffering inflicted by the Nazis on the Jews; and the personal acts of self-destruction compulsively repeated each decade. Plath stresses the public nature of the spectacle, so that her suicide attempts are no more private or personal than the Oberammergau Passion Play and its ritualized repetition of Christ's crucifixion and resurrection every ten years. Lady Lazarus's suffering is also a religious calling, a vocation. Her comeback is a "miracle" like Christ's resurrection of Lazarus, and the purpose is apparently the same: to provide visible proof of God's power over life and death to a skeptical audience. Once the brutish spectacle is over, the clothes strewn in Lady Lazarus's striptease, like the shroud left in the tomb by Christ's risen body, will be sold as religious relics with special healing and restorative powers.

Howe regards this use of Christian myth and the Jewish holo-

caust as illegitimate—bold but offensive devices for drawing attention to the poet's personal suffering. But Plath is not concerned
primarily with personal afflictions, except as they represent a wider
feminine condition. As she puts it in "Daddy," "Every woman
adores a fascist" (*Ariel*, p. 50); and Lady Lazarus, no less than the
daughter in "Daddy," has a masochistic relationship to the male god
who raises her from the dead. While Christian myth magnifies the
significance of the relationship between Lady Lazarus and her persecutor Herr God, Lady Lazarus's irony simultaneously undercuts
her Passion.

The story of Lazarus, ordinarily regarded, I suppose, as one of
the happier moments of divine intervention in human affairs, is
continually mocked by Lady Lazarus's name-calling. The deity is a
Nazi and addressed as Herr Doktor, Herr God, Herr Lucifer, and
"my Enemy," all of which deride the malignity of his purpose. His
most important attribute is his power over her. Initially he appears
as Herr Doktor, a physician in a Nazi concentration camp, and Lady
Lazarus makes her entrance as one of Frankenstein's monsters—an
experiment by Herr Doktor. As such, she is a bizarre amalgam of
inanimate objects, barely patched together into a living being—a
true monster-woman.

> A sort of walking miracle, my skin
> Bright as a Nazi lampshade,
> My right foot a paperweight,
>
> My face a featureless, fine Jew linen.
>
> (*Ariel*, p. 6)

There is little art to Herr Doktor's manufacture of paperweights and
lampshades. Only the Lady's sense of death and rebirth as an art of
self-creation instills these lifeless objects with any power to fascinate
a peanut-crunching crowd.

The circus setting, too, diminishes Herr God, providing him
with less than divine identities which alter our perception of his
control over her. Various lines suggest that he is a wild animal
trainer, a ringmaster, or a sideshow barker who displays Lady Lazarus like a carnival freak. Her special trick is suffering, dying, and

reviving for the amusement of an audience like that in the Roman Coliseum. In this version of the Biblical miracle, everyone is a collaborator: God is a flimflam man interested in drumming up money-paying suckers; Lady Lazarus enjoys baring her body and soul; and the audience won't avert its gaze until the show is over and they have seen it all. The more grotesque the spectacle, the better the effect and the bigger the "charge" for everyone.

Lady Lazarus's shifting relationship to Herr God and to her audience raises the question of complicity in her own suffering. Like her Biblical counterpart, she sometimes seems to be the passive medium for her creator's powers: "I am your opus, I am your valuable" (*Ariel*, p. 8). As the Jewess, she is an innocent scapegoat—"the pure gold baby that melts to a shriek" (*Ariel*, p. 8). But as a stripteaser in a sideshow, she participates in her degradation, a masochist who cultivates pain for the thrill of exhibition. Lady Lazarus's attitude toward the audience is equally unsteady. At times, she sounds flip and bored with the whole act: "What a trash / To annihilate each decade" (*Ariel*, p. 6). At others, she has a gift for the sarcastic understatement: "I turn and burn, / Do not think I underestimate your great concern" (*Ariel*, p. 8). And at one moment, an introduction to the audience turns into a painful supplication.

Gentlemen, ladies,

These are my hands,
My knees.

(*Ariel*, p. 7)

These shifts in tone are not inconsistencies in character so much as a wavering between unflinching pride and self-disgust. There is a perpetual antagonism between Lady Lazarus and her spectators, as though she wants and needs their sympathy, but will laugh in their faces if they dare to pity her. And so she both appeals to them and insults them with her casual attitude toward atrocity, as if to say, "Oh well, if you'd been to hell and back as I have, you'd look a fright, too."

Do I terrify?

The nose, the eyepits, the full set of teeth?
The sour breath
Will vanish in a day

And I a smiling woman.

(*Ariel*, p. 6)

These multiple, contradictory relationships between Lady Lazarus and both her audience and her creator are resolved in the last four stanzas of the poem. Still another Lady Lazarus emerges from the Nazi ovens, very different from the personalities we have seen so far.

Ash, ash—
You poke and stir,
Flesh, bone, there is nothing there.

A cake of soap,
A wedding ring,
A gold filling.

Herr God, Herr Lucifer,
Beware
Beware,

Out of the ash
I rise with my red hair
And I eat men like air.

(*Ariel*, pp. 8–9)

In the final invocation to Herr God, Herr Lucifer, there is no self-mockery. She is in deadly earnest. The warning "Beware" sounds as though a dangerous circus animal has escaped and refuses to perform anymore. The lioness turns on trainer and audience alike, baring her claws instead of her wounds, and revealing her untamed powers for the first time. She gives everyone a bigger "charge" than they wanted or expected.

With this shift in tone, there is a reversal on all levels of the action. Lady Lazarus is resurrected twice, first as the "opus," the "valuable" of Herr Doktor, the clumsy artist of paperweights and lampshades. Again he melts her down to the accumulated trash of her life—"A cake of soap, / A wedding ring, / A gold filling"—and pokes and stirs, thinking he might create something from the ashes. But "there is nothing there." He misses the flamelike exhalation from the oven and the incarnation of Lady Lazarus as a body of fire, a man-eating phoenix woman. The Jewess turns on her Nazi oppressor. The stripteaser who pleases men transforms herself into a man-eater. The scapegoat becomes a predator. And most important, the creator-creature relationship that supersedes all others in this poem is inverted. The creature takes over the task of resurrection and is her own miracle. It is as if Lazarus were to say, "I'd rather do it myself."

From this perspective, "Lady Lazarus" is an allegory about the woman artist's struggle for autonomy. The female creature of a male artist-god is asserting independent creative powers. Next to Lady Lazarus's miraculous rise at the end, the male god's art is an inept engineering feat. Where at the beginning of the poem the Lady merely manifests his potency—indeed, prostituting her imagination by playing the role of female exhibitionist—by the end of the poem she is a creator in her own right.

Given the shifting and complex set of relationships that Plath sets up in "Lady Lazarus," it seems a waste to dwell overlong on the poem's confessional aspects, to worry about whether this or that stanza refers to some incident in Plath's life, or to belabor the fact that Herr God may be a representation of her father or her husband. Whatever his origins in the circumstances of Plath's life, in this poem he is the usurper of Lady Lazarus's artistic powers, and he is defeated on those grounds.

It is important to note as well that Lady Lazarus is not simply an escape artist. She directly confronts and challenges Herr God at the end of the poem with her own self-resurrection, and this new self is surely less monstrous than Herr God's swaddled cadaver. As a poem about overcoming the woman writer's anxiety of authorship, "Lady Lazarus" provides a new reading of the monster-woman. She is neither mad nor "ugly and hairy," but a phoenix, a flame of released bodily energy. The insanity was her complicity in Herr God's sleazy sideshow, not in the choice of self-incarnation. Just as the male author allays his anxieties by calling their source bad names—witch, bitch, fiend, monster—so Plath allays her anxieties by identifying the father-god with Nazi brutality, calling him Herr Doktor, Herr Enemy, Herr Lucifer, or, in "Daddy," "a man in black with a Meinkampf look" (*Ariel*, p. 51). Plath also goes beyond simple name-calling; she manages to demonstrate his dependence on female passivity. His creative power is not his own, but derived from the woman's body and its capacity for rebirth. In this revision of mythology, both the male authorial will and "the angel in the house" are deconstructed. The angel is renamed a masochistic Jewess and she, rather than the madwoman, is the enemy within, the saboteur of woman's independence.

The Art of Incarnation

If we return now to that statement, "Dying is an art," its force is not canceled out, but complicated and qualified by other equally strong metaphors for Plath's creativity: resurrection, incarnation, rebirth. Indeed, Plath herself did not see Lady Lazarus as a woman gifted with the art of dying. Death was only a consequence of other talents. In a BBC reading of the poem, Plath describes Lady Lazarus as "a woman who has the great and terrible gift of being reborn. The only trouble is, she has to die first. She is the Phoenix, the libertarian spirit, what you will. She is also just a good, plain, very resourceful woman."[39] The mixture of everyday fortitude with political and mythic heroism gets at the quicksilver shape shifting of Lady Lazarus as she talks her way into freedom. And there is an inescapable ironic delight in Plath's description—as if enjoying the strength of her new voice.

Nor is "Lady Lazarus" an isolated instance of this theme of rebirth and incarnation. Many of Plath's finest lyrics are about the destruction and recreation of her self in new and vital forms. In

"Ariel," she unpeels "Dead hands, dead stringencies," an old skin
"flakes from [her] heels" and "the child's cry / Melts in the wall"
(*Ariel*, pp. 26–27), forgotten, as woman and stallion fuse into a
single being, flying toward the rising sun. The old self is annihi-
lated, but not without the appearance of a new identity as an agent
of apocalypse and revelation—"God's lioness." In "Purdah," the
harem wife tears away the veil over her mouth and reveals herself as
another "lioness," a Clytemnestra to an unsuspecting husband[40]; in
"Stings," the woman escapes her role as a female worker bee, a
"honeydrudger," and takes wing as a murderous queen bee in the
creative act of conception (*Ariel*, pp. 61–63); and in "Fever 103°," a
body sick with frustrated sexual desire is purged by these same fires
of lust, rising at the end of the poem as a lethal "acetylene virgin," a
paradox in that she is both too pure and too hot for any man to
touch (*Ariel*, pp. 53–55).

To be sure, none of these new selves achieves an aesthetic detachment from carnal experiences equal, say, to Yeats's golden bird
in "Sailing to Byzantium." They are never completely free from the
contradictory circumstances in which they are born. Lady Lazarus,
the acetylene virgin, the queen bee, and the lioness are distinctly
female, sexually aggressive, and bound to the past by a desire for
vengeance. Tainted with a need to destroy, reject, or rebel against
old selves and old loves, these new identities are forms of what
Richard Wilbur, in a poem about Sylvia Plath, calls the "brilliant
negative / In poems free and helpless and unjust."[41] That final judgment of Plath, "unjust," must be mitigated by a recognition of the
way Plath fuses the "brilliant negative" with an even more brilliant
affirmation of her creative powers. In all of these poems, there is an
inescapable buoyancy, a feeling of weightlessness, of sublimation
into fire and air, that is, in turn, a sign for the release of thwarted
energies and of a newly achieved emotional freedom. For Plath, art
is a physical elation, a new sense of the freedom of her body: these
poems are filled with metaphors of flight, ascension, and transubstantiation into new states of being. Ultimately, Plath's incarnation
poems are moments of awakening to the power of her art.

The group of poems in which self-transformation is so triumphantly achieved is small, but I believe it reflects an overall intention
in Plath's life and work. There are poems where the struggle to create

a beautiful self is defeated. In these, other claims on Plath's energy seem as strong or stronger than her art (e.g., see discussion of "Kindness" above). And there are many moments when death looks attractive and suicide is an even greater temptation since it would be both an act of defiance and control. Despite the mood of despair and tragic fatality in poems like "Edge," "Contusion," or "The Moon and the Yew Tree," Plath resists as often as she surrenders to self-destructive impulses. Ambivalence is her habitual attitude, so that even where death looks like a state of repose, ease, or perfection itself, as in "Edge" ("The woman is perfected," *Ariel*, p. 84), there is an underlying tension that is the sign of an ongoing conflict.

The circumstances of Plath's life at this time are crucial to understanding the emergence of these new poetic selves. As the earth mother figure is born out of her joy in being "this adam's woman," and wife to "the strongest man in the world . . . with a voice like the thunder of god—a singer, storyteller, lion and world-wanderer and vagabond" (*LH*, p. 233; April 17, 1956), so Lady Lazarus is born from Plath's alternate rage and despair at his desertion. Once she is born, however, she takes on a vivid poetic life of her own. Indeed, what this new voice captures is Plath's surmounting of a creative blockage Tillie Olsen believes is peculiar to women artists and particularly those born and raised in Plath's era.

> And the agony—peculiarly mid-century, escaped by their sisters of pre-Freudian, pre-Jungian times—that "creation and femininity are incompatible." Anaïs Nin's words:
>
>> The aggressive act of creation; the guilt for creating. I did not want to rival man; to steal man's creation, his thunder. I must protect them, not outshine them.
>
> The acceptance—against one's experienced reality—of the sexist notion that the act of creation is not as inherently natural to a woman as to a man, but rooted instead in unnatural aggression, rivalry, envy, or thwarted sexuality.[42]

Anaïs Nin's words—"I must protect them, not outshine them"— echo Aurelia Plath's description of her daughter.

> From the time Sylvia was a very little girl, she catered to the
> male of any age so as to bolster his sense of superiority. . . . She
> did not pretend the male was superior; she sought out those
> who were, and her confidence in her husband's genius was
> unshakable. (*LH*, p. 297n)

Plath's final letters home show that she was beginning to feel more
natural in the role of artist-creator. In contrast to her early apologies
over a small-time writing career, she speaks with assurance.

> I am a writer and that is all I want to do. (*LH*, p. 472; October
> 18, 1962)

> I amaze myself. It is my work that does it, my sense of myself as a
> writer. . . . Living apart from Ted is wonderful—I am no longer
> in his shadow, and it is heaven to be liked for myself alone,
> knowing what I want. (*LH*, pp. 478–79; November 7, 1962)

Statements such as these may be read as rationalizations for herself
and false reassurances for a worried mother, but the new sense of
writing as a vocation is also confirmed by the outpouring of poems
in the final months of Plath's life.

Lady Lazarus and Literary History

Although Plath's development as a poet, as we have seen, is marked
by distinctly feminine anxieties, in one important respect she is like
her male precursors. Plath's destruction and recreation of her self in
new forms resembles another "brilliant negative" in literature:
Stephen Dedalus's *non serviam*, "I will not serve," in *Portrait of the
Artist as a Young Man*. Stephen rejects the church and priesthood,
his Irish heritage, and his family. This is a conventional Oedipal
posture for the male artist who sees himself in opposition to forces
that threaten to use his creative energies for nonartistic ends.
Stephen resists the temptations of power over this world and the
next and chooses art as a greater power. His *non serviam* echoes

Lucifer's refusal to serve in heaven, and in this, Stephen embraces the tradition in masculine art of Satanic defiance to divine authority.

What can the woman artist reject? What great temptations can she resist? Nothing so grandiose as priesthood and politics, because they have not been options for a woman. Even a turn away from the security and dependent relationships of the family is not a literary model for the woman artist's coming of age—or at least not in the past. As for the masculine convention of rebellion against patriarchal authority, it does not, as we have seen, apply directly to the woman artist; woman has not played a part in the epic battles of literary tradition, except perhaps as helpmate, amanuensis, or nemesis.

What Plath does in many of her late poems is to mock, satirize, reveal as a fraud, the entire tradition of literary primogeniture. Lady Lazarus revolts against her role as the second sex in creation. As Northrop Frye explains, the archetype of poetic creation is the divine activity of a male god.

> As with other products of divine activity, the father of a poem is much more difficult to identify than the mother. That the mother is always nature . . . no serious criticism can ever deny. . . . But the poet, who writes creatively rather than deliberately, is not the father of his poem; he is at best a midwife, or more accurately still, the womb of Mother Nature herself: her privates he, so to speak.[43]

The representative poet is male; but the nature whose power he both imitates and wields as his own, Frye admits, is female. As in "Lady Lazarus," the male poet, according to Frye, is totally dependent on feminine passivity—Mother Nature's deference to the divine activity of the male. The myth rests on the assumption that woman is body, flesh, nature unredeemed, while man is the redemptive and controlling agency. Like Eve, woman's labor produces only pain, while man's manipulation of her "privates"—"the womb of Mother Nature"—is an aesthetic labor that produces beauty.

Such mythic assumptions are evident in Plath's early poem, "Two Sisters of Persephone," written shortly after her marriage to Hughes. Here she celebrates woman's secondary participation in creation.

Two girls there are: within the house
One sits; the other, without.
Daylong a duet of shade and light
Plays between these.

In her dark wainscotted room
The first works problems on
A mathematical machine.
Dry ticks mark time

As she calculates each sum.
At this barren enterprise
Rat-shrewd go her squint eyes,
Root-pale her meager frame.

Bronzed as earth, the second lies,
Hearing ticks blown gold
Like pollen on bright air. Lulled
Near a bed of poppies,

She sees how their red silk flare
Of petalled blood
Burns open to sun's blade.
On that green altar

Freely become sun's bride, the latter
Grows quick with seed.
Grass-couched in her labor's pride,
She bears a king. Turned bitter

And sallow as any lemon,
The other, wry virgin to the last,
Goes graveward with flesh laid waste,
Worm-husbanded, yet no woman.[44]

The first sister provides a sorry lesson for the intellectual woman. Mental activity is depicted as a barren, unnatural enterprise for a woman that leads to stunted growth and an early death, while

motherhood fulfills woman's creative potential. Despite the silly didacticism at work here, there are some disturbing tensions in the
poem—ambivalence that looks forward to Plath's later rejection of
the earth mother as a fraudulent identity. In the second sister's
sexual submission to the "sun's blade" on a green altar, there is
more than a suggestion of sacrificial violence in being a womanly
woman. The earth mother is not an agent in conception; in a half-
conscious state, "lulled" by the poppies (which resemble the female
genitals) into a mental stupor, she simply lies open to the sun—a
Danae or Amoret to a god's rape. She is but a medium for the male
sun's creativity.

The ambivalence of "Two Sisters" looks forward to Lady Lazarus's rejection of Herr God, Herr Lucifer's power over her body.
Lady Lazarus "will not serve," and the double-naming of divine
authority is itself an indictment of male artifice. Whether divine or
Satanic, Herr Doktor's magic is a form of violence practiced on
woman. The ideal of woman as vessel for the man's creative seed is
replaced in "Lady Lazarus" by woman as arbitress of her own fate
and perhaps most important as a theme of Plath's late poetry, the
ideal of woman as presiding genius of her own body.

The process of growth whereby Plath arrives at this final persona is the subject of this book. As I have demonstrated from *Letters
Home,* Plath tried to define herself against literary mothers, but was
unable to find a woman poet whose voice she might want to imitate
and then reject in the process of finding her own. Instead, Plath
envisioned her lyrical female voice coming out of the rich personal
life of a "normal" woman: "I'm not a Sara Teasdale type unhappy
writer—I'm only able to write when I'm living a rich, full life and
have an objective sense of humor" (Box 5, MSS II; August 10, 1956).

This frustration at not finding literary parents helps to explain
the "confessional" dimension to her work. Increasingly, Plath defines her imaginative self against personal history—against Otto
and Aurelia Plath and her life as it has been shaped under
"Daddy"-domination. There is, too, a self-conscious exaggeration—
what Bloom would describe as a purposeful misreading of her
past—in the various mythic and historical guises she gives her
"family romance." She sometimes plays Electra to Otto and Aurelia
Plath as the history-making colossus Agamemnon and the vengeful

mother Clytemnestra. Occasionally she adopts the role of Clytemnestra herself to her husband as Agamemnon. The Nazi holocaust
provides her with the prototypes for a sadomasochistic relationship
between man and woman in the figures of black-booted Nazi man
and Jewess and a dramatic and narrative design for her own self-
destructive collaboration in being victimized. The motive behind
such exaggerations is to allegorize—in extreme forms, to be sure—
the difficulties of women in making an imaginative space for themselves. I suspect this impulse may be representative of other
women poets as well: the turning away from received literary tradition as a significant context for defining themselves as creators and
a turning inward and backward, to the personal past and their
psychological development. As Gilbert and Gubar argue, it is not
the anxiety of literary influence so much as the anxieties of growing up female that are worked through in order for a woman to
assert herself as a creator. Despite this important difference, the
task is similar to the one described by Bloom. Poetic influence, he
argues, is "a variety of melancholy" induced by the loss of the
father-poet and the new poems produced by this melancholy both
return to that loss, reopening the wound, and show the poet wres-
tling "with their strong precursors, even to the death."[45] The "self-
saving caricature," "distortion," and "perverse, willful revision-
ism" of the younger artist's reading of the father-poet's life and
work is acceptable, for only "weaker talents idealize; figures of
capable imagination appropriate for themselves."[46] Bloom's description of the motives and techniques of the poet-son may be easily
transferred to Plath's appropriation of her personal history and her
willful misreading of Otto Plath in the bee poems and "Daddy."

Yet for woman poet, caricature, distortion, and revision may
not be enough. The whole myth must be retold from a feminine
perspective. If Plath's use of history and myth is self-aggrandizing,
it is also exemplary of woman as emerging artificer and no more
narcissistic or self-promoting than the male usurpation of woman's
body and its power to give birth for his divine activity. As birth is a
woman's special prerogative, so should it be a woman poet's special
metaphor for her creativity, and in many of Plath's poems, the action is to take back a fertile body that was originally her own. In
Plath's late work, the female body is the vehicle for imaginative

transformation and release. She translates social and psychological constraints on women into physical and sexual terms, so that we come to understand not only what it may feel like to live in a woman's body, but also how this affects her inventive freedom and control of the world around her. This theme, too, may well be representative of contemporary women artists. In *Of Woman Born*, Adrienne Rich claims,

> The repossession by women of our bodies will bring far more essential change to human society than the seizing of the means of production by workers. The female body has been both territory and machine, virgin wilderness to be exploited and assembly-line turning out life. We need to imagine a world in which every woman is the presiding genius of her own body. In such a world women will truly create a new life, bringing forth not only children . . . but the vision, and the thinking necessary to sustain, console, and alter human existence—a new relationship to the universe. Sexuality, politics, intelligence, power, motherhood, work, community, intimacy will develop new meanings; thinking itself will be transformed.[47]

Plath struggles in the *Ariel* poems to "imagine a world" where she is "the presiding genius of her own body," and the result is often a reshaping of the reader's perception of "sexuality, politics, intelligence, power, motherhood, work, community, [and] intimacy."

The following chapters unfold this argument in a variety of ways. Since biography is more significant than literary history for understanding Plath's poetic development, I have tried to interpret the links between person and persona, between life history and the life as it is portrayed in the poems, while also trying to preserve the essential separateness of Plath's life from her poems. Chapter 2 is primarily an analysis of Plath's relationship to her mother Aurelia and of how their extraordinary intimacy molded Plath's sensibility as both a woman and an artist. Bloomian poetics stresses the poet's relation to the father, but Plath's mother is the dominant parent in her life and may well have exerted a more unmanageable influence than Otto Plath on her poetry. While the main intention of chapter 3 is a reading of *The Bell Jar*, it also expands on my analysis of Plath's personality by exploring the role her dead father played in both her individual growth and in her ideas about male-female relationships.

This biographical context serves as a departure point for chapters 4 and 5, which focus on Plath's imagination. Chapter 4 is concerned with the poetic world and vision she creates for her reader and argues for a more generous reading of her engagement with humanity than previous critics have acknowledged. There are many poems—neglected, in some instances—that do not directly concern themselves with the issues of autonomy and creating a poetic persona—with the "Plath myth." I would like to demonstrate the breadth and richness of Plath's intellect and imagination and draw attention to subject matter in her work that, if not impersonal, reflects a mind engrossed with other concerns than the self. Chapter 5, the conclusion, concentrates on Plath's voice and its deliverance from a passive female body through a process of incarnation. It explores the strategies whereby Plath manipulates her body as a psychic and physical space; imaginatively transforms it into fantastic shapes; submits it to fire; freezes it into statuary; and translates it into figures of speed and flight. This "female body of imagination" she invents and gives voice to I see as her particular contribution to the lyric impulse in poetry.

As the title of my book suggests, I see Plath's life and work as typical in significant ways of "woman and the creative process." For this reason, I have tried to integrate literary criticism with Freudian psychoanalysis and social psychology, so that Plath's life no lor seems as unique, as peculiar to her alone, as it has sometimes been depicted in the past. Initially in my work on this book, this fusion created many strains—not only because of the reputed inadequacies in Freud's handling of female psychology, but because Freudian literary criticism tends to attach the stigma of the abnormal and neurotic to individual personality. As many feminists have pointed out, analysts who appeal to the Freudian paradigm for female psychological development have been especially harsh in their judgments on women who deviate from the "norm." I believe this stigma depends on a misreading of what Freud means by "normal" and on the frequent use of his terminology to prescribe rather than describe psychological conflict. Since I began my work on Plath, there have also been many modifications and refinements of Freudian thought on female psychology and women artists have begun to speak about the conflict between their culturally defined female roles and their perceptions of themselves as artists. My work has been strongly influenced by these new contributions, and I attempt to incorporate them into my reading of Plath.

Two. Perfection Is Terrible

Everywhere accountability is sought, it is usually the instinct for punishing and judging which seeks it.—Friedrich Nietzsche, *Twilight of the Idols*

They say she wrote the letters to keep me happy, to hide the darker side. Sylvia? Putting herself out day after day? The reason she wrote those letters was to get a reply, and she always did.—Aurelia Plath, *New York Times*, October 9, 1979

*I*N a letter dated July 6, 1966, Aurelia Plath complains to Ted Hughes about her daughter's notoriety in the media and the unwelcome attention she has received from journalists and critics. She feels unjustly accused of some terrible mistake in Plath's upbringing, as though her daughter's suicide were somehow her fault.[1] No doubt there is a sting for Aurelia Plath in critical commentary that blames Plath's suicide on "developmental failures" that occurred in infancy and childhood. According to Christopher Bollas and Murray M. Schwartz, for example,

> it seems that the dialectical interaction of mother and child, in which the child could see that she was seen and therefore develop the capacity to establish a rhythm of symbolic relatedness alternating with recognized absence was not firmly established.
>
> Plath's weird mirror experiences indicate a failure in the early months of her life to find herself consistently reflected in the human environment.[2]

As a result of this failure, we are told, "Plath seems helplessly enmeshed in a symbiotic mother-child matrix in which nurture is either inaccessible when needed or mutilative when feared."[3] Evidence for this destructive "mother-child matrix," as for Plath's "incapacity to

45

love," her "self-defeating" psychic activity, and her inability to handle the "crisis of motherhood" is found by Bollas and Schwartz in the poems and *The Bell Jar*, treated as projections of her "psychic and somatic states."[4] One is led to suppose from such analysis that Plath's life represents gross human failures by both Plath and her mother at every stage of her development. As with many psychoanalyses of artists, this one attaches the stigma of the pathological and neurotic to Plath's biography and her "weird" poetry.

It may come as a surprise, then, that I wish to use psychoanalysis as a critical tool for understanding Plath, given my opening argument about her paradigmatic nature as a woman artist. To many, these two lines of argument must seem contradictory: How can one use a method apparently designed to reveal abnormal and aberrant behavior and also argue for representative human qualities?

A Psychoanalytic Prologue

For me, the problem with Schwartz and Bollas's essay is in the rhetoric and not the method. It is a rhetoric of accountability rather than explanation. By this I mean that many of their insights exaggerate normal psychological development, such as Plath's jealousy when her brother Warren is born, or her "phallic identification with her father" (which Freud and other analysts describe as simply one stage or alternative in feminine psychological development) into blameworthy abnormalities. The ordinary passages—childhood, adolescence, motherhood—are all "crises" or "traumas" that Plath, unlike the rest of us, did not successfully manage. Likewise, the metaphorical language of the poet becomes "sick" language—proof, for example, of "the psychotic wish to re-enter the mouth" or "the deepest oral regression."[5] The words *psychotic* and *deepest* are the condemnatory words. They prescribe that "normal" people never feel such unconscious desires and are therefore cut off from sharing Plath's experience.

If we turn to Freud for some assistance in making the distinction between normal and abnormal behavior, we find something very different. In *Psychoanalysis and Feminism*, Juliet Mitchell responds to the common criticism of Freud that he prescribes "normal" behavior by noting that "the very nub of his work was the elimination of an absolute difference between abnormality and normality. Cases of neuroses gave him the clues to normal mental formations, dreams were everybody's everyday or every night psychoses: sexual perversions or inversions were both widespread and could constitute a choice."[6] Freud tells a mother disturbed by her son's homosexuality that "it cannot be classified as an illness; we consider it to be a variation of the sexual function" and that "if he is unhappy, neurotic, torn by conflicts, inhibited in his social life, analysis may bring him harmony, peace of mind, full efficiency, whether he remains homosexual or gets changed."[7] Freud implies that homosexuality, however divergent from culturally accepted norms for sexual behavior, may pose greater problems for the mother's well-being than for the son's.

"Normality," it turns out, is not a major issue of health or illness for Freud, except as an individual responds to the norms of the culture in which he or she grows up: "a normal ego . . . is, like normality, in general, an ideal fiction. Every normal person, in fact is only normal on the average. His ego approximates to that of the psychotic in some part or other and to a greater or lesser extent."[8] Freud's formula for health was a combination of the capacities for work and love. As Juliet Mitchell explains,

> if we want a rough definition of the signs of a state of mental health: health is the uninhibited quest for knowledge, mental illness the painful pursuit of secondary ignorance—a need not to know, though the knowledge will insist on making its presence felt. . . . Early on in his career Freud contended that an aspect of the psychoanalytic "cure" was the release in the patient of the ability to work at intellectual and creative pursuits, and the regaining of the curiosity which had been repressed by the difficulties of the Oedipus complex. This regaining could not be innocent, it had to acknowledge and know all that had happened.[9]

If we accept and pursue this line of reasoning with regard to Plath, a striking contrast emerges between her first and second "breakdowns." At the age of twenty, Plath retreats from her many accomplishments into a severe depression. One of her major symptoms is the inability to read or write.[10] She is dominated by the "need not to know" and becomes nearly catatonic in her inability to describe her anguish. During the final months of her life, though, she completes *The Bell Jar* and writes most of the poems in *Ariel*. She is insistent, too, about the new life she is making for herself and her children. In the top speed with which they were written and in their quest for self-knowledge, *The Bell Jar* and the *Ariel* poems do not look like evidence for a breakdown, but for an extraordinary "release" of "the ability to work at intellectual and creative pursuits." What is needed is a critical language that can at least make this distinction and, even more important, help the reader understand Plath's final effort "to acknowledge and know all that had happened" in her past. A rhetoric of accountability that assigns blame for a particular case of abnormal psychology and makes no attempt to distinguish Plath at the age of twenty from Plath ten years later—that sees the whole life as a botched effort—is inadequate to this task.

Psychoanalysis, a language and method for making what has been unconscious conscious, should be ideal for this purpose, except that Freudian theories of female psychological development are particularly designed to find sickness in women who deviate, as Plath did, from conventional expectations for femininity. The fact of being a poet is in itself a digression from presumably passive feminine aims, but her poems are also described by some psychoanalytic commentators as aggressive and man-hating, and, as in the Bollas and Schwartz essay, as reflections of her inability to deal with motherhood. Feminists argue that this is typical of psychoanalytic theory, that Freud is deterministic in his description of femininity ("Anatomy is destiny"), and that psychoanalytic language is loaded with "assumptions of the primacy of maleness."[11]

For these reasons, there was a period of almost total rejection of Freud and psychoanalytic theory by feminists. With the notable exception of Juliet Mitchell (*Psychoanalysis and Feminism*), feminists turned toward "social and cognitive psychology, which understands feminine development as explicit ideological instruction or formal coercion" (Chodorow, p. 33). According to many feminists, women are not women by nature, but are taught to accept their secondary, inferior roles by a male-dominated society, and orthodox psychoanalysis is one major ideological underpinning for such domination.

Only recently have feminists returned to psychoanalysis to account for the recalcitrance of our gender arrangements and our "ideal fictions," our norms for masculinity and femininity. In *The Reproduction of Mothering*, Nancy Chodorow argues that social conditioning is insufficient explanation for "the tenacity of self-definition, self-concept, and psychological need [by both men and women] to maintain aspects of traditional roles which continue even in the face of ideological shifts, counter-instruction, and the lessening of masculine coercion which the women's movement has produced" (p. 34). More specifically, Chodorow claims that women continue to be defined primarily as mothers. Despite women's supposed liberation from traditional expectations, "mothering" is still synonymous with femininity, and no amount of "counter-instruction" has been persuasive enough to disengage the biological fact of giving birth from the social role of mothering. Because mothering capacities seem to be built into female psychic structure, and not simply "behavioral acquisitions," Chodorow feels compelled to use psychoanalysis as her main critical tool: "psychoanalytic theory remains the most coherent, convincing theory of personality development available for an understanding of fundamental aspects of the psychology of women in our society, in spite of its biases" (p. 142). On a cultural level, as well, psychoanalysis helps to explain the perpetuation of "mothering" as woman's chief social role.

> The psychoanalytic account shows not only how men come to grow away from their families and to participate in the public sphere. It shows also how women grow up to have both the generalized relational capacities and needs and how women and men come to create the kinds of interpersonal relationships which make it likely that women will remain in the domestic sphere—in the sphere of reproduction—and will in turn mother the next generation. (P. 38)

In a similar vein, Dorothy Dinnerstein, in *The Mermaid and the Minotaur*, argues that there is an "unresolved core of ambivalence . . . that centers upon our species' most characteristic, vital, and dangerous gift: our gift for enterprise, for self-creation."[12] This ambivalence is expressed in our "normal" sexual arrangements between men and women, which support "enterprise" and "self-creation" in men, and restrain the exercise of these human gifts in women. As Dinnerstein queries, "What now keeps woman out of history? Why is her access to the public domain, even in the technologically advanced sectors of present-day society, still so restricted, her formally recognized creative contribution still so much slimmer than man's?" (p. 24). Instead of attacking the social and political superstructure which supports male privilege, Dinnerstein, like Chodorow, seeks answers to this question in human sexual development, and her first answer is "that *for virtually every living person it is a woman—usually the mother—who has provided the main initial contact with humanity and with nature*" (Dinnerstein's italics, p. 26). The substance of Dinnerstein's book is an argument that links the infant at the mother's breast with humanity's self-creation in time—man's peculiar place in nature as the history-making animal. The essential corollary to her argument is woman's virtual exclusion from this project, an exclusion almost as conspicuous as man's exclusion from the activities of mothering. The parallel question to "What now keeps woman out of history?" is Chodorow's, "So we can ask, why are mothers women? Why is the person who routinely does all those activities that go into parenting not a man?" (p. 11).

Chodorow and Dinnerstein reformulate both the questions and the answers psychoanalysis offers and the result may well be a radical change in the psychoanalytic account of development in both sexes, but particularly women. Both theorists are especially concerned with mothering and the source of cultural ambivalence toward women in the pre-Oedipal relationship between mother and child. By "ambivalence," I mean "contradictory emotional or psychological attitudes . . . often with one attitude inhibiting the expression of another."[13] On a social level, once again, this ambivalence is expressed in a man's right to enter and invent the world and woman's complementary segregation in the smaller, separate world of the home and nursery. Or, as Mrs. Willard, one of Plath's tradition-bound mother figures in *The Bell Jar* so succinctly puts it: "What a man is is an arrow into the future and what a woman is is the place the arrow shoots off from."[14] On an individual level, this ambivalence is "expressed in behavior by alternating obedience and rebellion, followed by self-reproach" and by the simultaneous attraction to and repulsion from an object, person, or action. The result is often guilt and paralysis—an inability to act upon either impulse.[15] While this ambivalence is common to both men's and women's attitudes toward the mother, it is a much stronger force in women's psychic disposition generally, according to Chodorow and Dinnerstein.[16]

As the Bollas and Schwartz essay on Plath illustrates, these two issues—woman's role as mother and feminine ambivalence—are central issues in psychoanalyzing Plath and judging both her own capacities as a mother and the mothering she received from Aurelia Plath. Chodorow and Dinnerstein's theories therefore have important implications for a revised, feminist psychoanalysis of both Plath's life and her art. *The Bell Jar* and many of the *Ariel* poems are concerned with the difficulties of autonomy and self-creation and with the competing claims of motherhood and art on a woman poet. Such poems reveal in Plath an "unresolved core of ambivalence" toward her femininity that is not so much a sign of her personal neurosis as it is a critical confrontation with the sexual differences described by Chodorow and Dinnerstein as built into feminine psychic structure and reinforced by our culture's sexual arrangements. As we shall see in a later chapter, Plath's ambivalence is nearly a governing principle in her poetry, which frequently explores a paralyzed or guilt-ridden state of consciousness where the speaker is simultaneously attracted to and repelled by an object, person, or situation. I will treat this habitual ambivalence, described by so many commentators as symptomatic of Plath's diseased mind, as inherent in feminine personality. Similarly, the frequent "boundary confusion and lack of sense of separateness from the world" in Plath's poems have been used by one critic as evidence for her schizophrenic perspective and relationship to the world,[17] while Chodorow's analysis of the daughter's pre-Oedipal relationship to her mother suggests that it is a typical characteristic of female psychology.[18]

In this chapter, I will show how Chodorow and Dinnerstein's stress on the pre-Oedipal period of development contributes to a fuller understanding of Plath's life, and especially her relationship to her mother, with whom she sustained an intimacy described by Aurelia as "psychic osmosis" (*LH*, p. 32). The two periods of Plath's life when she suffered greatest emotional disturbance are paradig-

matic of feminine psychological development, involved as they are
with issues of "separation, identification without merging, mitigation of dependency" on maternal nurture,[19] and in both instances,
there also seems to be an "internal emotional triangle" with her
mother and a man which contributes to the difficulty of this separation.[20] During her first breakdown, she retreats from a disillusioning
experience with a man to complete dependency on her mother.
When she emerges from psychiatric treatment, she rebels against
Aurelia and enters a phase of sexual experimentation that concludes
with her marriage to Ted Hughes.

Her marriage, as she describes it (see chap. 1), fulfills a pattern
of dependency on a man, home, and babies to give her a securely
feminine identity. When Hughes leaves her, she experiences many
of the old terrors—an emptiness and lack of identity similar to her
first breakdown—but instead of returning to her mother in America,
Plath struggles not "to go back to the womb or retreat" (LH, p. 469;
October 16, 1962) and "to make a life all my own as fast as I can"
(LH, p. 465; October 9, 1962). At the same time, she is fighting, she
says, for an artistic identity independent of Hughes. In her final
months, she returns in her art to the first breakdown. Fearing that
old patterns may repeat themselves, she intends to recover the past
and work it through to a new conclusion and a new life. Inevitably,
this personal struggle for an individual identity, dependent neither
on maternal nurture nor a husband, comes to mirror the larger problems women face when they venture outside a developmental pattern that is both strongly internalized and systematically reproduced
on the social level.

The discussion that follows therefore intertwines the unique
qualities of Plath's life and relationships with the norms for womanhood imposed on her by her culture. In this way, I hope that her life
and work will become available to the reader as exemplary rather
than abnormal expressions of woman and the creative process.

The All-American Girl

The adjectives that recur in portraits and anecdotes about Plath from
friends, relatives, teachers, even casual acquaintances, are "typical,"

"all-American," "bright," "eager," "well-rounded," "prim and pro-per," and "middle-class." There is no melodramatic villainy or hard-ship in her upbringing or education, and instead of "developmental failures," Plath's life history often looks from the outside like a female version of a Horatio Alger success story. In his introduction to Nancy Hunter Steiner's memoir of Plath, *A Closer Look at Ariel*, George Stade summarizes the years before her first suicide attempt.

> The social cast of her personality, anesthetic, frozen in a cover-girl smile, mother-directed rather than father-haunted, historical and local rather than mythographic, pragmatic in its protective coloring, fiercely self-denying and self-controlled, anxious, up-tight, and doomed, seems to have remained in charge during her first three years at Smith College.[21]

He concludes by describing Plath as "the American Girl as we want her"—"anxious to comply" with parental, institutional, and social demands made on her (*A Closer Look*, p. 31). Through her junior year at Smith, there was nothing outwardly unusual about Plath, except that "she continued to do what you were supposed to do, only better than anyone else" (*A Closer Look*, p. 30). She was, Plath says, "a rabid teenage pragmatist,"[22] someone who played by the rules. In high school, she received high grades, but she was also "popular" and "well-rounded."

> She played tennis, was on the girls' basketball team, was co-editor of the school newspaper, *The Bradford*, joined a high school sorority, Sub-Debs, painted decorations for class dances, went on college weekend dates, was Lady Agatha in the class play, *The Admirable Crichton*.[23]

Perhaps it is the perfection that is disturbing. If there is something idiosyncratic about her life, it is an extreme adherence to the expec-tations of relatives, friends, teachers, and benefactors. These exter-nal social pressures are matched by strong internal desires to con-form. Plath wholeheartedly embraces the norms for American women in the 1950s. In *Letters Home*, we get the portrait of a sunny

"Sivvy," a too-good-to-be-true voice of a young woman passing through familiar avatars of feminine perfection. A high school boyfriend describes her as a "supernormal teenager,"[24] and from her mother we learn that she frequently tried to hide her intelligence and achievements from high school dates for fear of being regarded as a "brain." She was apparently ecstatic at the success of her disguise (*LH*, p. 38). At Smith, her honors thesis advisor, George Gibian, praises her as a "wish-fulfillment" student[25] and her near-perfect academic record of mostly *A*s gives ample proof of the intellectual approval she won from her professors. She aspired to be the ideal "Smith woman," described by one of Plath's class-mates as "both efficient and well-rounded in her traditional role—that is, as someone who would eventually marry a professional man, raise a family, and yet be expected to converse about Rilke over a gourmet meal she had prepared herself."[26] As Adlai Stevenson's commencement address at Plath's graduation assured these overeducated future housewives, this was a worthy ambition for a Smith graduate.[27]

Plath's mental breakdown and suicide attempt in the summer after her junior year are but a brief lapse in her role of garnering awards and accolades and dating the best young men from the finest schools. Very soon,

> the false, flat, bright, insistent voice of the go-getter is back in the scrapbook to claim that "exams & papers proved I hadn't lost either my repetitive or my creative intellect as I had feared . . . a semester of reconstruction ends with an infinitely more solid if less flashingly spectacular flourish than last year's." (Quoted in *A Closer Look*, pp. 34–35)

Nancy Hunter Steiner, Plath's roommate in her senior year at Smith, had not yet met her before the breakdown, and reports their first meeting as a surprise. She expected someone socially maladjusted—a "maverick," a "rebel," someone "plain or dull or deliberately dowdy," or "a girl who rejected all frivolity in pursuit of academic and literary excellence" (*A Closer Look*, p. 55). Instead, Steiner says, Plath

could have been an airline stewardess or the ingenuous heroine
of a B-movie. She did not appear tortured or alienated; at times
it was difficult for me to believe that she had ever felt a self-
destructive impulse. She seemed eager to create the impression
of the typical American girl, the product of a hundred years of
middle-class propriety. (*A Closer Look,* p. 59)

For one semester, Plath dyes her hair and plays a platinum blonde
femme fatale; but when being interviewed for fellowships, she self-
consciously decides to return to her demure "nice girl" looks: "My
brown-haired personality is most studious, charming, and earnest"
(*LH,* p. 141; September 27, 1954), she explains to her mother.

Even after her marriage, when we might expect a less conventional, more Bohemian personality to appear in a literary London
milieu, she defeats us again. A. Alvarez reports that "Mrs. Hughes"
was "briskly American: bright, clean, competent, like a young
woman in a cookery advertisement." Fooled by her self-effacing
housewifery, Alvarez had no idea for some time that "Mrs. Hughes"
was Sylvia Plath, whose poems he had read, praised, and recom-
mended for publication in his job as editor for the *Observer*.[28]

There are suggestions in almost all the reported descriptions we
have of Plath that she wore a mask; that she could be as manipula-
tive as she seemed ingenuous; and that she sometimes doggedly
overplayed her role of "typical American girl." Her compulsion to
do everything right and to gain everyone's approval looked to some
cynical observers as coldly calculated. It is hard, though, to separate
envy from honest appraisal. There is a certain amount of carefully
dissimulated cattiness in Steiner's comparison of Plath's facade to
that of a stewardess or B-movie heroine, and from another, more
jaundiced Smith woman, we get outright nastiness: "You had the
feeling she would be in saddle shoes the rest of her life."[29] There is a
tinge of jealousy, too, in the description by Jane Kopp, her American friend at Cambridge (and competitor for attention), of Plath's
presence on campus: she "always dressed in the *Mademoiselle* idea of
American couture" and "she had a way in those days of gushing
and gurgling in the most typical American tourist style."[30] At the
same time, an English male friend, Mallory Woeber, remembers her

quite differently as turning heads wherever she went and living her life with the intensity of a genius.[31]

Rather than attempting to gauge whether Plath's public appearance was sincere or phony, it may be better to acknowledge how hard she tried to create herself according to accepted ideal fictions of young womanhood. She was certainly sincere about wanting to be perfect. In her high school diary, she writes,

> I think I would like to call myself "The girl who wanted to be God." Yet if I were not in this body, where would I be—perhaps I am destined to be classified and qualified. But, oh, I cry out against it. I am I—I am powerful—but to what extent? I am I. . . . How awful to be anyone but I. I have a terrible egotism. I love my flesh, my face, my limbs with overwhelming devotion. . . . I have erected in my mind an image of myself—idealistic and beautiful. Is not that image, free from blemish, the true self, the true perfection? Am I wrong when this image insinuates itself between me and the merciless mirror? . . .
>
> Never, never, never will I reach the perfection I long for with all my soul—my paintings, my poems, my stories—all poor, poor reflections. (*LH*, p. 40; November 13, 1949)

What Plath shows here is an extraordinarily grandiose ego-ideal: she wants nothing less than godlike perfection. This is matched by what Harriet Rosenstein calls a "terror of diffuseness," an insecurity detectable in that rather odd assertion of the limits of her body—"Yet if I were not in this body where would I be?"—and in the recognition of dualism—the "merciless" mirror reflection versus the ideal self in her mind's eye.[32] The desire for perfection and the equally strong impulses toward freedom from constraints are perhaps the most important polarity in this early confession. For "perfection," particularly a feminine kind of perfection, seems inextricably associated with social constraints in Plath's eyes. As Steiner describes Plath, "she wore the mantle of a bourgeois lady, as inhibiting and restraining as a straitjacket" (*A Closer Look*, p. 61), and she could be rigidly moralistic in her judgments of the foibles of her peers.[33] Cyrilly Abels, the editor at *Mademoiselle* where Plath worked for one month before her breakdown, also comments on her stiffness: "I never

found anyone so unspontaneous so consistently, especially in one
so young. She was simply all facade, too polite, too well-brought-up
and well-disciplined."[34] Plath's disciplined supernormality is frightening when we learn that some of her first words to her mother
after her suicide attempt were, "Oh, if only I could be a freshman
again. I so wanted to be a Smith woman" (*LH*, p. 126).

Abels's penetration of this studied perfection also shows that
Plath was having severe problems holding her mask in place—that
what she saw in the mirror before her breakdown was a merciless
image of herself that could "never, never, never" be like the "idealistic and beautiful" woman she had "erected in her mind." As in *The
Bell Jar* with the heroine Esther Greenwood, there was a serious
conflict between the public Sylvia, supposedly living out the dream
of the American Girl, and the internal Sylvia, who felt she could not
live up to her ideal self. Ostensibly, Plath's life looks fabricated out
of the glib magazine copy in the woman's slicks (indeed, after her
marriage to Ted Hughes, *Mademoiselle* does a little feature story on
her and her husband in their Boston writing garret). Why did Plath
feel such a strong need to be the *Seventeen* teenager, the *Mademoiselle*
and Smith girl, the American ingenue at Cambridge (she even mod-
els for the local stores), and the briskly competent wife and mother
who longs for subscriptions to *Ladies' Home Journal* and *Good House-
keeping* when she is pregnant and feeling "cowy"? The pressure of
doing everything right takes the shape of conforming to "teen tips
on popularity," "Can this marriage be saved?" (a regular feature in
Ladies' Home Journal), and *Reader's Digest* articles on virginity like
those Esther Greenwood's mother sends her; but the question is,
why does Plath feel such a strong need to respond to the authority
of American pulp?

"The Best Mummy a Girl Ever Had"

It is probably a truism in biography to assert that the parents, and
particularly the mother, are the most important formative influ-
ences on a person's life. But with Plath, this is an understatement.
Plath's desire for perfection was, at least in part, a personality trait
she learns from her mother Aurelia. I would like to avoid blaming

Aurelia Plath for her daughter's breakdowns and eventual suicide, because everything she did seems to be motivated by maternal devotion; and, it seems to me, she can only be seen as a rather remarkable figure for the way she managed to bring up two small children without the emotional and financial support of a father—and to raise them with all the advantages usually available to more wealthy families.

Aurelia's marriage to Otto Plath was not an easy one. In her introduction to *Letters Home,* Aurelia describes her marriage as happy, but not without some rather severe strains. Otto was twenty-one years her senior and her former professor. One suspects from Aurelia's worshipful attitude toward learning (which she would later instill in Sylvia) that the marriage was based as much on admiration and awe for Otto's intellectual superiority as on affection. On Otto's side, there seems to be an expectation that Aurelia would be an efficient secretary, research assistant, and editor for his scholarly work on bees as well as a wife and mother. Aurelia portrays Otto as an unsociable and autocratic figure who exercised a "rightful dominance" in arranging all aspects of their life. Fairly early, she decided that to keep a "peaceful home," she "would simply have to become more submissive" to "der Herr des Hauses" (*LH*, pp. 12–13). During the first eighteen months of their marriage, she helps to expand Otto's doctoral thesis into book form (*Bumblebees and Their Ways*), and a note of resentment slips into her narration when his "seventy-plus reference books" and scholarly writing take over the dining room: "No paper or book was to be moved! I drew a plan of the arrangement and managed to have friends in occasionally for dinner the one evening a week that my husband gave a course at Harvard night school, always replacing every item correctly before his return" (*LH*, p. 12). And the first years of marriage seem ruled less by romance or even simple domestic bliss than the silence of the library. She was disappointed in the shape their life was taking.

> Social life was almost nil for us as a married couple. My dreams of "open house" for students and the frequent entertaining of good friends among the faculty were not realized. During the

first year of our married life, all had to be given up for THE BOOK. After Sylvia was born, it was THE CHAPTER. (*LH*, pp. 12–13)

In the last four years of their marriage, Otto is even more remote because of his illness. Refusing to see a doctor, he mistakenly diagnoses his diabetes mellitus as lung cancer. As Aurelia describes these years, a grim fatefulness hangs over the household while Otto's health deteriorates. Sylvia's younger brother Warren, born two and one-half years after Sylvia (and as planned to the day by Otto), was also sickly and placed demands on Aurelia's time (*LH*, pp. 19–22). Some of the earliest correspondence between Sylvia and her mother dates from Sylvia's visits to Aurelia's mother, "Grammy" Schober, while Aurelia is nursing Warren through allergic asthma attacks. We can assume some jealousy from Sylvia, watching her mother's attention preoccupied with a sick father and brother. It is not until August, 1940, when Otto stubs his toe and it turns black, that his diabetes is discovered—but too late to save his leg, which is amputated for gangrene, and too late to save his life. In November of 1940, Otto Plath dies of an embolism, leaving a wife and two children, Sylvia, age eight, and Warren, age six. Aurelia narrates these events in a way that shows her frustration. When the diabetes is discovered, she can only think, "All this needn't have happened; it needn't have happened," and the doctor remarks, "How could such a brilliant man be so stupid?" (*LH*, p. 23). Otto Plath's death was the result of his stubborn conviction that he knew best. This obstinacy was an imposition of dread on his wife and children that could be interpreted, and eventually was by Sylvia in her poems, as a willful desertion.

However much he was loved, Otto Plath emerges from Aurelia's memoir as an oppressive ruler over their home life; and however much he was mourned, his death must also have provided some relief from this oppression. Aurelia, on the other hand, emerges as a supremely competent and self-sufficient young woman, whose capabilities are only enhanced by the death of her husband and the successful effort to support and raise Sylvia and Warren. Despite her avowed devotion to her father, Sylvia, too, must have felt her father's death as a relief. The day after Otto dies, Sylvia returns from school with a contract for her mother: "I PROMISE NEVER TO MARRY AGAIN. Signed: _____" (*LH*, p. 25). Aurelia signs the pledge as reassurance to her daughter, whose classmates raised the spectre of a stepfather. Did she not want another man to replace her father, because she loved him too much to accept a substitute? Or did she not want to share her mother's love, now that Aurelia had at last been freed from nursing Otto? Both motives were at work and would contribute later to the guilty ambivalence toward her parents that she explores in her art. Aurelia reports that Sylvia remembered the contract in later years and anxiously inquired whether it had prevented her mother's remarriage (*LH*, p. 25). She also justified her minimal mourning for Otto as an attempt to save her children from the trauma of their father's death. Later Plath will interpret this as lack of feeling and bitterness over Otto's leaving so little money to support them.

Aurelia Plath is an irresistible, if gentle pressure on her daughter in the early years. We have, for example, a letter to Sylvia dated April 8, 1939, when she was staying with "Grammy." The letter opens with a compliment on Sylvia's report card. Then Aurelia gives some instruction on how to color Goldilocks's hair. It concludes with a lesson on art that includes new vocabulary words. She mentions her daughter's art book and its illustration of a little boy making a bunny out of clay. Aurelia uses this as a way of teaching her daughter the meaning of the words *model* and *curve*. She goes on, as a good elementary school teacher might, to urge her daughter to find curves in the pictures hanging around Grammy Schober's house and particularly calls attention to a print of Whistler's mother, noting that he must have loved his mother very much to paint this portrait. Even this is not enough. By her own example of creating a story with "Dick and Jane" textbook characters drawing pictures of animals with curved lines, with the new vocabulary words underlined, Aurelia encourages the seven-year-old Sylvia to use her imagination, and perhaps to show, like Whistler, affection for her mother through art (Box 1, MSS II). What is curious about this is the didacticism—the seizure of an opportunity like letter writing to mold and educate her daughter. She prods her to try writing words instead of printing them, or encloses a poem that she hopes Sylvia will read if it is typed for

her (Box 1, MSS II; [1939]). Plath's obedient responses to this prod-
ding are equally remarkable: "In music I did the fingering just like
you told me to. And I kept saying to myself 'This is what mother
would want me to do' so I got along very well" (Box 1, MSS II;
January, 1943). In reading these letters, one is reminded of Cyrilly
Abels's comment on the nineteen-year-old Plath: "I never found
anyone so unspontaneous so consistently. . . . She was . . . too
polite, too well-brought-up and well-disciplined."

Plath's desire to please her mother and share everything with
her during these years is apparent in the voluminous correspondence from girl scout camp—or whenever she is away from her
mother, even for a few days. From camp, she writes nearly every
day, and not perfunctory "duty" letters, but fully detailed descriptions of what she did, almost moment by moment, from dawn until
dusk. The letters abound with lists—of expenses and budgets, how
many pieces of bread she eats at each meal, and of places and
camping itineraries. Plath sends inventories of her days, as if no
detail were too small to be insignificant or uninteresting to her
mother, and promises even more elaborate descriptions when she
returns home: "When I get home maybe you will go to bed when I
do some nights and I will tell you every detail about camp. It all
seems like a happy dream" (Box 1, MSS II; [1943?]). The fact that
Aurelia saved all these letters, plus childhood school papers, early
drawings, locks of hair and other scraps of memory for so many
years is, in itself, homage to the early bond between mother and
daughter. Plath is also a very prim little girl, expressing disapproval,
for example, of "two new girls" at camp, who say "ain't," "youse,"
"kids, guys": "It just hurts my ears. I long for my family's soft,
sweet talk" (Box 1, MSS II; [1943?]). She is everything a mother
could wish for, as Aurelia, in her encouragement and attention, is
everything a daughter could hope for.

Only in Plath's art do we discover any criticism of her upbringing. In "The Disquieting Muses," written while Plath taught at
Smith in 1957–58, the mother is accused of not preparing her
daughter to deal with life. As a result, she is haunted by

> . . . those three ladies
> Nodding by night around my bed,
> Mouthless, eyeless, with stitched bald head.[35]

These witchlike godmothers and what they represent are ambiguous. As we shall see, their featurelessness ("heads like darning eggs") is an ultimate horror in Plath's poetic world, which is filled with images of baldness, blankness, black-and-white voids. In this poem, however, they are pitted against the mother's conventional wisdom. The mother is an eternal optimist "whose witches always, always / Got baked into gingerbread." In minimizing the destructive energies outside her little home, she leaves her children vulnerable.

> . . . you fed
> My brother and me cookies and Ovaltine
> And helped the two of us to choir:
> 'Thor is angry: boom boom boom!
> Thor is angry: we don't care!'
> But those ladies broke the panes.
>
> (TC, p. 59)

The daughter wonders whether her mother can even see the muses or whether her charms—"Words to rid me of those three ladies"—are simply ineffectual to break "their vigil in gowns of stone" around her daughter.

At the end of the poem, the mother floats away, buoyed by her fool's vision,

> On a green balloon bright with a million
> Flowers and bluebirds that never were
> Never, never, found anywhere.
>
> (TC, p. 59)

There are no bluebirds of happiness, no happily-ever-afters for the daughter, who cannot dance or play the piano like other little girls: "I learned, I learned, I learned elsewhere / From muses unhired by you, dear mother." Yet the mother is also peculiarly responsible for their presence—"and this is the kingdom you bore me to, / Mother, mother"—as though the only alternative to her mother's flimsy "soap bubble" world is a place of long shadows in the "setting sun / That never brightens or goes down" (TC, p. 60). The word "bore" also implies birth, as if to say, "So this is the world you gave me at birth," a world of death, where the shadow she casts looms larger than her body.

Yet the daughter's final attitude is one of obedience both to the ladies and her mother. Like the darning egg faces of the three muses, she wears an expressionless mask: "But no frown of mine / Will betray the company I keep" (*TC*, p. 60). For her mother, this unfrowning mask is unquestioning, obedient, and uncritical of her mother's Mary Poppins vision of the world. The poem appears to record a moment in Plath's life when she forever left behind her mother's hopes that she would be like other little "schoolgirls"—a princess in the "twinkle-dress" for the "glow-worm song." Inwardly, she is "heavy-footed," "Tone-deaf and yes, unteachable," while outwardly she sustains the illusion of being a docile princess for her mother.

At least one answer to the question of why Plath wore the mask of an all-American "golden girl" is that it pleased her mother. In "The Disquieting Muses," as in *The Bell Jar* later, considerable hostility is expressed toward Aurelia, but in the correspondence, an endless and occasionally disturbing stream of devotion and gratitude is directed to "the best Mummy a girl ever had." We know from Aurelia's introduction to *Letters Home* that her own family was too poor to send her to a place like Smith—she went to business school instead—or to provide music and drawing lessons, girl scout camp, or any of the cultural advantages Aurelia lavished on her own children. We also know that Aurelia was determined to be a "textbook" mother—to follow all the advice on childrearing available and to give Sylvia and Warren everything she could to make their future success and happiness possible.[36] It is more than likely that Aurelia was living out her own fantasies of an ideal girlhood—of what she wanted for herself as a child—through her daughter.

Despite Plath's poetic assertion that she was "unteachable," in her letters she sounds like a "textbook" child. During her first two years at Smith, the letters continue to be exceptionally rosy and innocent, with problems no darker than school assignments and what to wear at the next big college weekend. If Plath is worried about anything, it is how to succeed as a Smith girl.

One sure thing, I'll have to learn bridge and knitting during
next summer. They are nice "small" ways of conforming.
There's so much I "can't wait for"—the Nov. *Seventeen*, the
right boy (whoever he is poor thing) for my Freshman year, my
first English theme to come back.—Life here is lovely—. (Box 1,
MSS II; October 20, 1950)

[The Honor Board's members are] . . . poised, lovely, assured. I
wondered how so many people could devote all their energy to
extracurricular activities and still be brilliant, beautiful, popular.
They are perfect Smith girls. I just hope I can contribute in some
small way to this huge city. (Box 1, MSS II; October 25, 1950)

Such letters are no doubt exactly what Plath felt her mother wanted
to hear from her "well-adjusted" daughter, and Plath is ardent
enough about being a Smith girl that it is difficult to discount her
own desire to conform and excel. As a scholarship student, Plath
was especially grateful and desirous of showing her worthiness. She
pressures herself continually to live up to her many opportunities.

Now I will plunge into those darn critical English themes with
renewed vigor and go through my art exercises with that
"means-to-an-end" gleam in my eye. If only I can meet all the
opportunities. . . . I just can't stand the idea of being medi-
ocre. . . . I'll be studying and sleeping all Thanksgiving, I
fear. . . . I am so busy finding out about Smith that I have no
time to be either homesick or lovesick. . . . If only I'm good
enough to deserve all this! (*LH*, p. 57; October 31, 1950)

When Plath discovers that her scholarship is endowed by Olive
Higgins Prouty, the writer who created Stella Dallas, she sends off a
letter of gratitude that wins her a lifelong friend and another mother
figure with whom to share her life.

I wonder . . . if I have revealed even a small part of my love for
Smith. There are so many little details . . . the glimpse of Paradise from my window. All this and so much more. . . . I just
want you to understand that you are responsible, in a sense, for

the formation of an individual, and I am fortunate enough to be that person. (*LH*, p. 62; December 1, 1950)

Esther Greenwood's drop-dead cynicism and wicked little caricatures in *The Bell Jar* tell us that Plath must have been looking at people and situations around her with some irony; but her letters are lacking in humor, much less wit, and abundant in this earnest, girlish enthusiasm. Plath's satiric streak—what Ted Hughes later describes as "the vivid, cruel words she could use to pin down her acquaintances and even her close friends"—is totally suppressed.[37] The omission of this sharper side from *Letters Home* leads some commentators to question their validity as self-revelation. Peter Davison, although commenting on a postbreakdown Sylvia, suggests something close to fraud in the way Plath "managed" her relationship with Aurelia: she was "cozy with her and would talk one way in her presence, another outside."[38]

"Lovely, Immoral, Radical" Eddie and the "Sweet Wonderman"

"Sivvy" is not so much a fraud as she is Plath's "normal" version of herself, an ideal fiction for budding young womanhood. There is evidence of another, less well adjusted, more rebellious young woman than Aurelia's ingenue. Simultaneously with her letters home, Plath has what seems to be a substantial correspondence with Eddie Cohen, a student at Roosevelt University in Chicago, initiated by his fan letter for one of her stories in *Seventeen*. While Aurelia is the guardian for Sivvy, Eddie Cohen becomes the confidant for the less-than-perfect and vulnerable Sylvia. Immediately, Plath's irony crops up in this correspondence, showing another personality than the one we meet in *Letters Home*. At the same time that she is declaring to her mother how eager she is for the next issue of *Seventeen*, and how proud she is of her publications in that magazine, she writes to Eddie, "I consider my story not far from the usual 'Seventeen' drivel" and "other stories I considered better, less trite, less syrupy, came home with those horribly polite little slips" (Box 1, MSS II; August 6, 1950).

Only a few of Plath's replies to Eddie are available, but Eddie is fond of quoting and responding to specifics in her previous letters, so that the content of their dialogue is apparent. Almost all of their letters are about sex: virginity, promiscuity, the pros and cons of premarital sex, marriage, the double standard, and Plath's difficult search for an ideal and "idealistic" husband—idealistic meaning a virgin himself. In one early exchange, it is obvious that Plath has been using Eddie as a sounding board for questions about the social risks of giving up her virginity. He answers, "I not only did not advocate promiscuity, I think I very specifically said the person who indulges in it is likely to be unhappy. . . . You say that everyone sets on the girl like buzzards. Is it worth it, you ask? Chances of getting an idealistic husband are damaged? The only thing I can say to that is just plain old-fashioned B.S." (Box 1, MSS II; September 15, 1950). Plath is also worried about the implications of marriage, and Eddie rather skillfully sums up the future options of a Smith woman.

> I guess, though, that the main knot exists in your indecision as to whether you want to be tied down. . . . Also, why does marriage necessarily have to interfere with your chosen career? . . . You might as well face it—we "radicals" believe that a wife should share her husband's life and experiences, but for most of the world a woman has a definite social role in marriage which will not permit the existance [sic] which I am inclined to feel you want before you start on the home and kiddies and dinner-every-night stuff. If I may get bitter for a moment, the nice clean boys of your acquaintance (you know, the ones who want the mother of their kids to be a virgin, etc.) would probably faint dead away at the thought of their wife living in the jungles of Mexico or on the left bank of Paris. Which means only this—that the type of individual who believes in what I somewhat contemptuously refer to as conventional morality also leads the type of life which is apt to be somewhat conventional. Literarywise, such a situation is likely to be rather sterile. (Yes, I've heard of Emily Dickinson.) You can have your career, or you can raise a family. I should be

extremely surprised, however, you can do both within the framework of the social structure in which you now live (Box 2, MSS II; September 16, 1951)

These letters show that while outwardly Plath may appear perfectly content with the shape her life is taking, inwardly she is balking at its limited possibilities. The mention of Emily Dickinson is intriguing, too. Was Plath already wondering whether she would have to sacrifice a "normal" woman's life if she wanted to be a poet? The reference suggests that Plath envisioned a choice—a life as either an Emily Dickinson recluse or a Wellesley matron fitting Eddie's description.

It is reasonable that a girl raised in the 1950s would not discuss her sex life with her mother, since she was not expected to have one. Yet it seems unusual that Plath would not choose someone closer to her as a counselor and intimate—unless, which seems probable, she regarded sex as an unacceptable topic for "nice" girls to discuss. For the well-brought-up young lady from Wellesley, Eddie Cohen was not the "right boy" for her freshman year, but he was a "lovely, immoral, radical" outsider (Box 1, MSS II; May 19, 1951; Eddie Cohen quotes Sylvia)—a safe because distant sharer of Plath's multiplying questions, doubts, and fears about men and sex and the life that seemed plotted out for her. When Plath is given the opportunity to introduce her pen pal to Aurelia in the spring of 1951, she is extremely rude and fends off anything more than a brief introduction. As Ed Cohen describes this first meeting with Plath, it was a "fiasco," and it becomes clear that she preferred his letters to his physical presence in her life—the reminder, perhaps, of a less well adjusted personality

> I did not, foolishly, tell her or anyone else of my plans. I borrowed my parent's [sic] car on the pretense of visiting relatives in Detroit, which I did, for about one hour. Then I drove across Canada, pausing only to admire Niagara Falls, and on to Smith. I arrived, unheralded, just as she was preparing to leave for home. I drove her home, and we made desperate attempts at conversation.

Picture the situation. I had just dropped out of the gray New England sky. Syl was still a teen-ager, and a rather sheltered one at that. I was four years older, and a somewhat evil older man, to boot. (Put my living with a woman in the context of 1950s morality.) While her contact with literary society consisted largely of teas with Auden, I had been drinking in disreputable bars with the likes of Algren and Motley. Ann Davidow [a classmate of Plath's at Smith] may have been the only other Jewish person she had ever met. I was probably unshaven, and certainly hadn't slept in two days.

Now, on top of all that, there was *the* problem that faced us both: to maintain, and yet step beyond, the unchallenged images of ourselves we had created on paper, and build a real relationship. I know that I was frightened. I suggest that she was, too, and for the reasons cited above, considerably moreso. *Not* of having to integrate me into her mother's world, but just of dealing with me, period.

With sophisticated hindsight, I can speculate that I might have broken the tension between us by touching her, and thus possibly introducing the fact that I was indeed real and corporeal. However, I didn't, and this finally led to the scene on her mother's doorstep. . . . she did *not* really introduce us. I learned later that Mrs. Plath was horrified when she learned that I was "that" Eddie, and that Syl had not invited me to stay. . . .

Strangely enough, none of this seemed to effect [*sic*] the tremendous rapport Syl and I had on paper, and we very shortly had the Post Office working overtime. We made plans to meet again, and did, the following spring. I came with a friend, and we double-dated with Syl and a friend. This time there was no trauma—nor anything else. Our relationship seemed as sterile in person as it was fertile via the mails.[39]

The counterpoint of Eddie's "fertile" correspondence with Plath's letters to her mother, particularly when the subject is Dick Norton, her "steady" during her first two years at Smith, illuminates the conflicts which contribute to her eventual suicide attempt. Eight months before Plath's attempted suicide, Eddie predicts a nervous breakdown and advises her to see a psychiatrist.

I am not striving to be an alarmist, although such may be my
effect. I am merely taking cognizance of the fact that all the
danger signals which I have noted in you from time to time
have suddenly all popped up at once. The Yale Man [i.e., Myron Lotz], peculiarly enough, is one of them. From time to time
you have related to me stories of incidents in which a handsome
stranger has popped up and you have established an immediate
and miraculous rapport with him. Then, after a rapturous few
days, he fades out of your life, temp. or perm. There have been
at least a half dozen such occurances [sic] (The Mad Russian,
The Biologist on the Bus, to name a couple). You attach tremendous significance to these meetings, and what their real meaning may be, I haven't the foggiest notion. The fact that they
invariably happen, (or at least are related to me) during periods
of stress seems more than a mere coincidence. (Box 2, MSS II;
January 2, 1953)

The "period of stress" Eddie alludes to is brought on by Plath's disillusionment and breakup with "Allan," the pseudonym she assigns to
Dick Norton in her letters to Eddie. Ostensibly, Norton is the perfect
mate for Sivvy. He is the boy next door, the son of one of Aurelia
Plath's best friends, and a Yale medical student with a promising
future—"the foremost-doctor-to-be-in-the-next-decades" as Plath
describes him to her mother (Box 1, MSS II; February 23, 1951). He is
handsome in a clean-cut, all-American way, and taller than the anxiously five-foot-nine-inch Plath. Later, she will compare his height
and weight unfavorably to a new beau: "Dick is barely 6 feet &
weighs 190; Myron is 6'4" and weighs 185. Also can carry women
weighing 140 lbs" (Box 3, MSS II, February 28, 1953); but at first, he is
the "sweet wonderman" (Box 1, MSS II; April 16, 1951), and she is
fond of extolling his many mental and physical virtues. To her mother
she writes, "He knows everything. . . . He has an amazing mind and
a remarkable group of highly developed skills—dancing, skating,
swimming, & so on. . . . He's the most stimulating boy I've ever
known. . . . I adore him and worship his intellect and keen perceptions in almost every field" (Box 2, MSS II; [February, 1951]). Eddie,
however, is skeptical both of Allan and of Plath's adoration: "Some of
the things you tell me about Allan, and what Allan says, tempt me to

open up with my broadest satire—You know, more neurotic women get that way because some dream or other of theirs has never been fulfilled" (Box 2, MSS II; November 21, 1951). Here, and in other letters, Eddie notes a pattern of overidealization in Plath's relationships with men. New boyfriends are briefly inflated as perfect— "golden gods," as Eddie calls them (Box 2, MSS II; December 28, 1951)—and then discarded or forgotten for some blemish. Such overidealization is quite common for young women without fathers (Chodorow, p. 118) and, in Plath's situation, suggests that she was seeking a superior male figure to initiate her into adult femininity. When Dick Norton, a senior at Yale while she is a freshman at Smith, begins to court her, she is overcome with awe and delight.[40] He seems to be the mental and physical giant she has been searching for.

Despite her early enthusiasm for Norton, there is an undercurrent of competition between them. For awhile, Plath accedes to his superiority. He is experienced in all things, while she is a novice. While he is multitalented, she lists (like Esther Greenwood) her inadequacies: she does not know "how to skate, swim, charleston, *or* cook and sew"—the latter two being special embarrassments since they are customarily skills women have over men, and Norton, trained by his superefficient mother, outdoes Plath here as in everything (Box 1, MSS II; February 23, 1951). They are rivals, too, over the merits of the sciences versus the humanities, and Norton persuades Plath of science's preeminence.

> He regards me as an indulgent older cousin would. He even memorized some poetry & read aloud some—as much as he does not credit emotional expression as valuable without scientific knowledge. (Box 1, MSS II; February 20, 1951)

> He knows everything. I am so firmly convinced that knowledge comes through science that I would like to get some elementary books of physics or chemistry. . . . I don't care if I am not "mathematically minded." All that I write or paint is, to me, valueless if not evolved from a concrete basis of reasoning, however uncomplex it must be. . . . There's no reason why I can't learn a few physical laws to hold me down to something nearer truth. (Box 1, MSS II; [February])

Once again, this does not last. Later, she will develop an unreason-
ing hatred for science and try to be released from courses in chemistry and physics. Her anxiety over science courses is so extreme as to
alarm Aurelia (*LH*, pp. 96–97; November 19, 1952).

Norton is only too willing to be Plath's mentor. He assures her,
"You won't be badly off, Syl, if she [i.e., Aurelia] can teach you
shorthand [he already has his certificate] and if I can impart some
enthusiasm for natural science. One or both may come in time" (Box
1, MSS II; March 1, 1951). His long letters are filled with anatomy
lessons and profuse diagrams of his cadaver dissection (Box 2, MSS
II; September 25, 26, and October 3, 1951); and on a date when they
watch a baby being born, he promises, "I'll bring my microscope
back to the room from the lab and show you slides of blood cells.
Then you will be ready for the clinic next morning" (Box 2, MSS II;
October 17, 1951). As if sizing Plath up as a future homemaker,
Norton often compliments her on her frugality—her "practical gab-
ardine coat" (Plath to Aurelia, Box 1, MSS II; February 20, 1951)—
and writes to her mother about one of their shopping excursions.

> Whose resolve to-peer-and-not-purchase weakened first? not
> hers. We emerged with a physics text (49¢) that I had decided I
> needed for summer scientific review, that was all!
>
> Now you can be a proud parent. I would be. (Box 1, MSS II;
> May 12, 1951)

One is tempted, like Eddie, to "open up" with the broadest satire at
Plath's avuncular lover. His most ardent expression of love in these
long letters is, "I think of you often, when it can't be avoided" (Box
1, MSS II; May 19, 1951). Eddie's letters also hint that Norton shows
little sexual interest in Plath and that she is puzzled. Eddie tries to
reassure her that this is not abnormal: "His-er, physical reticence is
more likely to be a result of his being unsure of himself and you
rather than anything else" (Box 2, MSS II; September 16, 1951).

Plath's acquiescence in training for future housewife and scientific home companion comes to an end when she discovers that
Norton is not a virgin. She cannot break up with him immediately or
finally, though, both because he is a family friend and because Norton becomes seriously ill with tuberculosis. He leaves Yale medical

school for a sanitorium in Lake Placid, believing that Plath is still pledged to him. She is, meanwhile, drawing Aurelia into a league against Norton and his mother, who are pressuring her into a summer job near the sanitorium.

> I discovered that Mrs. Norton has decided (at this late date) that she doesn't want me for her precious courageous boy anyway, because, number one, my summer plans show what a Selfish Person I am. I was really appalled and very hurt. Not only is my not ruining my health as a waitress at Saranac proof that I'm Selfish, but so is my going to Harvard SS [summer school], because I should be working so that you wouldn't have to. (Box 3, MSS II; May 12, 1953)

For her mother, Plath depicts Norton as a blackguard, interested only in compromising her sexually: "He told me of a cabin not far away which is signed up by desirous couples: a bed and a locked door. He also wrote a poem about raping Ann in said cabin" (Box 3, MSS II; February 28, 1953). Rape? This doesn't fit the poem Norton sends her, although he is belatedly showing a physical attraction for Plath and he continues to cling to her with long, and now passionate, letters.[41] He is apologetic, too, about his former scientific browbeating, and tries to show his love by developing literary interests. He sends her love poems and a critical essay on William Carlos Williams, but these incursions into Plath's province only seem to threaten her.[42]

The moral indignation she displays for her mother—"I was so broken up about the fact of Dick's hypocrisy in setting himself up as a paragon when he'd gone out and slept with other girls all the time. . . . I wonder if his parents still think he is a virgin" (Box 3, MSS II; February 28, 1953)—takes a rather peculiar turn in her letters to Eddie. She seems determined to lose her virginity and in this way avenge herself. Eddie responds,

> It is hard for me to believe that the discovery of the Mr. Hyde in Allan's hitherto sterling character will set you to flinging yourself bodily at every male that crosses your path. As for the

comment about your being an unfaithful wife---again $$$$$. . . .
But do climb down off this Cross of Wantoness . . . and you
really are not in such a hurry to sacrifice your maidenhead upon
the altar of Allan's hypocrisy. . . . One just *doesn't* say: I wanted
to go out and *lie* with someone else. . . . And what, may I ask,
is this sudden preoccupation on your part with having your
chastity taken from you by force? You must have used the word
rape in this letter five times. (Box 2, MSS II; December 28, 1951)

Plath casts herself as a sacrificial victim to Norton's imperfection, as
if to say, "If he is not the perfect future husband, then I will be
promiscuous." As Eddie interprets Plath, this "Cross of Wanton-
ness" is a disguise for other motives. He describes her relationship
to Norton in one letter as always "vicious, biting, and competitive"
and her new "preoccupation with the brutishness of Physical Science" and view of sexual intercourse as violent rape are, Eddie feels,
ways of suppressing her envy and anger (Box 2, MSS II; January 2,
1953). Eddie also understands the self-destructiveness in Plath's behavior. Because she cannot express her rage openly, she breaks her
leg on a visit to Norton at the sanitorium. Eddie tells her, "Inciden-
tally, you are going to be a mighty maimed sort of person if you
make a habit of substituting broken legs and other forms of violence
for the colds which have been your psychological catharsis in the
past" (Box 2, MSS II; January 26, 1953). Plath feels she ought to
remain a faithful little woman to her ailing future husband and at
the same time has a strong and growing aversion to him. Hence, she
punishes herself for Norton's "crime," since it is the only way simultaneously to satisfy her guilt for deserting him and her anger at
his infidelity. Even in her letters to Aurelia, this suppressed rage
surfaces. Plath is unsuccessful at transforming her anger into pity,
even though it would be the proper and ladylike response. Marriage
to Norton is described as an "overwhelming bear trap": "I feel a
great *pity* for him, and a sad sort of maternal fondness: but you
know how fatal that has been to love in the past. I feel, ever since I
made the irrevocable decision not to marry him last summer, that I
am suddenly blissfully free of an overwhelming bear trap" (Box 3,
MSS II; February 28, 1953).

Before Plath actually reveals Norton's crime to Eddie, he guesses that "Allan" is not the "sweet wonderman" of Plath's fantasies and that she feels obligated but incapable of loving him.

> Which is to say that I wonder who you think you are kidding about Allan—thou or me. I have heard gals come up with all kinds of reasons for not getting hooked up with a guy, but never, absolutely never, have I heard anyone say, "He's handsome, brilliant, personable, athletic, and generally simply wonderful, but I doubt if I could come up to the subconscious set of standards he expects me to emulate.". . . What sounds extremely more probable to me is that Allan does not come up to your standards for some reason or other. (Box 2, MSS II; October 26, 1951)

If anything, Norton's infidelity provides Plath with an excuse for releasing herself from a future role as a perfect housewife—a role too much like that of her mother's and Mrs. Norton's. If Norton had been as perfect as her fantasy, she may have been intimidated into marriage. Since he is not, she feels betrayed. As Eddie analyzes her disappointment, "Does it occur to you that your reaction to the falling out with Allan is less that of a woman disappointed in love than it is that of an engineer whose latest airplane design didn't quite come up to specifications in performance?" (Box 2, MSS II; December 28, 1951).

The complexity of Plath's feelings toward Norton can be explained by the double role he seems to play in her psychological development. In his close connection with Aurelia and Wellesley, he represents a continuation of the maternal bond. He is the ideal future husband, offering financial security and the gracious life of the well-educated bourgeoisie. Plath's marriage to Norton would be close to an acting out of the kind of life, one senses, Aurelia might have chosen for herself—another "happy dream" to share with her mother for the years of self-sacrifice that went into Sivvy's creation. At the same time, Plath overidealizes Norton as a superior male, a father figure who will initiate her into a life independent of Aurelia, a life in the "huge city," as she calls it, of college, maturity, academic success, and accomplishment. It is a male world—logical and scientific—

where she is at a disadvantage because of her dreamy literary and artistic inclinations. Norton must be perfect in order to substitute for such an intense mother-daughter bond—to justify her desertion of Aurelia for a man. In this he also symbolizes sexual independence—a "sweet wonderman," affirming her femininity and helping her to negotiate her transition to heterosexuality from a neuter and childish dependence on the mother. This is, as Chodorow describes it, also the father's role in shaping a female child's gender identity. Through her attachment to the father and later to other men, eventually a husband, the developing woman experiences independence vicariously—but not complete autonomy (Chodorow, pp. 138–39). That Plath feels she needs a man to do this for her is evident in the correspondence with her mother during the summer when she finds out that Norton is not a virgin. She describes her reaction to a date, who, like Norton, is "so gifted in all physical attributes—skiing, swimming, football, charlestoning, singing, pool playing. . . . I suddenly envied him very much—for the life he leads. Boys live so much harder than girls, and they know so much more about life. Learning the limitations of a woman's sphere is no fun at all" (LH, p. 72; August 4, 1951). At the same time, she is depressed over imaginary inadequacies, telling her mother that whenever she thinks, "I'm a worthless, ungifted lummox," she takes out the approving letters from Seventeen to remind herself of her accomplishments as a writer (LH, p. 72; July 7, 1951). In a veiled way, I surmise, Plath is revealing her sense of inferiority to Norton and to men generally. Like her heroine in The Bell Jar, she feels fraudulent in her attempts to be independent because she doesn't know enough about life; she has no sexual experience, because this is unavailable for "nice" girls. She becomes obsessed, as Eddie Cohen notes, with losing her virginity, because it represents this superior male knowledge—"they know so much more about life."

Plath's extreme and contradictory reactions to Norton's infidelity are comprehensible in light of these motives. As a father figure, he is no longer perfect, no longer the strong, idealistic man who will initiate her into what she describes to Eddie as an "intellectual elite" (Box 2, MSS II; August 25, 1951). His severe illness weakens him further in her eyes and exacts her unwilling devotion. Perhaps his illness triggers hostility because it touches on repressed anger to-

ward her father's nursing demands on Aurelia. He is a philandering
"husband," too, and not only to Plath, but to her mother and Mrs.
Norton as well, which explains her moral indignation and desire for
her mother and his parents to know of his blemish. His crime is an
affront to her fragile sense of mature femininity, and this accounts
for her assertion to Eddie that she is doomed to become an unfaithful wife: she will prove herself an equal to Allan and become wan-
ton, if only to affirm that she is attractive enough, womanly enough,
to command a man's sexual interest. Finally, it is a blow to her sense
of independence and maturity. Because of her disillusionment with
Norton, she turns her back on the "brutishness" of the male world,
retreating from sex by seeing it as violent rape, and from scientific
knowledge as a male province. After two years of separating herself
from her mother, Plath regresses to the original, childish symbiosis
with Aurelia. Instead of a future as a wife to a successful doctor, or
even as an independent woman, with a writing career of her own,
she imagines a life with her "twin" Aurelia, both of them as creative
writers: "I am elated by the way you are to be a ghost-writer. Dob-
bin nothing! You have a gift in your own line, and between the two
of us we should make a lovely life. I owe all I am to you anyway, for
you have made all possible, from my life to my Smith career" (Box 3,
MSS II; May 5, 1953).

An even more extreme assertion of this mother-daughter bond
occurs a few months later after Plath's guest editor stint with *Mademoiselle* in New York City. Plath is refused entrance into Frank
O'Connor's writing seminar at Harvard Summer School—a rebuff
that she regards as proof of her inadequacy—and, with no other
plans, she is forced to spend the summer with her mother in Wellesley. As Aurelia describes Plath's reaction,

> From that point on, I was aware of a great change in her; all her
> usual *joie de vivre* was absent. My mother tried to reassure me
> that this was no doubt temporary. . . . At home, she would
> sunbathe, always with a book in hand, but never reading it.
> After days of this, she finally began to talk to me, pouring out
> an endless stream of self-deprecation, self-accusation. She had
> no goal, she said. As she couldn't read with comprehension
> anymore, much less write creatively, what was she going to do

with her life? She had injured her friends, "let down" her spon-
sors—she went on and on.

Sylvia's self-recrimination even extended to reproaching herself for having published "Sunday at the Mintons'," one of the
two prize-winning stories in the August 1952 edition of *Mademoiselle*. She felt it had been unkind to the young friend who
supplied the germ of the characterization of Henry, one of the
two characters in the story. . . .

One unforgettable morning, I noticed some partially healed
gashes on her legs. Upon my horrified questioning, she replied,
"I just wanted to see if I had the guts!" Then she grasped my
hand—hers was burning hot to the touch—and cried passion-
ately, "Oh, Mother, the world is so rotten! I want to die! Let's
die together!" (*LH*, pp. 123–24)

Aurelia Plath offers nothing more as reasons for her daughter's suicidal depression than the Harvard rejection and guilt over exploiting
a friend for one of her stories. Here, as elsewhere, she seems honestly puzzled by her daughter's illness—the one illness, she tells
Olive Prouty later, that she could not afford (Box 3, MSS II; August
29, 1953). She does not pursue the death pact, although it reveals
the nature of Plath's withdrawal from the world: she returns to the
only certain, unconditional love she has known. Nor does Aurelia
mention Norton as the friend wounded by Plath's story, even
though Plath's guilt and self-deprecation would then become explicable as the psychological costs of her suppressed rage at him.

Henry Minton is as surely modeled after Norton as Buddy Willard is in *The Bell Jar*. One of Plath's strategies for dealing with her
anger at Norton is to cast him in her story as a smug, scientific,
domineering and "always right" older brother to Elizabeth Minton,
the dreamy, intuitive alter ego for Plath herself. Like Norton, Henry
is only too eager to teach his wayward sister what the world is all
about.

She visualized Henry in the center of the map, which was
quartered like an apple pie under the blue dome of a bowl. Feet
planted firmly he stood with pencil and paper making calcula-
tions, checking to see that the world revolved on schedule. . . .

"I suppose telling direction is something anyone can learn," Elizabeth murmured at last.

"Of course," Henry told her, beaming at her humility. "I would even lend you a map to use for practice."

Elizabeth sat quite still . . . cherishing the world the way she would a dear, slandered friend, the vague, imprecise world in which she lived.

Hers was a twilight world, where the moon floated up over the trees at night like a tremulous balloon of silver light and bluish rays wavered through the leaves outside her window, quivering in fluid patterns on the wallpaper of her room. The very air was mildly opaque, and forms wavered and blended one with the other. . . .

She winced under the benevolent brightness of Henry's patronizing smile. She wanted to say something brave and impudent, then, something that would disturb the awful serenity of his features. (*Johnny Panic*, pp. 300–301)

Like Esther Greenwood in *The Bell Jar*, who longs for an unanswerable retort to Buddy Willard's pronouncement that a poem is nothing but a piece of dust,[43] Elizabeth Minton would like to confront Henry with "something rather shattering and dreadful," something "disrespectful and frivolous" that would leave "Henry for once nonplused, Henry faltering, wavering helplessly, without words" (*Johnny Panic*, pp. 298–99). Instead, she fantasizes Henry's death by drowning as he stoops to retrieve the brooch she drops in the ocean on their afternoon stroll. Momentarily, the reader is led to believe that Elizabeth triumphs over her brother, "borne along beneath her on the outgoing tide," and only in the final lines does Plath retrieve him from his watery death.

The afternoon was shading into twilight. There was a sudden tug at Elizabeth's arm. "Come along home, Elizabeth," Henry said. "It's getting late."

Elizabeth gave a sigh of submission. "I'm coming," she said. (*Johnny Panic*, p. 305)

Norton is mocked and briefly "killed off" in Plath's art as a way of satisfying her aggression. Even while she is dating Norton, Plath's poems focus on her antagonism to his scientific superiority. She writes sonnets "about the mechanical age as versus the natural world. . . . Wistful imagination is excluded by scornful logic" (Box 2, MSS II; November 13, 1951); and she defeats him intellectually in verse with one of her Emily Dickinson imitations.

> If you dissect a bird
> To diagram the tongue
> You'll cut the chord
> Articulating song.
>
> If you flay a beast
> To marvel at the mane
> You'll wreck the rest
> From which the fur began.
>
> If you pluck out the heart
> To find what makes it move,
> You'll halt the clock
> That syncopates our love.
>
> (LH, p. 110; April 30, 1953)

One cannot help but see this as a response to Norton's voluminous letters describing his cadaver dissection. Such indirect assaults on Norton eventually intensify Plath's sense of guilt and lead to the self-deprecation her mother describes.

Plath herself came to see this breakdown as a failure to achieve separation and a mature sexual identity independent of her mother. Butscher reports that while in treatment at McLean's, "Sylvia had confided to a visitor that she believed her mother had never wanted her to become a woman, but rather remain a neuter creature dependent on her for love's nourishment."[44] The letters do not show that Aurelia actually attempted to assert such control over her daughter—only that the nature of their intimacy did not permit her to discuss her sexual feelings or to communicate fully her reaction to Norton, because Plath herself does not seem to comprehend her ambivalence. What is more likely is that Plath feared as much as she needed to retreat to her pre-Oedipal dependency on mother love and that this accusation is a projection of the dread of being enveloped by maternal devotion, permanently losing her sense of self to that primal bond. In this, it is like the accusation of rape against Norton—a projection of her worries about sex and her inevitable role as female victim to male brutality. Much later at Cambridge, Plath complains that she misses relationships with father figures and mother figures, but also tells her mother she will seek them only "as long as there is no perilous and ambivalent dependence or over-domination involved" (Box 5, MSS II; March 5, 1956), again showing how much she has learned from her first breakdown. There is also that seemingly absurd statement, "Oh, if I only could be a freshman again. I so wanted to be a Smith woman!" upon awakening from her abortive attempt at self-destruction. In this context, it assumes new meaning as a wish to begin anew the task of growing up.

Shortly before Plath returns to Smith, Aurelia reports that she has found her confidence again and claims, "I know I can do it, Mother! I know I can do it!" (LH, p. 129), as if she can once again attempt to enter an adult world. As she writes in a letter to Eddie Cohen, "I long to be out in the wide open spaces of the very messy, dangerous real world which I still love in spite of everything" (LH, p. 132; December 28, 1953). Plath saves a copy of her letter because it records her feelings immediately before the suicide attempt. As with her other statements, it documents a sense of failure at entering adulthood.

> To top it off, all my friends were either writing novels in Europe, planning to get married next June, or going to med. school. . . . The one or two males I knew were either proving themselves genii in the midst of adversity . . . or were not in the market for the legal kind of love for a good ten years and were going to see the world and all the femmes fatales in it before becoming victims of wedded bliss. (LH, p. 130; December 28, 1953)

Aurelia deletes the description of Norton after "genii in the midst of adversity (e.g., Allan, who was becoming a writer, a buddy of W. C. Williams, and a researchist at the sanitorium)" (Box 3, MSS II), which reveals how much Norton was still on Plath's mind as an intellectual rival, competing with her on her own turf, and how

guilty she felt at not being faithful to him in his "adversity." Without a fiance or husband to be a guardian and give her a place in
the "messy, dangerous, real world" and with a growing sense of
the fraudulence of her writing, her one claim to an independent
self, she decided, "I would spare them all by ending everything at
the height of my so-called career while there were still illusions
among my profs, still poems to be published in *Harper's*, still a
memory at least that would be worthwhile" (*LH*, p. 132; December
28, 1953).[45]

"A Certain Healthy Bohemianism"

When Plath reenters the "dangerous" world in January of 1954,
virtually the first thing she does is lose her virginity. She dyes her
hair blonde and wears it a la Veronica Lake to assert a new, femme
fatale personality. She proceeds to collect men with the same ease
with which she formerly collected high grades. For a while, she
dates two roommates at Yale simultaneously—J. Melvin Woody
(Mel) and Richard Sassoon—and carries on a steamy correspondence with both. While with Woody she seems to be a sexual tease
(he writes to her that "the interrupted love ritual can only appear to
me as a terribly perverse thing . . . in somewhat the same category
as homosexuality," Box 3, MSS II; April 28, 1954), with Sassoon she
establishes an on-again, off-again affair that continues up to her
meeting with Ted Hughes. The French Sassoon seems to attract her
because of his total difference from the all-American Norton she was
formerly destined to marry. She describes him to Aurelia as a de-
monic, romantic figure: "He's a very intuitive wierd [*sic*] sinuous
little guy whose eyes are black and shadowed so he looks as if he
were an absinthe addict . . . all of which helps me to be carefree and
gay" (Box 3, MSS II; April 19, 1954).

Sassoon's letters to her are written in an illegible breakneck
scrawl of French and English, and he cultivates an image of decadent diabolism. He is a disciple of Rimbaud and Baudelaire: "I too
love the flowers of evil, but I shall prefer pyramids of evil" (Box 3,
MSS II; April 28, 1954). Perhaps Plath finds in Sassoon a man who
satisfies her fantasy of male violence and domination. Like Norton,

Sassoon is fond of playing a fatherly role, but his is a different kind of paternal dominance. He is the father who will not spare the rod and spoil his headstrong child.

> . . . and I doubt I could love a child who was not capable of making me angry once in a while and I doubt not that there must be something very strong and very wrong in anything that can make me angry, and I love you very much because you do not run away if you are punished, for which I have scorned so many. . . . (Box 4, MSS II; [1954?]).

> Do not think I am scolding you, my love, for I have recently decided you are a quite grown up child and that I may not henceforth chide you in the manner to which I am used, nor even probably spank you. Such it is that if you ever anger me greatly I shall have but two alternatives, one of which is to beat you, which is a very different thing from spanking.

> P.S. Do not take me too literally about not spanking you any-more. . . . (Box 4, MSS II; February 11, 1955)

While it would be an exaggeration to describe this as sadomasoch-ism, there are disturbing hints throughout their correspondence that Plath enjoys playing a submissive female child to a sexually punish-ing father. As Nancy Hunter Steiner describes Plath's attraction to Sassoon, she also reveled in his deformity.

> She endowed him with the qualities of a Byronic hero: an air of mystery and an almost sinister melancholia that she found fasci-nating, even though she seemed also to regard him, at times, as an amusing toy. Because he was small and slightly built she admitted to a feeling of physical revulsion in his presence. "When he holds me in his arms," she confided, "I feel like Mother Earth with a small brown bug crawling on me." (*A Closer Look*, pp. 77–78)

It is as if Plath decided to meet her former fears directly, immerse herself in her former revulsion for sex, and by so doing conquer that fear. During the spring and summer of 1954, the correspondence with Eddie Cohen also shows that she was experimenting with sex. Eddie replies to one of her letters, "I find it to be the first letter I have received from you in a long, too long time, which does not either float on a cloud of sensuality or wallow in a morass of it" (Box 3, MSS II; May 6, 1954). Steiner, too, reports that Plath is preoccupied with sexual experiment of a rather perilous kind. She narrates an incident that appears in *The Bell Jar* as Esther Greenwood's bloody deflowering. According to Steiner, Plath was eager to make a conquest of "Irwin," a brilliant biologist, even after Steiner, who dated him a couple of times, refused to see him anymore because of his aggressive sexual advances. To Steiner's mind, Plath was attracted to the danger. Even after a bloody ordeal that Plath attributes to being raped, she continues to see Irwin: "She was seeing Irwin again before the week was over and also boasting that she had become innocently involved with a Harvard professor whose wife, jumping to an erroneous conclusion, called her 'the blond bitch.' Syl found the epithet, as well as the circumstances, curiously amusing" (*A Closer Look*, p. 96). One cannot help but wonder if Plath did not find in Irwin a man who would execute the rape fantasies she had before her breakdown, and so fulfill the desire to see herself as a female victim to brutish men. There is also a resemblance between Irwin and Plath's biologist father and the scientific Norton. Plath's peculiar attraction to and conquest of Irwin may well be an acting out of her repressed fury at unreliable father figures—a way of confirming their ungodlike vulnerability to sexual impulse.

At the end of her Smith years, Plath reflects on this adventurous period of her life in a letter to her mother. She sought, she says,

> a sense of "fun," which I think has been a family weakness. . . . I know that underneath the blazing jaunts in yellow convertibles to exquisite restaurants I am really regrettably unoriginal, conventional and puritanical, basically, but I needed to practice a certain healthy bohemianism for awhile to swing away from the gray-clad, basically-dressed, brown-haired, clock-regulated, responsible, salad-eating, water-drinking, bedgoing, economical, practical girl I had become. (Box 4, MSS II; October 12, 1954)

Despite this experiment with another personality, Plath continues to see herself as a conventional young woman, and in this letter reassures her mother that Sivvy is still very much in control. That Plath is living out her fantasies of a more rebellious self while Sivvy is still the dominant personality is apparent in a number of descriptions by friends. While dallying with several men who are clearly not marital prospects for "studious, brown-haired" Sivvy, she carefully sustains a relationship with Gordon Lameyer, a naval officer whom she considered her fiance. According to Peter Davison, who also claims a summer affair with Plath before her Cambridge years, she kept Lameyer in ignorance of her "healthy bohemianism": "He remained convinced that his exasperating, unstable Sylvia was still chaste and totally committed to him alone and that he was that one who would have to make a decision regarding their future."[46] Steiner also reports a finickiness to Plath's personal habits that suggests she kept the perfect Sivvy "separate and inviolate" while donning a looser, breezy persona with men. While living with her in Cambridge, Steiner noticed "her preoccupation with possessions." Plath labeled a bottle of inexpensive nail polish to distinguish it from Steiner's identical bottle, and when she gave a party, "Sylvia meticulously wrote her name on every leftover box of crackers and bag of potato chips" to assure that her roommates would leave them untouched. Plath is outraged at a stranger who "steals" her Veronica Lake hairstyle and "once, when she was in the bedroom putting away laundry, I remarked about the neat, almost mechanical arrangement of the contents of her drawers. 'Yes,' she confessed, 'if anyone ever disarranged my things I'd feel as though I had been raped intellectually' " (*A Closer Look*, p. 75). Plath seems aware of the doubleness, the ambivalence in her impulses, and the need for containment of her risk taking by a careful, even obsessive regimentation of other areas in her life.

"In Plaster," though written much later, is about the divided self—a plaster saint with female virtues ("Her tidiness and her calmness and patience") and an "ugly and hairy" "old yellow one" whose "habits offended her in some way."[47] Old yellow is the assertive, and, surprisingly, the beautiful one, and the poem is in her voice.

I gave her a soul, I bloomed out of her as a rose
Blooms out of a vase of not very valuable porcelain,
And it was I who attracted everybody's attention,
Not her whiteness and beauty, as I had first supposed.

(CTW, p. 16)

But old yellow needs her "mummy-case" for support: "I was quite limp" and "I still depended on her." Without the plaster cast, the defenses of perfect control, Plath implies, old yellow might die, and the saint, without old yellow's humanity, would be nothing but an empty shell, "the face of a pharoah" mummy. The poem hints at the pattern Plath shows both before and after her breakdown. The always-good-little-girl Sivvy hides a self Plath prefers—the questioning, witty young woman she shows to Eddie Cohen and the femme fatale she later permits to take sexual gambles for the sake of experience. But she is afraid of this personality, who represents too much of a breach with her upbringing, with her ideal and normal self, and ultimately with her mother.

"Her Letters Are Such a Heavy Weight on Me"

The "normal" Sivvy whom Plath preserves so carefully in her relationship with her mother may be understood as a gift or compensation for Aurelia's self-sacrifice—even, perhaps, for her promise never to marry. In this, Plath's relationship to her mother is an extreme form of a common condition between parent and child: how does one repay one's parents, especially a paragon of maternal nurture like Aurelia? Plath may deride her mother's fairy-tale world as deficient in "The Disquieting Muses," but in the letters she praises her unreservedly as "the best Mummy a girl ever had, and I only hope I can continue to lay more laurels at your feet" (LH, p. 94; October 6, 1952). Her scholarly achievements; her effusive descriptions of debutante parties, weekends with Yale and Harvard men, and new "princess" clothes; her writing prizes and growing list of published-and-paid-for stories; her intellectual, social, and artistic achievements are glowingly shared with Aurelia, as if her own life's fullness and richness might substitute for the mother's generous sacrifice of her own: "I . . . want more than anything to make you proud of me so that some day I can begin to repay you for all the treats you've given me in my two decades of life" (*LH*, p. 104; February 28, 1953).

Suggestions of "payment" abound in *Letters Home*, taking the form of lists—her stories in one column, the payment recorded next to it; her budgets for clothes, books, writing supplies. A regular accounting of her finances often seems as important as the mother-daughter confidences, and this joyless frugality reminds us constantly of Plath's "debt" of gratitude, a debt that often seems too large ever to repay. As Plath writes to her brother Warren,

> You know, as I do, and it is a frightening thing, that mother would actually kill herself for us if we calmly accepted all she wanted to do for us. She is an abnormally altruistic person, and I have realized lately that we have to fight against her selflessness as we would against a deadly disease.
>
> After extracting her life blood and care for 20 years, we should start bringing in big dividends for her. (*LH*, pp. 112–13; May 12, 1953)

This would appear to be another example of Plath's exaggeration-prone praise, until we learn, for example, that Aurelia, because of a recent operation on her chronic ulcers, must be carried to Plath's graduation on a litter, because she would not miss her daughter's day.[48] The burden of Aurelia's love, carried to the extreme that it is felt by Plath as a "deadly disease," can only create strong feelings of ambivalence. On the one hand, Plath wishes to justify her mother's martyrdom with the gift of her own "perfect" life; on the other, such a tie, as we have seen, prolongs her dependency on maternal nurture and creates extreme guilt whenever imperfections mar the value of her gift. There is a double bind to such intimacy: Plath expects and needs her mother's self-sacrifice, but simultaneously cannot ask for help openly at crucial times of weakness in her life. This will increase the burden of gratitude—and the need for guilty repayment. This guilt contributed to her first breakdown and helps to explain Plath's mean caricature of Aurelia in *The Bell Jar*, written at a time in Plath's life when she feared very much that she might, once again, feel compelled to retreat to her "neuter" and infantile tie to Aurelia. Indeed, many of Plath's last angry letters home seem like strategies for fending off this dependency.

In the last months of her life, when Plath is in a state of despair over her broken marriage, she alternately complains of poverty and insists that her mother not help her with loans. Aurelia rightly, to my mind, understands this financial strain as a reflection of Plath's emotional insecurity: "Actually, this emphasis on her lack of funds may have been an exaggeration intended to convey her sense of urgency. Ted Hughes says that he borrowed money from his family when he left and between September and early February gave her over £900" (*LH*, p. 461). As in *The Bell Jar*, where money becomes equated with maternal nurture and its deprivation, so in *Letters Home* we see Plath needing money as proof of her mother's continuing love. Like the *liebestod* Plath offers her mother after her first breakdown, she expresses her need for Aurelia's unqualified love as a substitute for the loss of her husband-lover, but she also tries to deny this need. Unlike the first breakdown, Plath is aware of the dangers in her appeal. This is a natural enough reaction—to wish a return to the secure love of the mother when affection is withdrawn by the husband—and equally natural that as a mature woman, Plath now fears her regression: "I must not go back to the womb" (*LH*, p. 469; October 16, 1962). Plath is ill with the flu—"the flesh has dropped from my bones" (*LH*, p. 465; October 9, 1962)—and she must care for an infant and two-year-old in a medieval manor house with a thatched roof. It was so cold that she had chilblains her first year in Devon. Plath obviously needs help to make a new life, but she persistently resists her mother's support. In this her extremes of desire and denial take a destructive form, and money is the vehicle for her ambivalent impulses.

Plath is angry with her mother's behind-the-scenes financial arrangements with Winifred Davies, a local midwife in Devon. Aurelia stayed with Davies the previous summer while Plath and Hughes were in the throes of their marital breakup. Aurelia asks Davies to provide help with the children, Frieda and Nicholas, and to watch over her daughter as a maternal presence. Plath cruelly chides Aurelia for this interference. Later, when Aurelia sets up a bank account in London for her daughter, Plath tells her mother angrily to save for her retirement and to leave her alone (*LH*, p. 473; October 21, 1962). At the same time, Plath accepts money from mother surrogates like Olive Prouty and her mother's sister Dot, and then describes their generosity at great length to Aurelia, whose generosity is rebuffed. The previous suicide attempt is a Damocles' sword over Aurelia, who is pulled by her daughter's entreaties, but left helpless to respond.

Plath's incessant recitation of bills and debts occasionally looks petty, but this is a vehicle for what she is trying to say: "You must give me your complete support, but I cannot accept it because I already owe you too much." One senses behind all her heartrending cries of needing a woman to help her—at one point even requesting that her brother's new wife, Maggie, someone she has never met, come to England—a demand that Aurelia come at once. And this is in contradiction to her resolution that she will not come home and her insistence that she cannot face her mother.

In addition to her repeated accusation that Hughes is spending all of their joint savings, leaving her with nothing, Plath frightens her mother regularly with stories of his hatred. She tells Aurelia and her brother that Ted and "his woman" taunt her with her previous breakdown and suicide attempt (Box 6, MSS II; October 16, 1962), and that she suspects him of wanting to provoke a similar act of desperation in hope of gaining custody of the children (Box 6, MSS II; to Warren, October 18, 1962). Such extreme accusations seem calculated to arouse Aurelia's deepest fears for her daughter and are highly suspect when, at the same time, she persistently warns Aurelia not to worry excessively: "don't say 'unless you are safe & reasonably happy, I can't live anyway'! One's life should *never* depend on another's in *that* way. Why do you identify so with me? . . . That sort of statement only makes me chary of confiding any difficulties in you" (Box 6, MSS II; November 29, 1962). Aurelia's anguish seems completely explicable given the nature of her daughter's confidences. These are the maneuvers of someone who will make her mother guilty whatever course of action is taken, and who, in turn, is angry and guilty about her own dependence. The maneuvering is not, I believe, consciously calculated, not a deliberate punishment of her mother and herself, but out of control, as out of control as the suicide itself, which inevitably leaves a heavy load of guilt on the surviving loved ones. Indeed, those whom the suicide loves the most are the persons meant to suffer the loss most intensely. Aurelia's brief marginal note on this letter, expressing her regret for this declaration of deep love and concern for her daughter, is poignant evidence of the difficulty of her position and the pain Plath's suicide inflicted on the mother she loved.

The Gorgon's Stare

Plath often expresses something close to shame in these final letters. She cannot go home; she cannot face her mother: "I haven't the strength to see you for some time. The horror of what you saw and what I saw you see last summer is between us and I cannot face you again until I have a new life" (*LH*, p. 465; October 9, 1962). The previous July Aurelia saw the final fights between Plath and Hughes before he left her, and for Plath, this was a "horror," as if she saw her shame through her mother's eyes. The gift of her life had become soiled, imperfect, and she could no longer sustain the illusion of a sunny Sivvy. She writes to Olive Prouty, "I am so glad you have seen the dream I have made—as far as it got" (Box 6, MSS II; September 29, 1962). It may seem like stretching it a bit, but this recalls the desire in her letter from girl scout camp to share the "happy dream" of her summer with her mother. The analogy is apt if *Letters Home* is a "happy dream," a self-creation for her mother, and a gift of a successful life that her mother never had. By "successful," I mean an ideal fiction: the achievements of high school and college; marriage with a man Plath often describes as a physical and mental colossus and at one point, as compensation for the loss of Otto Plath; a writing career that fulfills Aurelia's own oft-expressed literary aspirations; and, finally, the womanly consummation of children. Babies were, as Aurelia perceives, crucial to Plath's sense that she was creative, evidence that she was not a barren intellectual, and therefore superior to the childless Assia Gutman, the woman Hughes deserts her for. They, too, are a part of the gift to the mother. When she miscarries in January, 1961, she promises, "All I can say is that you better start saving for another trip another

summer, and I'll make sure I can produce a new baby for you then!"
(*LH*, p. 409; February 9, 1961). An appendectomy follows this miscarriage (February, 1961), and the poem "Tulips," written shortly
after Plath's hospital stay (March, 1961), records feelings quite different from the indefatigable optimism of *Letters Home:* "I only wanted /
To lie with my hands turned up and be utterly empty."[49]

Plath must have felt not only that her "gifts" were marred, but
that she was repeating her earlier breakdown. The situation is similar to and worse than the earlier one: Hughes is an unfaithful
"brute" as Norton was, and in both instances, Plath feels her femininity, her mature sexuality, undermined. She sees herself as a
"hag in a world of beautiful women just waiting for him" (Box 6,
MSS II; October 9, 1962). Evidence in *The Bell Jar* also shows that
male desertion and infidelity arouse dread because they recall her
father's "desertion" of her as a child—a desertion which nourished
the mother-daughter identification that dominates Plath's psychological development. Her situation strongly reinforces this identification. As a young woman alone with two small children to raise,
Plath might well see herself as bound—unwillingly—to the model
of self-sacrifice provided by Aurelia. Plath would live out her years
like her mother, without men, sexually "neuter," and without an
identity apart from her children's. Much of Plath's assertive femininity in the final poems reflects a determination not to recapitulate
Aurelia's self-effacement.

According to Judith Kroll, Plath transcribed the following passage from Jung's essay, "The Development of Personality," showing
that these issues were on her mind.

> Parents set themselves the fanatical task of always "doing their
> best" for the children and "living only for them." This clamant
> ideal effectively prevents the parents from doing anything about
> their own development & allows them to thrust their "best"
> down their children's throats. This so-called "best" turns out to
> be the very things the parents have most badly neglected in
> themselves. In this way the children are goaded on to achieve
> their parents' most dismal failures, and are loaded with ambi-
> tions that are never fulfilled.[50]

The concluding sentence implies something more than parents trying to fulfill their lives through their children. It also implies that the martyrdom of parents creates a burden of resentment that dooms children to repeat their failures. The identification is complete and runs both ways. On October 18, 1962, Plath complains in a letter to her brother Warren that Aurelia "identifies too much with me, and you must help her see how starting my own life . . . here—not running, is the only sane thing to do" (*LH*, p. 472). If the identification runs both ways, then Plath may also be saying that she identifies too much with her mother. The project of starting her own life, without Ted Hughes, a surrogate for Otto Plath, is also to begin a new life separate from Aurelia. The gift of Sivvy, her ideal self, was spoiled; a rigid form of symbiosis with her mother had been forcibly broken; and Plath must create her self on new terms.

At the same time Plath expresses this urgent need for a new life, she composes the poem "Medusa" (October 16, 1962).[51] This is an obscure poem that only begins to come clear when one discovers that *medusa*, a stage in the life cycle of the jellyfish, is synonymous with *aurelia*.

> *aurelia* . . . A genus of . . . Hydromedusae, . . . The name is synonymous with Medusa regarded as a genus. . . . The adult state of any medusa, . . . (*Century Dictionary*)[52]

As Judith Kroll describes the poem, it is a companion piece to "Daddy" and "presents the exorcism of an oppressive parent—in this case the speaker's mother."[53] Kroll notes the bell-shaped form of the jellyfish—"I shall take no bite of your body / Bottle in which I live"—as a parallel to Esther Greenwood's oppressive bell jar and draws an analogy between the way Plath portrays her father's body in "Daddy" and her mother's body in "Medusa": "The body of the jellyfish thus appears as a 'ghastly Vatican,' which, with its implication of paralyzing and overwhelming authority, parallels the image of her father as a 'ghastly statue.' "[54] In her footnotes, Kroll also infers an important connection between Plath's shame at her mother's presence during her marital breakup and the phrase, "overexposed, like an X-ray" in "Medusa": "That her mother witnessed Plath's traumatic discovery in July 1962 meant that Mrs. Plath herself became a repository of terrible knowledge. Plath was overexposed, like an X-ray before her mother, who could now 'see through' the illusion of her marriage."[55] "The horror of what you saw and what I saw you see last summer is between us." The horror of her husband's infidelity stands between them. This seems to me a peculiar and rather extreme form of shame between mother and daughter, and the poem "Medusa" a heavily disguised explanation for this breach. It may be, as Kroll argues, a "mommy" poem—a companion piece to "Daddy"—but the stylistic differences between these two works are instructive.

In "Daddy," Plath is conscious of her complicity in creating and worshiping a father-colossus.

> You stand at the blackboard, daddy,
> In the picture I have of you,
> A cleft in your chin instead of your foot
> But no less a devil for that, no not
> Any less the black man who
>
> Bit my pretty red heart in two.
> I was ten when they buried you.
> At twenty I tried to die
> And get back, back, back to you.
> I thought even the bones would do.
>
> (*Ariel*, pp. 50–51)

The photograph is of an ordinary man, a teacher, with a cleft chin. She imaginatively transforms him into a devil who broke her heart, and she tells her audience precisely what she is doing. As Plath describes "Daddy," it "is spoken by a girl with an Electra complex. Her father died while she thought he was God. Her case is complicated by the fact that her father was also a Nazi and her mother very possibly part Jewish. In the daughter the two strains marry and paralyze each other—she has to act out the awful little allegory once over before she is free of it."[56] The poem is a figurative drama about mourning—about the human impulse to keep a dead loved one alive emotionally. And it is about mourning gone haywire—a morbid inability to let go of the dead. The child was unready for her father's death, which is why, she says, she must kill him a second time. She resurrected Daddy and sustained his unnatural existence in her psyche as a vampire, sacrificing her own life's blood, her vitality, to a dead man. The worship of this father-god, she now realizes, is self-destructive.

There is nothing unconscious about the poem; instead it seems to force into consciousness the child's dread and love for the father, so that these feelings may be resolved. Plath skillfully evokes the child's world with her own versions of Mother Goose rhymes. Like the "old woman who lived in a shoe and had so many children she didn't know what to do," she has tried to live in the confines of the black shoe that is Daddy. Like Chicken Little, waiting for the sky to fall in, she lives under an omnipresent swastika "So black no sky could squeak through." And Daddy is a fallen giant toppled over and smothering, it seems, the entire United States. He has one grey toe (recalling Otto Plath's gangrened appendage) dangling like a Frisco seal in the Pacific and his head lies in the Atlantic.

The Mother Goose rhythms gradually build to a goose step march as the mourning process turns inward. She feels more than sorrow, now guilt, for Daddy's death and this guilt leads to feelings of inadequacy, acts of self-abasement, and finally self-murder. Nothing she can do will appease the guilt: she tries to learn his language; she tries to kill herself; she marries a man in his image. It will not do.

The self-hatred must be turned outward again into "*You* do not do" by a very self-conscious transformation of a mild-mannered professor into an active oppressor. Her emotional paralysis is acted out as a struggle between Nazi man and Jewess, and, I would argue, the Jewess wins. The poem builds toward the imaginary stake driving, the dancing and stamping and "Daddy, daddy, you bastard, I'm through." Not necessarily through with life, as many critics have read this line, but through with the paralysis, powerlessness, guilt. At last Daddy—the Nazi Daddy she frightened herself with, and not the real one, the professor—is at rest.

Plath's control over ambivalent feelings toward her father is probably the result of their availability for conscious artistic manipulation. She had already written several poems about her dead father when she composed "Daddy," and we also know from a conversation recorded by Steiner that she had "worked through" her emotions in therapy. "She talked freely about her father's death when she was nine and her reactions to it. 'He was an autocrat,' she recalled. 'I adored and despised him, and I probably wished many times that he were dead. When he obliged me and died, I imagined that I had killed him' " (A Closer Look, pp. 62–63). The result in "Daddy" is a powerful and remarkably accessible allegory about her adoration and dread, which ends in emotional catharsis.

"Medusa" has neither the psychological clarity nor dramatic ease of "Daddy," which suggests that the effort for control through language—the "talking cure"—is not completely successful. The poem's imagery is heavily overdetermined and the love-hate of "Daddy" looks relatively simple to disentangle next to the feelings in "Medusa." Here, there is no love, only loathing for the mother's hold on her. The umbilical cord between mother and daughter is stronger than Daddy's iron-fisted dominance because it poses a subtler threat and is an older, primal connection. Where sacrificial death is the payment exacted by the psychic vampire Daddy, in "Medusa," the mother's claim is that of a devoted parasite to its host. The parasite may maim or slowly destroy its victim, but it wants to keep its host alive as long as possible.

The central metaphor of the poem is the medusa. As already noted, this is the immature form of the adult jellyfish, aurelia, so that it works as a code for her mother's name; but it also applies to the child, to Plath as an immature medusa to the adult aurelia. The double meaning contributes to the symbiotic relationship Plath explores in "Medusa." Medusa is also the mythological Gorgon, an "unnerving head" with snakes for hair, and a "God-ball" with the paralyzing powers of the Gorgon's stare. Both of these metaphors—mother as jellyfish and Gorgon—help to define the tie between mother and daughter, in imagery drawn from birth and infancy: they are bound together by an "old barnacled umbilicus"; the jellyfish mother is "Fat and red, a placenta"; and the "hot salt" of the sea water is like amniotic fluid. What Plath explores, then, is the emotional effect of this primary mother-infant relationship on her adult life.

The jellyfish engulfs and paralyzes its prey, like a large, sucking mouth. An "unnerving head" is an apt if ghastly image of the jellyfish, with its umbrella-shaped head and trailing tentacles, like dangling nerve ends. Like the hydra and sea anemone, the jellyfish is nothing more than a digestive cavity, an amorphous creature that moves rhythmically with the impulsion and expulsion of water, a movement Plath captures in "You steamed to me over the sea, / Fat and red, a placenta." This seems to be an invitation back into the womb and a fetal state, where the infant is fed by the mother; but there is a contradictory menace of being eaten by this creature. It only looks like a nourishing placenta, when it is actually a devouring mouth. The "unnerving head" pursues the speaker

> . . . in my keel's shadow,
> Pushing by like hearts,
> Red stigmata at the very centre,
> Riding the riptide to the nearest point of departure,
>
> Dragging their Jesus hair.
>
> (*Ariel*, p. 39)

Plath loads her images with a religious meaning: the "red stigmata" (recalling the mottled membrane appearance of the jellyfish) are the marks of the saint, of Jesus' wounds on the cross, and the tentacles are like lashing Jesus hair, implying self-flagellation. Ostensibly, this pursuit signifies that the mother offers to die for her child and to be a sustaining "communion wafer" and a nurturing intercessor—a "blubbery Mary." The invitation to "eat me" veils another motive: the child must be consumed with guilt and confess her sins to partake of communion with the mother. This psychological predation emerges in comparisons of the mother to a strangling and "eely tentacle," a fish "at the end of my line," "dazzling and grateful," "Touching and sucking" at the daughter's "water rod" (a fishing pole? a divining rod?). The daughter reverses the mother's self-sacrificial feeding situation so that the daughter's guilt apparently nourishes the suckling mother.

All of this may seem rather bizarre—an unnatural mother-daughter bond. From a psychoanalytic perspective, though, the poem struggles to express a common complex of feelings. The first love and the first painful loss of love centers in the mother.

The child's bodily tie to the mother, then, is the vehicle through which the most fundamental feelings of a highly complex creature are formed and expressed. At her breast, it is not just a small furnace being stoked: it is a human being discovering its first great job, handling its first major social encounter, facing its first meeting with a separate creature enormously more powerful than itself, living out its first awareness of wanting something for which it must depend on someone else, someone who is imperfectly benevolent and imperfectly reliable because she is (although the infant, of course, has no way of knowing that she is) also a human being. This is the prototype of the tie to life. The pain in it, and the fear of being cut off from it, are prototypes of the pain of life and the fear of death. (Dinnerstein, p. 34)

As a result, the infant is ambivalent: envious of "other people with a claim on the mother's intimate concern"—most importantly, the father and siblings—and grateful for the moments when the mother's attention is focused solely on the infant.

Melanie Klein explores an even more primal "envy and gratitude" in the infant's feelings at the mother's breast. As Dinnerstein summarizes Klein's argument,

The infant, for example, may have a grievance that the milk comes too quickly or too slowly; or that he was not given the breast when he most craved for it, and therefore, when it is offered, he does not want it anymore. She writes of "the infant's desire for the inexhaustible, ever-present breast . . ." and of its "feeling that the mother is omnipotent and that it is up to her to prevent all pain and evils from internal and external sources. . . ." The resulting attitude of destructive rage, which she calls envy, "spoils and harms the good object which is the source of life," for the child believes—and on some level continues to believe—that angry thoughts damage their target. If envy of the feeding breast is strong . . . full gratification is interfered with because . . . envy . . . implies robbing the object of what it possesses and spoiling it. As a result, *a part of the self is felt as an enemy to the ego as well as to the loved object* and the child feels "recurrent anxiety that his greed and his destructive impulses will get the better of him. . . ." (Dinnerstein, p. 96; emphasis added)

In Plath's biographical sketch, "Ocean 1212–W," she remembers her feelings at the age of two when her brother was born. What she records is similar to the envy-gratitude phenomenon described above, and the resulting split in her ego of good and bad selves. She remembers walking along the beach and suddenly recognizing the "*separateness* of everything. I felt the wall of my skin: I am I. That stone is a stone. My beautiful fusion with the things of this world was over" (*Johnny Panic*, p. 23). The "I am I" echoes the high school diary entry with its similar terror of diffuseness and recognition of dualism—the "merciless mirror" image and the perfect self, "free from blemish." This day on the beach, she says, was "the awful birthday of otherness." Like the phenomenon described by Klein where "a part of the self is felt as an enemy to the ego as well as to the loved object," Plath describes the form this "otherness" takes as a split into an envious second self: "My rival, somebody else" (*Johnny Panic*, p. 23). There is another Sylvia who is angry with her mother and the new baby, a competitor for the mother's attention: "How could she, so loving and faithful, so easily leave me?" (*Johnny Panic*, p. 23).

Such feelings of separateness, of two selves—one envious, one grateful—are, according to Klein, also projected onto the mother. The split in the infant's ego is matched by a dual perception of the mother.

The sense of having harmed "the breast" leads by a process of projection to "persecutory anxiety": ". . . the object that arouses guilt is turned into a persecutor," becomes the "earliest internalized persecutory object—the retaliating, devouring, and poisonous breast."

Threatened by bad feelings from within and (projected) hostility from without, the child is in danger of being cut off from its "good object"—that is, from its sense of connectedness to a benevolent and lovable outside force. The child comes to feel "that a good and bad breast exist." The good breast remains intact, unsullied by badness, but it disappears altogether from time to time and the bad breast is there instead: ". . . early emotional life is characterized by a sense of losing and regaining the good object." (Dinnerstein, pp. 96–97)

The "retaliating, devouring, and poisonous breast" is an apt description of the Medusa "God-ball" in Plath's poem. There are, in fact, startling similarities in the ambivalence and projection Klein describes and Plath's feelings of persecution by the mother. The opening line of "Medusa"—"Off that landspit of stoney mouth-plugs"—suggests that the mother's Gorgon stare ("the horror of what you saw and what I saw you see") has turned the nipples into "stoney mouth-plugs" and made "connectedness to a benevolent and lovable outside force" impossible.

In this sense, too, we might understand how starting a new life, separate from Hughes, was also to start a new life rid of her mother's devotion. If the mother-infant relationship is the prototype for later loving relationships, then the loss of Hughes would echo the feelings of loss Plath suffered as a child on that "awful birthday of otherness," when her mother became bound to another infant; and Plath might redirect her anger toward Hughes against her mother, who would then suffer the loss of love that her daughter suffers. The envious "rival" self and the devouring mother, or in Klein's words, "the bad breast," would both resurface. Something akin to this happens when Plath as a child acts out her anger against Aurelia and the new baby: "Sometimes I nursed starfish alive in jam jars of sea water and watched them grow back lost arms. On this day, this awful birthday of otherness, my rival, somebody else, I flung the starfish against stone. Let it perish. It had no wit" (*Johnny Panic*, p. 23). As Plath describes herself here, *she* takes on the role of a bad mother. In refusing to nurse these fetal starfish, she also rejects a mothering female role for herself.

The feelings in "Medusa" are similarly complicated by a rejection of a nurturing role. She does not want to be nursed by her mother or to feel gratitude for the mother's protective body, so she projects it as a loathsome and predatory jellyfish. Out of envy, as

Klein describes this emotion, Plath repudiates her love and allows the rival ingrate to speak: "Off, off, eely tentacle! / There is nothing between us."

The most difficult lines in "Medusa" are those which establish a connection between Plath's infantile relationship to her mother and the loss of her husband. Plath seems to blame her mother in some peculiar way for the marital breakup: the jellyfish mother is

. . . a placenta

Paralyzing the kicking lovers.
Cobra light
Squeezing the breath from the blood bells
Of the fuchsia. I could draw no breath,
Dead and moneyless,
Overexposed, like an X-ray.

(Ariel, pp. 39–40)

The last two lines accurately describe Plath's feelings after Hughes leaves her and her shame when she remembers her mother's presence. The first four imply that the mother's Gorgon stare stifles sexual enjoyment and suffocates her daughter—that her mother has created this predicament. Like Plath's earlier breakdown, when she felt her "mother had never wanted her to become a woman, but rather remain a neuter creature dependent on her for love's nourishment," she dreads being devoured by mother love. The lines above imply that the mother's presence at the marital breakup exerts an equally baleful influence. In such a situation, a sympathetic mother inevitably becomes a partisan and refuge, providing "love's nourishment" to substitute for the unfaithful husband, the untrustworthy male.

This accusation against Aurelia, of wanting to paralyze her daughter's sexual development and enjoyment, is also illuminated by an understanding of the female child's original loss of the mother. In the Oedipal situation, the little boy's rivalry with the father for the mother's love does not require a "central shift of erotic allegiance," as it does for the little girl.

She is the parent with whom the boy has been physically intimate from the outset, and to whom he is likely still to be much
more attached, in this way, than to his newly vivid father; and
now his growing awareness of bodily and social maleness tells
him that she is a member of the sex for whose affections he is
destined to compete with other males.

In the girl's case, this jealous concern about one's place with
the parents is typically much more deeply two-edged. The
father's animal allure is likely to be more powerful for her than
it is for the boy. . . . At the same time, the mother is for the girl,
as for the boy, the parent around whom bodily based tender
passion was first organized. This means that for her, love of this
kind is more evenly directed toward both parents than it is for
the boy, and rivalry with the mother for the father's love is
more evenly balanced against rivalry with the father for the
mother's. The growing insight that this balance is scheduled to
tip mainly in the father's direction is on some level wounding.
To realize that one is female, destined to compete with females
for the erotic resources of males, is to discover that one is
doomed to renounce one's first love. (Dinnerstein, pp. 45–46)

The "wounding" Dinnerstein describes as inevitable to the little
girl's recognition of her femaleness is what Freud defines as penis
envy, the female analogue to the little boy's castration anxiety over
his rivalry with the father. Penis envy is the little girl's recognition
that her original bodily fusion with her mother can never be physically recovered. In contrast, the little boy, in possession of a penis,
might still have access to a woman *like* his mother, although castration anxiety is a recognition of the father's exclusive access to her
body. Both sexes are equally wounded in the loss of the mother, but
the ultimate effect on their mature sexuality is quite different. The
result in the woman is a blunting of her sexual passion; it is a gift of
guilt for deserting the mother for a man.

Woman's need for penance and her sense of primal loss are
complicated, moreover, by the other large fact about the girl's
Oedipal situation . . . : the fact that the infidelity to her first
love [i.e., her mother] that began in this period typically went

far deeper than her shift toward the second [i.e., the father]
actually required. The sacrifice of full bodily pleasure with man,
which I have heard described as "the gift to the mother," atones
for something more than the partial desertion of her that the
girl's growth toward heteroerotic susceptibility would in itself
inevitably entail. What the girl has been guilty of is lavishing
upon her father—that is, upon man—not only the erotic recognition, and the warmth and trust, that he on his own could
inspire in her, but also much of the physical affection and filial-
romantic gratitude that would have remained attached to her
mother—that is, to woman—if they had been integrated with
the child's inevitable antagonisms toward her. What she has
done is to give away to someone else love that a part of her
knew belonged rightly to the mother. . . . The result is that she
has cut herself off from a continuity with her own early feeling,
for which she now mourns. It is in part to propitiate her fantasy
mother, to punish herself, and thereby to regain some of this
inner continuity that she holds back the final force of her "selfish" carnal passion for man. She holds it back . . . out of anger
at herself and at him: anger at a gratuitous betrayal of her oldest
root in life, a betrayal for which she was responsible but of
which he (in the form of his original parental predecessor) was
the instrument. (Dinnerstein, pp. 64–65)

Certain features in Plath's life history may well have exacerbated the
kind of guilt Dinnerstein defines and made the mother's claim on
Plath's sexual enjoyment, on her marriage to Ted Hughes, seem
oppressive. If woman's "sacrifice of full bodily pleasure" is a "gift to
the mother," for Plath it must also have been payment for the
mother's even larger gift of sexual abstinence. Aurelia's promise
never to marry again, backed by her maternal self-sacrifice, was a
pact of absolute fealty to Sylvia. This might explain why Plath felt,
in periods of emotional stress, that her side of the bargain was to
remain sexually "neuter" and dependent on Aurelia. Plath's sexuality would be a sign of infidelity to her mother. Likewise, Hughes's
infidelity must have been a horrific and double betrayal (like Norton's) to both Plath and her mother: Plath broke her childhood pact
to her mother when she married Hughes, but compensated for this

breach by promising a man who would take the place of Otto Plath.
As she describes the husband in "Daddy," he is a "model of you."
Many critics interpret this exclusively as a repetition of the father-
daughter relationship; but, as we have seen, Plath's perfect marriage, her genius of a husband, her babies, her life itself were a gift
to the mother for the sacrifice of her own. When Hughes betrays
her, he is also, as a father substitute, betraying Aurelia.

That Plath unconsciously felt she was betraying her mother by
marrying Hughes may be seen in the exaggerated way she first describes him to her mother, brother, and Olive Higgins Prouty in her
early letters. She does not only present him as an idealized father
figure; she also portrays him as a hulking giant. She stresses his
overpowering intellect and imaginative powers, but also his barbaric
temper and his violence, so that Olive Higgins Prouty is surprised by
Aurelia's report of his gentle demeanor when she first meets him.
After Aurelia meets Hughes, she tells Prouty that he is "gentle" and
"understanding," quite different from the "impetuous" and "tem-
peramental" soul Plath had led Prouty to imagine (Box 5, MSS II;
September 12, 1956). In the process of trying to convince her mother
and Olive Prouty that she has found a superlative match for herself,
Plath lavishes rather frightening virtues on Hughes. When she first
meets him she writes to Aurelia that he is "the only man I've met yet
here who'd be strong enough to be equal with" (LH, p. 221; March 3,
1956) and that he has an "iron will to beat the world across" (Box 5,
MSS II; April 17, 1956); but he is also "arrogant, used to walking over
women like a blast of Jove's lightning. . . . He is a breaker of things
and people. . . . No other man could breed supermen, with all the
vigor of mind and body in this world of cerebralism and with the
primitive force too, which has spilt off in our pale white-collared
race" (Box 5, MSS II; April 19, 1956). To her brother, she writes that
he is "a force that breaks windows when he stalks into a room. . . .
He has done nothing but write, rave, work, and desert women for 10
years" (Box 5, MSS II; April 23, 1956). After they marry, she claims to
have calmed his tempestuous nature: "Gone is the tortured black
cruel look, the ruthless banging gestures" (Box 5, MSS II; May 26,
1956); but Olive Prouty wonders just what sort of man she has found,
because Plath has described him to her "as bashing people around."
Prouty also questions whether a man of his age can be reformed and

gentled, if he is as violent as Plath depicts him (Box 5, MSS II; June 3, 1956). It is as if she needs to dramatize Hughes as someone who can dominate her—a man who will be strong enough to break her bonds with Aurelia. Such masculine dominance is an excuse for her own lack of resistance—her infidelity to Aurelia. How can she resist a superman?[57]

Plath's strange paranoia about her marriage is also comprehensible in this context. She feared terrible reprisals from the spinsterish woman dons at Cambridge, women Plath sees as neuter "bluestocking grotesques." She regarded her marriage as illicit and kept it secret for several months, although when she finally does tell her tutor Dorothea Krook, there is no punishment, and Krook cannot understand her hysteria.

> But now the hour of reckoning had come: she had got married without tutorial permission, and had to now keep it from tutorial knowledge (this is what she meant by saying she had done it secretly, which I had at first not understood), she was afraid that her outraged college would recommend that her Fulbright scholarship be taken away, in which case she would have to leave Cambridge and come away without a degree, and please *what* was she to do?
>
> I was a little taken aback, by the intensity of her fear and agitation, and, even more perhaps, by what I sensed to be a strong suppressed resentment: presumably, at Cambridge rules and practices, perhaps. It was the first and the only time I glimpsed in Sylvia (without, of course, at the time recognizing it for what it was) a small touch, oh ever so small, of the passionate *rage* which Elizabeth Hardwick and others have come to see as a dominating emotion of her later poetry.[58]

Perhaps the fear and the rage would not have been so overwhelming if Plath did not believe that she had committed some terrible crime by marrying. Plath saw her marriage as a crime against the prim women dons (who sound more than a little like her mother), against the rules this well-brought-up girl never broke because she wanted never to displease her mother.

There is still another aspect to the overdetermined imagery of

"Medusa" that needs elucidation. At one point, Plath describes her mother as a fish.

> Tremulous breath at the end of my line,
> Curve of water upleaping
> To my water rod, dazzling and grateful,
> Touching and sucking.
>
> (*Ariel*, p. 39)

She depicts her own body as male, with a phallic "water rod" and the mother as touching and sucking at the end of her line. This is not surprising if Plath's early contract with her mother is a way of offering herself as a male substitute for the father. The Oedipal rivalry with the father for the mother's love was not resolved conventionally, with the daughter conceding the father's right to the mother's body or acknowledging her female "wound"—her physical incompatibility with the mother's body. Instead, she gained complete dominance over her mother. In doing so, she could identify with the father's power and delay recognition of her femininity. She could be the little boy for her mother; indeed, she had to be as part of the unspoken contract, to make up for his loss. In "Medusa," though, this maleness becomes one more demand on Plath's body, one more payment exacted by a devouring mother, and one more reason for loathing her dependence.

According to Freud, this is not an uncommon outcome of Oedipal conflict for the female child, even when the father is still alive: "Analysis very often shows that a little girl, after she has had to relinquish her father as a love-object, will bring her masculinity into prominence and identify herself with her father (that is, with the object which has been lost), instead of with her mother."[59] Freud's description of the male child's terror at the sight of his mother's genitals also echoes the dread of sexual paralysis in "Medusa" and suggests that Plath is returning to an old identification with her father's masculinity.

> To decapitate=to castrate. The terror of Medusa is thus a terror of castration that is linked to the sight of something. Numerous analyses have made us familiar with the occasion for this: it

occurs when a boy, who has hitherto been unwilling to believe the threat of castration, catches sight of the female genitals, probably those of an adult, surrounded by hair, and essentially those of his mother.

The hair upon Medusa's head is frequently represented in works of art in the form of snakes, and these once again are derived from the castration complex. It is a remarkable fact that, however frightening they may be in themselves, they neverthe-less serve actually as a mitigation of the horror, for they replace the penis the absence of which is the cause of the horror. This is a confirmation of the technical rule according to which a multi-plication of penis symbols signifies castration.

The sight of Medusa's head makes the spectator stiff with terror, turns him to stone. Observe that we have here once again the same origin from the castration complex and the same transformation of affect! For becoming stiff means an erection. Thus in the original situation it offers consolation to the specta-tor: he is still in possession of a penis, and the stiffening reas-sures him of the fact.[60]

What Freud finds most startling about the image of the Medusa head is its hermaphroditic character, which mitigates the horror of castration. The snakes around the head are a substitution for the feared loss of the male genitals, and the Gorgon's stare causes stif-fening or paralysis, which Freud interprets as a displacement for erection, the lost male function. The decapitated head itself is a symbol of castration.

In "Medusa," there is the same fusion and confusion of male and female bodies in the depiction of a "phallic mother." The jelly-fish is a large, sucking cavity, but with tentacles like "Jesus hair." It is a "placenta," but also a "cobra light." A dilated, erect cobra ready to strike is phallic, but its "Squeezing the breath from the blood bells" is more like the female genitals. The threat of being eaten or paralyzed and connected by an "eely tentacle" is com-bined with the threat of being castrated, unsexed, and deprived of sexual satisfaction.

"Medusa" translates the horror of what Aurelia saw and what Plath saw her mother see during that final summer into the mythological Gorgon's stare. From a psychoanalytic perspective, the "sight" is the "shame" of being female, the shame of a wounded, inadequate body that can only fulfill itself through a feeding, devouring symbiosis. Plath attempts to exorcise this shame through a form of bold exhibitionism.

> If Medusa's head takes the place of a representation of the female genitals, or rather if it isolates their horrifying effects from the pleasure-giving ones, it may be recalled that displaying the genitals is familiar in other connections as an apotropaic act. What arouses horror in oneself will produce the same effect upon the enemy against whom one is seeking to defend oneself. . . . To display the penis (or any of its surrogates) is to say: "I am not afraid of you. I defy you. I have a penis."[61]

The display is akin to the goddess Athena's, who wore this emblem of horror on her dress "and rightly so, for thus she becomes a woman who is unapproachable and repels all sexual desires—since she displays the terrifying genitals of the Mother."[62] The contradiction here is peculiar; by displaying the female genitals of Medusa, Athena asserts at once both her father's power (the origins of her godhead), since she is the motherless goddess who emerged full-blown from Zeus's head, and her own fearful femaleness. As in so many of Plath's final poems, where female sexual powers represent inviolability, so in "Medusa" we may see Plath attempting to assert such self-possession.

The assertion is not successful. Even though I have tried to disentangle the poem's imagery to satisfy the critical need to know what the poem is about, "Medusa" remains incoherent, inadequate to the feelings toward her mother that Plath is struggling to express. Unlike "Daddy," where the real professor-Daddy is distinguished from the fantasy Nazi-Daddy and where the love-hate combat is allegorized, as if Plath knew what she wanted to say before she says it—as if she formulated the idea and then found a poetic drama emotionally sufficient to its utterance—in "Medusa," I would argue, the ideas have not been reality tested. The real mother is not distinguished from the Gorgon, and Plath's own body is indistinguishable from her mother's. This is what Freud, I believe, designated "dreamwork"—the body itself residing in the poem and making its pain felt in fantastic shapes and forms that elude rational discourse.

Despite this incoherence, the poem reflects a struggle for personal and imaginative autonomy in Plath's final months. It is an example of what Adrienne Rich, I believe, would call "writing as re-vision," with her connotations of an alteration in visual perception.

> If the imagination is to transcend and transform experience it has to question, to challenge, to conceive of alternatives, perhaps to the very life you are living at that moment. You have to be free to play around with the notion that day might be night, love might be hate; nothing can be too sacred for the imagination to turn into its opposite or to call experimentally by another name. For writing is re-naming. Now, to be maternally with small children all day in the old way, to be with a man in the old way of marriage, requires a holding-back, a putting-aside of that imaginative activity, and demands instead a kind of conservatism. I want to make it clear that I am not saying that in order to write well, or think well, it is necessary to become unavailable to others, or to become a devouring ego. This has been the myth of the masculine artist and thinker; and I do not accept it. But to be a female human being trying to fulfill traditional female functions in a traditional way *is* in direct conflict with the subversive function of the imagination. The word traditional is important here. There must be ways, and we will be finding out more and more about them, in which the energy of creation and the energy of relation can be united.[63]

The tension between the energy of creation and the energy of relation, between a woman artist's imaginative freedom and her "mesh of relationships" and allegiance to children, husband, mother, and father, is likely to create guilt. As Rich reflects on herself at twenty-nine, she sounds very much like Plath: "I always felt the conflict as a failure of love in myself. I had thought I was choosing a full life: the life available to most men, in which sexuality, work, and parenthood could coexist. But I felt, at twenty-nine, guilt toward the people closest to me, and guilty toward my own being."[64]

In poems like "Daddy" and "Medusa," Plath attempts to rename the relationships with her parents and to release her guilt through anger. With "Daddy," the effort is successful, and a daughter with knowledge of how a fantasy father propitiated her powers emerges at the end of the poem. With "Medusa," Plath renames her relationship with her mother as an identification with Aurelia's sacrificial femininity. She tries to exorcise this identification, to avoid repeating her mother's martyrdom in her own life and to break free from guilty obligations to "the best Mummy a girl ever had." This mother love would not be such a threat, so fervently denied by Plath, if the original tie were not so strong and such a temptation—a temptation she succumbed to once before in her life, with disastrous results. "Medusa" is not a complete renaming, perhaps because of all the reasons Chodorow and Dinnerstein offer as inherent in female psychology. Women define themselves as successful primarily in terms of relationship—to men, to children, to family—in terms of their ability to support and sustain others. "Medusa" depicts these traits solely as predatory and ignores the pleasure-giving aspect to motherly love. In cutting herself off in this way from Aurelia and what Aurelia represents, Plath may well have felt herself cut off from all benevolent outside sources, and also from Sivvy, the ideal fiction created for her mother in the image of her culture—the old perfect self, free from blemish. As a result, only old yellow, the rival ingrate, was left to speak, and Plath was not yet strong enough to manage all the guilt in giving her voice.

Three. *The Bell Jar:*
The Past as Allegory

Re-vision—the act of looking back, of seeing with fresh eyes, of entering an old text from a new critical direction—is for women more than a chapter in cultural history: it is an act of survival. Until we can understand the assumptions in which we are drenched we cannot know ourselves.—Adrienne Rich, "When We Dead Awaken: Writing as Re-vision"

UNTIL the publication of *Letters Home* and *Sylvia Plath: Method and Madness*, *The Bell Jar* was the primary source of biographical information on Sylvia Plath. For many critics, it is a fairly accurate account of a central event in her life: a mental breakdown, suicide attempt, and eventual recovery during the summer and fall of 1953. Although it is less often treated as a novel, when it is, critics often type *The Bell Jar* as an adolescent crisis narrative in the style and mood of Salinger's *Catcher in the Rye*.[1] Despite the categorizing of critics, there are interpretive problems in dealing with *The Bell Jar* either as straightforward autobiography or as a familiar subgenre of the novel.

In some ways, Plath's attitude toward *The Bell Jar* while she wrote it is more crucial to an understanding of her life and artistic development than the novel's contents. Her motives for writing *The Bell Jar* are a puzzling combination of financial opportunism and a desire to work through and master her personal history. *Letters Home* shows that Plath is almost always worried about money (as her heroine Esther is in the novel), and is particularly beset with financial pressures brought on by her separation from Hughes while preparing *The Bell Jar* for publication. For years, she contemplated the riches of a best-seller and started many novels with the hope of achieving financial security like that of her benefactor, Olive Higgins Prouty. To her mother she speaks quite frankly of prostituting her talent to write a "potboiler"[2] and warns her brother Warren that "no one must read it!"[3] This is the ostensible reason for not disclosing the title and nom de plume, Victoria Lucas, when the novel is published in England.

At the same time, she writes a friend that *The Bell Jar* is a serious effort—"an autobiographical apprentice work which I had to write in order to free myself from the past"[4]—and despite her mother's claim that she did not wish to publish the novel in America, there is evidence that Plath offered the book to Harper and Row but that it was initially rejected.[5] From this perspective, her secrecy looks more like an attempt to hide her feelings about the past from relatives and friends. *The Bell Jar* upset the image of a loving Sivvy with whom they were more familiar. Many of the portraits—of her mother, Olive Prouty (as Philomena Guinea), neighbors, and old boyfriends (Dick Norton as Buddy Willard) and girlfriends—are exaggerated caricatures and so unflattering that Plath could be regarded, as her mother feared she would when the novel was eventually published in America under her real name, as ungrateful and unjust. Shortly before *The Bell Jar's* appearance in the United States, Aurelia Plath made a last-ditch effort to persuade the editors at Harper and Row to stop publication.

> Practically every character in *The Bell Jar* represents someone—often in caricature—whom Sylvia loved; each person had given freely of time, thought, affection, and, in one case, financial help during those agonizing six months of breakdown in 1953. . . . As this book stands by itself, it represents the basest ingratitude.[6]

Plath's mixture of motives in writing the novel suggests an unresolved confusion about what the novel was supposed to do for her. She could probably excuse her mean portraits (which are also very funny) as necessary for the creation of a best-seller, but there must also have been emotional release in venting her anger toward people who cared for her. The anger is complicated by equally strong feelings of guilt for her ingratitude, which is why Plath alternately worries about the novel's publication and is desperate for its success. The unforgiving heroine, Esther Greenwood, and pervasive sourness of the novel also show that past feelings have not been mastered so much as spewed forth—ugly testimony to a continuing undercurrent of hostility. If Esther is placed next to the Sivvy of *Letters Home* as her "double," one is also reminded of a similar conflict between two female personalities in so much of Plath's work. Esther Greenwood's voice is similar to old yellow's of "In Plaster," or the rival ingrate in "Ocean 1212-W" and "Medusa." The enthusiastic, sentimental Sivvy of *Letters Home* disappears to leave behind the contemptuous voice of Esther and the often vengeful voice of the woman in the *Ariel* poems. *The Bell Jar* gives the most literal expression to an old yellow demanding to be heard. But as in the poems, so in Plath's letters to friends and relatives about *The Bell Jar* there is an ambivalence toward letting old yellow have her say— permitting the "ugly and hairy" side to emerge from the plaster mask of bright cheerfulness.

Formally, *The Bell Jar* bears the marks of Plath's confused feelings and motives. An adolescent crisis novel "in the Salinger mood" is a salable commodity. But this rubric simplifies the narrative perspective and structure of the novel. In these terms, Eileen Aird describes the novel as having a tripartite structure corresponding to Esther's movement from New York City to Wellesley to the mental asylum: the first part is Esther's confrontation with "the wilderness of city life" and the "adult world"; the second, a "growing inability to take decisions which culminates in an unsuccessful suicide attempt"; and the third, "hospital treatment and eventual recovery" with Esther emerging as a mature woman.[7] This summary assumes a clarity and resolution that the novel does not, in fact, attain.

The structure of the novel is episodic and digressive, with many individual climaxes, and the first part moves freely backward and forward in time. The flashbacks reveal that Esther's depression is not brought on solely by new experiences in the big city and the adult world, but also by a series of events from her past now having a cumulative effect and distorting her vision of the present. Frequently, the recollections are ruled by free association and transitions are arbitrary because the precise causes for Esther's depression are unclear. She does not know what is wrong with her and her behavior is symptomatic rather than explanatory. This is captured in Esther's own bewilderment at her emotional detachment. She describes herself as feeling "very still and empty, the way the eye of a tornado must feel."[8]

Esther's recovery and entry to adulthood are also dubious. One would suppose from Aird's description that the novel ends more brightly than it opens. It does not—at least not much. Esther sounds the same. She is as hostile at the end as she was at the beginning: self-absorbed and indifferent to the suicide of one of her fellow inmates; as ironical and disdainful toward the women she leaves behind in the asylum as she was toward her girlfriends in New York City; and if anything, even more contemptuous of men. The only difference seems to be that she is capable of demonstrating her hatred openly, because her psychiatrist forgives and encourages free expression of her hostility. There is no movement from a naive to a more mature and complex point of view, and Esther's loss of virginity is not a coming of age (though she feels part of a "great tradition"). Instead, this act evens the score with her unfaithful boyfriend Buddy Willard with a tit-for-tat infidelity. It was an irrational vengeance she sought at the beginning of the novel, made no more rational by its final success.

Instead of a controlled movement in voice from deranged to normal or youthful to mature, we get a few odd shifts forward at the beginning of the novel that show Esther looking backward in time as she tells the story: "I got such a kick out of all those free gifts showering on to us. For a long time afterward I hid them away, but later, when I was all right again, I brought them out, and I still have them around the house. I use the lipsticks now and then, and last week I cut the plastic starfish off the sunglasses case for the baby to play with" (p. 3). These brief glimpses of Esther ten years later tell us that she is a wife and mother—two possibilities that look remote if not impossible from what we see of the youthful Esther, who says children disgust her and claims that she won't marry. As a result, these disclosures of Esther's future sound inconsistent with what we learn about her.

Furthermore, despite the similarities of time and place and the neat correspondence of the events in the novel with Plath's life— right down to her spectacularly sanguinary deflowering—the novel does not offer a direct experience of life, from either a normal or a deranged perspective.[9] The novel is closer in form and style to allegory than autobiography. By allegory, I mean quite simply in this instance a narrative or description conveying a hidden meaning. Esther is someone who sees each event in her life as teaching a lesson of some kind. Even a short story she casually picks up and reads has a glaring application to her own situation. When Esther is not pointing a moral, the episodes themselves are shaped in order to impart lessons.

As an allegory, *The Bell Jar* is about femininity, and more specifically, three aspects of femininity: the woman's place in society; her special creative powers; and finally, her psychological experience of femininity. This may sound too abstract, but if we look at any one of Esther's relationships to other characters or any of the various predicaments she finds herself in, we find a "moral" concerning one or more of these subjects. Esther's desire for revenge on Buddy Willard, for example, is motivated first by the hypocrisy of a social double standard that gives him the privilege of premarital sex (indeed, encourages such experience as necessary for later guiding his wife into the mysteries of sex), but denies women the same freedom of sexual expression. "Nice" girls remain pure for marriage, according to Esther's mother, Buddy Willard's mother, and Esther's friends. As if these social pressures on Esther are not strong enough, her mother sends her an article from the *Reader's Digest*— the final authority on such matters, it would seem—called "In Defense of Chastity," as a less-than-subtle warning to remain pure. Second, Esther is provoked to vengeance by Buddy's frequent threats to her creativity. He tells her that she will not want to write poems when they are married, because home and children will satisfy her creative desires; and Esther spends much of her time inventing unanswerable retorts to Buddy's belittling description of a poem as nothing but a piece of dust. Finally, Plath strongly suggests that Esther is motivated by penis envy in her vendetta against Buddy. On one of their dates, he proudly exhibits his genitals to her, and Esther, while outwardly not very impressed (she compares his member to a turkey neck and gizzards), is also reminded of her college entrance physical. She had to stand in the nude for a photograph and receive a grade for her posture. We may suppose by this analogy that Plath means us to read Esther's refusal to exhibit herself to Buddy as reluctance to be "graded" next to him. Other evidence in the novel, as well as Esther's return to this incident as the source for her disillusionment with sex, support this reading of Plath's intentions.

The Bell Jar is also an anatomy of Plath's mental breakdown—a self-analysis that attempts to reveal the causes for her self-destructive impulses. In this, the novel is muddled, largely because all aspects of Plath's feminine allegory are not resolved. While her psychiatrist convinces her that purity is social propaganda and Esther worries no longer about her creativity being destroyed in marriage (she becomes, she says, her "own woman"), her psychological experience of womanhood is ambivalent. At the end of the novel she seems intent on exploiting and punishing men, outsmarting them to prove she is not inferior. Her attitude toward other women is equally charged with negative feelings. She separates herself from her fellow inmates at the asylum by seeing herself as the exceptional survivor, the one woman who slips out from under the thumb of a man. Her final farewell is to Valerie, the girl who has been deprived of her anger by a lobotomy and lives permanently in a bell jar. Unlike Valerie, Esther still has her anger and she remembers every distorted vision she suffered.

> A bad dream.
> I remembered everything.
> I remembered the cadavers and Doreen and the story of the fig tree and Marco's diamond and the sailor on the Common and Doctor Gordon's wall-eyed nurse and the broken thermometers and the Negro with his two kinds of beans and the twenty pounds I gained on insulin and the rock that bulged between sky and sea like a gray skull.
> Maybe forgetfulness, like a kind of snow, should numb and cover them.
> But they were part of me. They were my landscape. (P. 194)

The bad dream has taken the familiar shape of reality, but Esther has not fully awakened. The landscape is still as threatening.

One suspects that Esther's supposed "cure" for feelings of inadequacy has been only artificially induced by shock treatments and the purchase of a diaphragm that she carries around as a secret badge of her liberation. The real sources for these feelings of inadequacy remain submerged and inaccessible to Esther's conscious mind. This uneasiness in the resolution to the novel is hinted at in Esther's question, "But I wasn't sure, I wasn't sure at all. How did I know that someday—at college, in Europe, somewhere, anywhere—the bell jar, with its stifling distortions, wouldn't descend again?" (p. 197). Esther's doubts seem more than justified by her lack of self-knowledge. At no point in the novel does she explain her suicide attempt to herself or another character for the benefit of the reader. Instead, Plath gives us a deflowering and the suicide of Joan Gilling as symbolic events marking the end of Esther's illness, and the reader must interpret their meaning for Esther . . . and for Plath.

As we have seen, Plath's own "return from the dead" restored her to a life not at all different from the nineteen years of straight As, scholarships, and prizes that preceded her illness. Outwardly, she seems little changed by her devastating experience. The only difference we have noted is the brief donning of a more aggressive sexuality. This is in full accord with Esther's new adventurousness at the end of the novel. The deflowering incident is, in fact, a reshaped version of the experience with Irwin during the time she lived with Nancy Hunter Steiner in Cambridge, Massachusetts, during the "platinum summer."

What Plath seems to be doing is a return to these incidents in her life in a new attempt at self-understanding, as if she herself were unsure of the causes and motives for her behavior. The problem with this cathartic psychological dimension to Plath's allegory is that it is difficult to determine how much artistic control she has over it. She presents Esther's (and by extension, her own) depression as a result of the inequities of the double standard and the male usurpation and abuse of female creative powers, and these two lines of action are well developed and to a certain extent resolved. Plath seems to have gained a new, and what we might now call feminist, awareness of how her life has been shaped under male domination. But the most important source of anxiety is Esther's supposed Electra complex. Plath plants a good deal of evidence for this reading of Esther's character, but somehow it never coalesces, and the conclusion of the novel heads in another direction altogether. Because of this confusion, Plath's self-analysis demands revision through a sustained psychoanalytic study of Esther's character. In what follows, therefore, there will be a double interpretation of Esther's character—both a review of what Plath discovers and intends to reveal about herself through her heroine, and a more thorough analysis supplemented by evidence from the poems that shed light on Esther and, by extension, Plath herself.

The Allegory of the Double Standard

The structure of *The Bell Jar* is more like a Chinese box than a linear narrative with a distinct beginning, middle, and end in their proper order. Plath begins with the outward circumstances of Esther's depression—her reactions to New York City, the Rosenberg trial, new acquaintances, and her job as a college editor of *Mademoiselle* magazine—and then moves inward and backward in time, revealing incidents from the past that are presumably related to Esther's anxiety. This Chinese box mode of development is exemplified by Esther's progressive recognition of her isolation from other people and in her regression back to the time of her father's death. Her suicide attempt is a further regression; it is depicted as a retreat into the womb and nonentity. While there is considerable overlap and interdependence of the social, artistic, and psychological allegories, their development is similarly like that of a Chinese box. Plath begins with social oppression—the limitations on Esther's future ambitions because she is a woman—moving to the specific threats against her creativity by friends and relatives, to, finally, the ways in which she victimizes herself. This multilayered, self-enclosed form works very well for allegory, each box as a separate episode with a lesson attached to it, and to articulate the movement of Esther's consciousness. In this movement, there are many missing links between episodes, but it is downward and inward to the single hope that the puzzle has been solved, the last box has been opened, and she may crawl in and extinguish her pain. After the suicide attempt, there is a reversal of this process. Esther reaches out first to an inmate at the asylum who is catatonic, and gradually ventures outward again.

Together, the first two episodes of *The Bell Jar* are an allegory about the divided image of woman that emerges from the double

standard. Esther's companions are Doreen and Betsy, the stereotypical "bad" girl and "nice" girl of this social ideology. Esther plays
each part in turn, both unsuccessfully. This temporary adoption of
alternative identities is also one of the major structuring devices of
the novel. All of the female characters are doubles for Esther—possible roles she tries on and then discards, because they do not fit her
self and because her own sense of self is so fragmented. This desire
to be someone else is primarily a form of escape from a feeling of
fraudulence and failure.

> All my life I'd told myself studying and reading and writing and
> working like mad was what I wanted to do, and it actually
> seemed to be true, I did everything well enough and got all A's,
> and by the time I made it to college nobody could stop me . . .
> and now I was apprenticed to the best editor on an intellectual
> fashion magazine, and what did I do but balk and balk like a
> dull cart horse. (P. 26)

> I wondered why I couldn't go the whole way doing what I
> should anymore. This made me sad and tired. Then I wondered
> why I couldn't go the whole way doing what I shouldn't . . .
> and this made me sadder and more tired. (Pp. 24–25)

In the orgy with Doreen and then at the *Ladies' Day* banquet
with Betsy, Esther first tries to "go the whole way doing what I
shouldn't" and then "the whole way doing what I should." The
"bad" girl Doreen is sophisticated, bored, sexy, and representative
of a "marvelous, elaborate decadence" that draws Esther "like a
magnet." Doreen's "perpetual sneer" at the other girls and their
lack of worldly wisdom attracts Esther, who is equally incapable of
responding with energy and enthusiasm to her "golden opportunity." The "nice" girl Betsy, on the other hand, is the ingenue—a
pure, corny, all-American girl from Kansas, intent on saving Esther
from Doreen's influence. Betty co-ed. She is the "should" for Esther,
and Betsy wants marriage, a big farm, and lots of children. Betsy
will be rewarded for her conformity later by becoming a "model"
matron in B. H. Wragge advertisements—a media image for every
woman's aspirations. As polar opposites, Doreen and Betsy repre-

sent the successful vamp and the future homemaker, and Esther, at least for awhile, envies each of the girls for the security of their identities.

Doreen's wise cynicism, however, evaporates when she is in the presence of a man, and she transforms herself into a tawdry little sex goddess—a diminutive version of Marilyn Monroe. She permits herself to be squeezed and touched by the cowboy disc jockey, Lenny, while pretending not to notice: "She just sat there, dusky as a bleached-blond Negress in her white dress, and sipped daintily at her drink" (p. 9). As Doreen sits there being stared at and fondled, Esther, now alias Elly Higginbottom, does all the talking and tries to sound as worldly as Doreen does when she isn't with a man. At the beginning of the evening, Esther even feels like Doreen—"wise and cynical as all hell" (p. 6)—but as the evening progresses Esther finds herself fading into a shadow-self: "It was so dark in the bar I could hardly make out anything except Doreen. With her white hair and white dress she was so white she looked silver. I think she must have reflected the neons over the bar. I felt myself melting into the shadows like the negative of a person I'd never seen before in my life" (p. 8). There is something enviable about Doreen's total passivity as a sex object, but the Doreen identity fails because it does not give Esther the rebellious feeling of release she hoped for. Plath's comparison of Doreen to a Negress, with its connotations of slavery, tells the reader that she is nothing but a sexual possession. It was the combination of witty sarcasm and decadent sexual experience in Doreen that promised independence and superiority. Without her sneer and her wit, Doreen looks like a "great white macaw" (p. 9) with beautiful plumage but a birdbrain—a stereotypically dumb blond.

Although it is Doreen who passes out in her own vomit before Esther's door, Esther is the one who feels dirtied by the experience of watching Lenny's seduction and Doreen's sexual teasing. She ritualistically bathes after returning to the hotel, and the next day says, "I still expected to see Doreen's body lying there in a pool of vomit like an ugly concrete testimony to my own dirty nature" (p. 19). And, in fact, Esther regurgitates what Doreen represents as unwholesome: "I made a decision about Doreen that night. I decided I would watch her and listen to what she said, but deep down

I would have nothing at all to do with her. Deep down, I would be loyal to Betsy and her innocent friends. It was Betsy I resembled at heart" (p. 19).

Innocence, however, proves equally unwholesome. In the next episode, Esther attends a lavish banquet at the promotional expense of *Ladies' Day* magazine. With Betsy, she enters the world of the homemaker, with its helpful hints on cleaning and cooking, new recipes, and "peach-pie" faces of contented domesticity. Nothing could be more hygienic than the spread put out for the guest editors as a "small sample of the hospitality" of the Food Testing Kitchens at *Ladies' Day*. The feast, however, proves to be "chock-full of ptomaine." Esther's attempt to "go the whole way doing what she should" with Betsy, like her attempt to play the bad girl with Doreen, ends with nausea and a sickening vision of the appetizing but poisonous kitchens at *Ladies' Day*.

> I had a vision of the celestially white kitchens of *Ladies' Day* stretching into infinity. I saw avocado pear after avocado pear being stuffed with crabmeat and mayonnaise and photographed under brilliant lights. I saw the delicate, pink-mottled claw meat poking seductively through its blanket of mayonnaise and the bland yellow pear cup with its rim of alligator-green cradling the whole mess.
>
> Poison. (P. 39)

The neon and silver seduction of Doreen is nothing compared to this deadly cuteness. The images suggest a sickeningly coquettish domesticity. The crab claws poke above the mayonnaise like a coy woman peeping over a blanket, and the avocado holds its poison lovingly like a mother cradling a baby.

In this comic-book feminist allegory, girls like Betsy are rewarded with marriage, while girls like Doreen, who willingly give men their bodies without marriage, eventually end up empty-handed. This is the lesson Esther learns from her experience. To round off these first two episodes, Esther and Betsy attend a movie based on that moral: "Finally I could see the nice girl was going to end up with the nice football hero and the sexy girl was going to end up with nobody, because the man named Gil had only wanted a mistress and not a wife all along and was now packing off to Europe on a single ticket" (p. 34). We can be thankful that it is precisely at this moment that the ptomaine overwhelms Esther and she has the urge to puke, but the nausea over this wholesome fare is also a signal that Esther cannot share in the innocent naiveté of Betsy, or, as she says later, in scornful Doreen tones, the stupid simplicity of "Pollyanna Cowgirl."

What she cannot, quite literally, swallow is the limitation imposed on her by a double standard and the sexual hypocrisy permitted men in this arrangement. When Esther's mother sends the *Reader's Digest* article "In Defense of Chastity," Esther refuses to accept "the main point" of her culture's sexual arrangements: "that a man's world is different from a woman's world and a man's emotions are different from a woman's emotions and only marriage can bring the two worlds and the two sets of emotions together properly." Instead, she decides that justice demands a quid pro quo.

> I couldn't stand the idea of a woman having to have a single pure life and a man being able to have a double life, one pure and one not.
>
> Finally I decided that if it was so difficult to find a red-blooded intelligent man who was still pure by the time he was twenty-one I might as well forget about staying pure myself and marry somebody who wasn't pure either. Then when he started to make my life miserable I could make his miserable as well. (P. 66)

One of Esther's chief preoccupations is how she can sidestep the rigors of the double standard without becoming a Doreen. Yet every man she meets seems to think of women in these terms. The male imagination in *The Bell Jar* has room for only the pure and the impure. Her college friend Eric tells her that "if he loved anybody he would never go to bed with her. He'd go to a whore if he had to and keep the woman he loved free of all that dirty business" (p. 64). Esther considers Eric a likely candidate for spoiling her purity until he tells her that she reminds him of his older sister, "so I knew it was no use, I was the type he would never go to bed with" (p. 65).

In New York, Esther is fixed up with a malevolent version of Eric—the Peruvian woman-hater Marco. He, too, divides women into Madonnas and whores. He is in love with his first cousin, a pure beauty who intends to be a nun, and as if guessing Esther's secret purpose, treats her as a slut, flinging her into the mud and threatening to rape her.

Despite her best efforts, Esther remains "pure" until the end of the novel. It is important to note that the origins of Esther's obsession with purity are presented as social.

> When I was nineteen, pureness was the great issue.
> Instead of the world being divided up into Catholics and Protestants or Republicans and Democrats or white men and black men or even men and women, I saw the world divided into people who had slept with somebody and people who hadn't, and this seemed the only significant difference between one person and another. (P. 66)

For a young woman, the great social division is between girls who "do" and girls who "don't." Esther's perception of her culture is not a distortion. It is confirmed later by Esther's benefactor, Philomena Guinea, who is willing to help Esther as long as her problem, it is implied, isn't an illegitimate pregnancy.

> My mother said that Mrs. Guinea had sent her a telegram from the Bahamas, where she read about me in a Boston paper. Mrs. Guinea had telegrammed, "Is there a boy in the case?"
> If there was a boy in the case, Mrs. Guinea couldn't, of course, have anything to do with it.
> But my mother had telegrammed back, "No, it is Esther's writing. She thinks she will never write again." (P. 151)

Ironically, Esther's "purity" saves her from a state institution, and her loss of it later will help to cure her. All of this may seem to be an exaggeration of the issue on Plath's part, except that the first question newspaper reporters asked when Plath herself attempted suicide was whether there was a boy involved in the case.[10]

The Allegory of Female Creativity

The allegory of the double standard gives way to and is complicated by Esther's relationship with Buddy Willard. In recompense for the ptomaine, *Ladies' Day* distributes a volume of short stories to the victims. One of them applies to Esther's vendetta against Buddy. It is about a "Jewish man and a beautiful dark nun" who meet at a fig tree growing between the man's house and a convent,

> until one day they saw an egg hatching in a bird's nest on a branch of the tree, and as they watched the little bird peck its way out of the egg, they touched the back of their hands together, and then the nun didn't come out to pick figs with the Jewish man anymore but a mean-faced Catholic kitchen maid came to pick them instead and counted up the figs the man picked after they were both through to be sure he hadn't picked anymore than she had, and the man was furious. (P. 45)

The Edenic innocence of the love between the Jewish man and nun is symbolized by the fruit and the baby bird. The maid's entry, which is like that of the serpent in the garden, introduces lust, jealousy, and small-mindedness. The story reminds Esther of her relationship to Buddy and a similarly blighted innocence and disillusionment with sex: "We had met together under our own imaginary fig tree, and what we had seen wasn't a bird coming out of an egg, but a baby coming out of a woman, and then something awful happened and we went our separate ways" (p. 45). In this little allegory, the kitchen maid is both the waitress with whom Buddy has an affair and Esther, who keeps a balance sheet on sexual encounters. Like the kitchen maid who counts figs to make sure everything is even, Esther is determined that Buddy will not remain one up on her. We discover that Esther is not chafing under the oppression of a double standard so much as she is outraged by Buddy's new power over her. In the past, she basked in the sexual sophistication Buddy told her she had.

> From the first night Buddy Willard kissed me and said I must go out with a lot of boys, he made me feel I was much more sexy

and experienced than he was and that everything he did like hugging and kissing and petting was simply what I made him feel like doing out of the blue, he couldn't help it and didn't know how it came about.

Now I saw he had only been pretending all this time to be so innocent. . . .

What I couldn't stand was Buddy's pretending I was so sexy and he was so pure, when all the time he'd been having an affair with that tarty waitress and must have felt like laughing in my face. (Pp. 56–57)

Esther feels duped into a false confidence in her sexual attractiveness and potent femininity. The balance of power in their relationship has shifted from an uneasy equality (while Buddy may effectively have put down the impracticality of Esther's artistic ambitions, she could assert her sexual dominance) to a situation where Esther is clearly bested by Buddy's experience.

Her feeling of inferiority is compounded by Buddy's already mentioned exhibition of his genitals—she has never "seen" a man before, only statues, she says—and even more seriously by her attendance with Buddy at the birth of a child. What she sees is another instance of male control over women.

I was so struck by the sight of the table where they were lifting the woman I didn't say a word. It looked like some awful torture table, with these metal stirrups sticking up in mid-air at one end and all sorts of instruments and wires and tubes I couldn't make out properly at the other.

The woman's stomach stuck up so high I couldn't see her face or the upper part of her body at all. She seemed to have nothing but an enormous spider-fat stomach and two little ugly spindly legs propped in the high stirrups, and all the time the baby was being born she never stopped making this unhuman whooing noise.

Later Buddy told me the woman was on a drug that would make her forget she'd had any pain and that when she swore and groaned she really didn't know what she was doing because she was in a kind of twilight sleep. . . .

I thought it sounded just like the sort of drug a man would invent.

I didn't feel up to asking if there were any other ways to have babies. For some reason the most important thing to me was actually seeing the baby come out of you yourself and making sure it was yours. I thought if you had to have all that pain anyway you might just as well stay awake.

I had always imagined myself hitching up on to my elbows on the delivery table after it was all over—dead white, of course, with no makeup and from the awful ordeal, but smiling and radiant, with my hair down to my waist, and reaching out for my first little squirmy child and saying its name, whatever it was. (Pp. 53–54)

The problem, as Plath dramatizes it here, is that men have usurped the privilege of giving birth from women. The doctors are all male and they are entirely responsible for the emergence of a new creature into the world. To Esther's mind, they have deprived the woman of her consciousness of both the pain and pleasure of birth and used her body for their own purposes, their own ends. The woman and her baby are their opus, their engineering feat.[11] The mother has been made mindless with drugs invented by men, incapable of seeing or comprehending the birth of her own child. Esther, too, is deprived of that vision of herself as a strong woman, enjoying the powers of her own body.

Ultimately, this episode becomes part of the allegory on female creativity in *The Bell Jar*. Men take over women's powers and use them for their own pleasure. Such is the lesson Esther learns in watching a birth and it is reiterated in a second episode, while she is on another date with Buddy.

Once when I visited Buddy I found Mrs. Willard braiding a rug out of strips of wool from Mr. Willard's old suits. She'd spent weeks on that rug, and I had admired the tweedy browns and greens and blues patterning the braid, but after Mrs. Willard was through, instead of hanging the rug on the wall the way I would have done, she put it down in place of her kitchen

mat, and in a few days it was soiled and dull and indistinguishable from any mat you could buy for under a dollar in the five
and ten.

And I knew that in spite of all the roses and kisses and res-
taurant dinners a man showered on a woman before he married
her, what he secretly wanted was for her to flatten out under-
neath his feet like Mrs. Willard's kitchen mat. (P. 69)

Esther's little allegory here may be interpreted in sexual terms. This
is only one more instance of sex being associated with filth in *The
Bell Jar:* Esther's ritualistic bathing to cleanse herself after the orgy
with Doreen; Eric's disgust over the dirty surroundings of his sexual
initiation by a prostitute; Marco's attempted rape of Esther in a
muddy ditch; Irwin's shower after "deflowering" Esther; and here
the analogy between the marital relationship and a man wiping his
feet on a doormat. But there is also an allegory about the abuse of
female creative powers in this incident. Mrs. Willard gleans the materials of her art from clothes cast aside by her husband, but once
she transforms them into something beautiful, they return to male
use. The moral is as old as the cliché, "You treat me like your
personal doormat, and I let you step all over me." The woman
acquiesces in her own slavery.

From what she has seen, Esther fears that marriage will destroy
her desire to write, that her artistic energies will be channelled into
the humdrum activities of a housewife: "I also remembered Buddy
Willard saying in a sinister, knowing way that after I had children I
would feel differently, I wouldn't want to write poems anymore. So
I began to think maybe it was true that when you married and had
children it was like being brainwashed, and afterward you went
about numb as a slave in some private, totalitarian state" (p. 69).
Esther's fears are confirmed by Mrs. Willard's homely wisdom:
" 'What a man wants is a mate and what a woman wants is infinite
security,' and 'What a man is is an arrow into the future and what a
woman is is the place the arrow shoots off from' " (p. 58). But
Esther wants "to shoot off in all directions myself, like the colored
arrows from a Fourth of July rocket" (p. 68). Her mother, too, warns
Esther that

nobody wanted a plain English major. But an English major who knew shorthand was something else again. Everybody would want her. She would be in demand among all the up-and-coming young men and she would transcribe letter after thrilling letter.

The trouble was, I hated the idea of serving men in any way. I wanted to dictate my own thrilling letters. (Pp. 61–62)

Servitude, brainwashing, numbness, drugs that wipe the mind clear, shock treatments—all of these are closely associated in Esther's mind with the connubial state and its threat to her creativity. Later, this victimization is made a part of her experience as a mental patient, and a bell jar that descends over all women, suspending them forever in a state of arrested development, like "the big glass bottles full of babies that had died before they were born" (p. 51) at Buddy's medical school. The women she meets at the mental asylum are analyzed and given insulin injections, shock treatments, or lobotomies, depending, it seems, on the degree of their rebelliousness. Mrs. Savage appears to have committed herself for no better reason than to "louse up" her daughters' debutante parties with the public shame of a crazy mother. As they get better, the women return to their old lives, filled with shopping and bridge, unfaithful husbands and catty chitchat. In fact, the society of women at Belsize reminds Esther of the "normal" girls in her college dormitory: "What was there about us, in Belsize, so different from the girls playing bridge and gossiping and studying in the college to which I would return? Those girls, too, sat under bell jars of a sort" (p. 194). The nurses and inmates respond with the same envy and excitement at the news of a male visitor and amuse themselves in the same ways. Their docility is symbolized by the lobotomized Valerie, who apparently passes her confinement in complete contentment, watching other women come and go, not so much as a mental patient but as a prim old "Girl Scout Leader" (p. 154) watching her "girls" grow up and leave childish things. Occasionally, there is a pathetic display of creativity and independent spirit: Dee Dee composes a tune on the piano and "everybody kept saying she ought to get it published, it would be a hit" (p. 169). But female society in *The Bell Jar*, whether it's the Amazon Hotel in New York City (an obvious, but clever transformation of the Barbizon for women), a college dormitory, or a mental asylum, is a state of waiting for the "right" man to come along and time is passed with "harem" activities.

Esther is surrounded by women like dolls, zombies, and mannequins. The epitome of this condition is Hilda, another guest editor in New York. She is a mindless mannequin for the stylish hats and other accessories she creates in accord with shifts in fashion (another example of female creative energy channeled into a socially acceptable, and absurdly insignificant, activity). Her narcissistic habit of gazing at herself in shop windows is compensation for nonentity: "she stared at her reflection in the glassed shop windows to make sure, moment by moment, that she continued to exist" (p. 82). Behind her "vacant, Slavic expression" is a "blind cave" (p. 81). She does not, in fact, exist, except for a cavernous voice that reminds Esther of a dybbuk when she responds to Esther's pity for the Rosenbergs: "It's awful such people should be alive. . . . I'm so glad they're going to die" (p. 81). As Esther falls deeper into depression, she comes to resemble Hilda. She is surprised by her reflection in mirrors, as if an unknown "other," flattened out and distorted by the mirror's flaws, stares back. She later sees her suicide like the Rosenbergs' trial and execution as a lurid newspaper headline, and similar to Hilda, is curiously detached from the human pain.

The electrocution of the Rosenbergs is at first simply a recognizable feature in the novel's American landscape. Eventually, Esther's obsession with their case is linked to the shock treatment she is given, which she does not see as therapy, but as a punishment for some terrible, unknown crime.

> Then something bent down and took hold of me and shook me like the end of the world. Whee-ee-ee-ee-ee, it shrilled, through an air crackling with blue light, and with each flash a great jolt drubbed me till I thought my bones would break and the sap fly out of me like a split plant.
>
> I wondered what terrible thing it was that I had done. (Pp. 117–18)

It is as if God bent down to smite her. Esther wants to confess to a priest, to be cleansed of her sins, and at one point, even thinks of entering a nunnery; but she has no idea what her "sins" are. Later she tells her nervous Unitarian minister, who has come to call on her in the mental asylum, that she believes in hell. She must live in it before she dies, she says, "to make up for missing out on it after death," and this is a punishment, in turn, for not believing in a life after death (p. 166).

This circular reasoning is symptomatic of Esther's anxiety and is similar to Freud's description of patients in "Analysis Terminal and Interminable," who, out of an unconscious sense of guilt, punish themselves by never getting well.[12] It is an inner inhibition (i.e., they do not consciously reject health). Likewise, we begin to suspect that Esther's sudden halt after years of accomplishment is motivated by guilt, rather than the opposite cause-effect sequence. It is guilt that leads to failure, rather than, as we normally expect, failure that leads to guilt. And this unusual process of self-victimization casts doubt on both the allegories of the double standard and female creativity as the sole explanations for Esther's depression and her feelings of inadequacy. We must probe deeper still.

Living under the Bell Jar

In a defense of the political nature of feminist criticism, William Morgan complains that

> it is permissible . . . to teach Huck Finn or even Native Son as an indictment of American society since the larger cultural tradition has taken care to dissociate itself (hypocritically, in the case of the latter) from the "bad" guys in both books. But it is not, not yet anyway, permissible to teach The Bell Jar as a novel about a world, our world, structured so as to drive the talented woman into insanity or straitjacket domesticity.[13]

In part, my discussion of The Bell Jar answers to Morgan's complaint, and it is a justifiable one. The novel has not received very much attention except as autobiography, and while social, feminist issues have persistently surfaced in discussions of *The Bell Jar*, they have not received sustained analysis. But I believe there are good reasons—in the novel itself—for this reluctance to make *The Bell Jar* into a feminist melodrama about whether or not society will turn the talented Esther into a zombie or a domestic slave to Buddy Willard or to some other equally wretched male specimen.

Plath is not a feminist—or at least not a feminist in the sense that Morgan means in his description of *The Bell Jar*. She complicates the sociocritical thrust of the novel with the presence of two characters: the career woman, Jay Cee, and the simultaneous interpreter, Constantin. Jay Cee is the one female character in the novel who may be characterized as "liberated." She is proof that marriage and a successful career are not incompatible. But Esther does not want to identify with her.

> I tried to imagine Jay Cee out of her strict office suit and luncheon-duty hat and in bed with her fat husband, but I just couldn't do it. I always had a terribly hard time trying to imagine people in bed together.
> Jay Cee wanted to teach me something. All the old ladies I ever knew wanted to teach me something, but I suddenly didn't think they had anything to teach me. (P. 5)

From what we see of Jay Cee, she wishes to make Esther a protegé, but in Esther's psychological state, Jay Cee's advice and encouragement sound like criticism, and she is further repelled by Jay Cee's "plug-ugly" appearance. Esther would prefer to look like Doreen and have some sexual power over men. Later, Esther will unreasonably lash out at her mother for not being like Jay Cee—"I wished I had a mother like Jay Cee. Then I'd know what to do" (p. 32)—but like Esther's later wish that she had continued living with her grandmother and grown up to be a contented housewife, wearing wash dresses and making pots of coffee, like her fantasy of being a nun or gentle Elly Higginbottom, this wish is just one more instance of Esther's confusion. She is trying, unsuccessfully, to find someone to blame for her depression; this, at least, provides some relief from her own feelings of guilt. Having a mother like Jay Cee—mentor and role model that she is for Esther's literary ambitions—would not, in fact, help Esther.

Esther is her own victim. She acknowledges as much at the end of her date with the simultaneous interpreter, Constantin. For a moment, she knows that social inequities are less threatening than her own self-destructive impulses. Like Jay Cee, Constantin's presence in the novel refutes the case for Esther being downtrodden by insensitive men. He proves that all men are not "out for one thing"—to separate "bad" girls from "nice" girls by trying to seduce them all. He is a thoroughly pleasant companion (despite his association with Mrs. Willard), and even though their date ends up in his room, he makes no move to deflower Esther. Instead, he innocently falls asleep by her side and his one sexual gesture is an affectionate stroking of her hair. In this pleasant mood, Esther fantasizes about marriage to Constantin and concludes with a vision of herself in housewifely servitude. There is nothing in Constantin's behavior to warrant this fantasy, which turns inevitably from idyll to nightmare about the future, but Esther sees herself as a victim in every situation. It is only when she returns to the hotel and goes to bed that it dawns on her that she is her own worst enemy.

> Every time it rained the old leg-break seemed to remember itself, and what it remembered was a dull hurt.
> Then I thought, "Buddy Willard made me break that leg."
> Then I thought, "No, I broke it myself. I broke it on purpose to pay myself back for being such a heel." (P. 70)

She then remembers a visit to Buddy in a sanitorium for patients with tuberculosis and her callous treatment of him at a time when he was weak and dependent on her. Unlike every other episode in the novel, where Esther manages to distort the situation so that she is the one who is badly treated (we have just seen this in her reverie about being married to Constantin), in this flashback she acknowledges her culpability. She treated Buddy badly and injured herself in recompense.

It is significant that this revelation occurs after the only healthy encounter that Esther has with a man in the novel. This points to the way in which external social conditions—men with a sensibility like Buddy, Eric, and Marco—complement and contribute to Esther's feeling of being oppressed. Finally, though, the oppression is, as she perceives here, not only the fault of others or outside pressures.

Plath is, indeed, concerned with what Morgan calls the structure of Esther's world, but it is a mental structure: the bell jar. The bell jar defines a multitude of relations between Esther and the world. It represents her sense of self and it divides her, cuts her off, makes her different from other people. It is a metaphor for her inner life: she exists in the bell jar as a stillborn baby. Because Esther's mental life reflects in a transformed way what culture, society, has already done to her as a human being, the bell jar does eventually serve as a symbol of social oppression, and Plath, as we have seen, uses it in this way in the final chapters of the novel to define the female condition. But before we can accept Esther's easy generalization about all women living under a bell jar, we must take into account the origins for Esther's feeling that she is "pickling" in her own foul air. These, it turns out, can be better understood in psychological than in social terms.

The Fraudulent Father and the Electra Complex

One explanation for Esther's depression can be found in Freud's essay on "Mourning and Melancholia." Her symptoms fit a pattern described by Freud.

> In grief the world becomes poor and empty; in melancholia it is the ego itself. The patient represents his ego to us as worthless, incapable of any effort and morally despicable; he reproaches himself, vilifies himself and expects to be cast out and chastised. He abases himself before everyone and commiserates his own relatives for being connected with someone so unworthy. He does not realize that any change has taken place in him, but extends his self-criticism back over the past and declares that he was never any better. This picture of delusional belittling— which is predominantly moral—is completed by sleeplessness

and refusal of nourishment, and by an overthrow, psychologically very remarkable, of that instinct which constrains every
living thing to cling to life.

The distinguishing mental features of melancholia are a profoundly painful dejection, abrogation of interest in the outside
world, loss of the capacity to love, inhibition of all activity, and
a lowering of the self-regarding feelings to a degree that finds
utterance in self-reproaches and self-revilings, and culminates
in a delusional expectation of punishment.[14]

The last two symptoms—a severe fall in self-esteem and the expectation of punishment—differentiate melancholic depression leading to
suicide from normal grief for the loss of a loved one. These are
Esther's most striking characteristics—her incessant self-reproaches
and her obsession with the electrocution of the Rosenbergs, which
eventually becomes associated with the "punishment" of shock
treatment. When she is not "wondering what it would be like, being
burned alive all along your nerves" (p. 1), she is chastising herself
for not living up to her own and others' ambitions for her.

I was supposed to be having the time of my life. (P. 2)

I was supposed to be the envy of thousands of other college
girls. (P. 2)

It was my first big chance, but here I was, sitting back and
letting it run through my fingers like so much water. (P. 3)

I should have been excited the way most of the other girls were.
(P. 3)

She is also fond of indicting herself with fraud—dishonestly maneuvering herself out of a required course on chemistry or writing
"factitious" poems and short stories for her creative writing courses
in college.[15] Much of the time she reviews and adds to a long list of
things she cannot do: cooking, shorthand, singing, horseback riding, skiing, foreign languages—especially German (her father's lan-

guage)—geography, tennis. The absurdity of the combination shows that the object is not healthy self-criticism, but irrational self-denigration. She ends her list by noting, "The one thing I was good at was winning scholarships and prizes, and that era was coming to an end" (p. 62).

As Esther retreats more and more from any activity, the self-accusations coalesce into a little chorus of voices warning her, "You'll never get anywhere like that" (p. 120). Except for Jay Cee (who displays, in fact, a motherly concern), no one accuses Esther of being a laggard or failure except Esther. How could they, with her nineteen years of hard work, straight As, and long list of scholarships and poetry prizes? There is, in Freud's words, "no correspondence . . . between the degree of self-abasement and its real justification."[16] But "if one listens patiently to the many and various self-accusations of the melancholiac, one cannot in the end avoid the impression that often the most violent of them are hardly at all applicable to the patient himself, but that with insignificant modifications, they do fit someone else, some person whom the patient loves, has loved, or ought to love."[17]

Do Esther's self-revilings fit someone else? Her most violent self-accusation is that she is a fraud, a despicable intellectual phony. When her boss Jay Cee asks what her future ambitions are, Esther cannot respond with her usual enthusiasm and assurance, "Famous poet and English professor." Instead, she says,

> "I don't really know" . . . . I felt a deep shock, hearing myself say that, because the minute I said it, I knew it was true.
>
> It sounded true, and I recognized it, the way you recognize some nondescript person that's been hanging around your door for ages and then suddenly comes up and introduces himself as your real father and looks exactly like you, so you know he really is your father, and the person you thought all your life was your father is a sham. (P. 27)

Esther's strained comparison of her "unmasking" to the discovery that a common loiterer is her real father is a Freudian slip revealing the identity of the person she "loves, has loved, or ought to love," who is also the true object of her self-castigation.

This is borne out by an episode at her father's grave later in the novel. She has been trying to decide how to kill herself: with a razor? by hanging herself with her mother's bathrobe cord? by hara-kiri? or perhaps with morphia powders? This indecision, which is alternately terrible and grotesquely funny, makes the final choice, the when and how, of crucial import for understanding the psychological nature of the attempted suicide. She "knows just how to go about it" immediately after the visit to her father's grave. She cries over the pitifully untended grave of her father and says, sorrowfully, "I had a great yearning, lately, to pay my father back for all the years of neglect and start tending his grave" (p. 135). This sentence hides a barb of resentment. It can also be read, "I had a great yearning, lately, to *pay* my father *back* for all the years of *neglect.*" His neglect, not hers; and vengeance—to pay back—not mourning, is the disguised wish in this sentence. It echoes all the other situations in *The Bell Jar* where Esther wants to "pay back," get even, with Buddy, Marco, Mrs. Willard. How dare her father die and desert her, when as she says earlier, she was his favorite, and the nine years before his death were the only time when she was truly happy? He is a sham as a father. With a simple change in tone, we recover the feelings of a child who did not forgive her father for dying and deserting her. This is at least one of those terrible, unknown crimes that causes guilt in Esther Greenwood and ultimately leads her to attempt suicide.

Plath is acutely aware of her supposed Electra complex both here and in her poems—of her suicide being an act of love and longing for union with a dead father who has, in her imagination at least, become a god, a colossus. I would like to digress a moment to look at one of these poems, because Plath is purposely vague, I believe, about Esther's feelings at her father's grave (if Esther knew the precise nature of her feelings, she would probably not attempt suicide). Plath is also not completely clear about why a feeling of fraudulence should be Esther's major complaint.

In "Electra on Azalea Path," Plath recalls the same incident: the pilgrimage to her father's grave shortly before her attempted suicide. Unlike *The Bell Jar*, which simply leaps without intervening explanation from this event to the final decision to kill herself, the poem delves into the daughter's new knowledge.

The day I woke, I woke on Churchyard Hill.
I found your name, I found your bones and all
Enlisted in a cramped necropolis,
Your speckled stone askew by an iron fence.

In this charity ward, this poorhouse, where the dead
Crowd foot to foot, head to head, no flower
Breaks the soil. This is Azalea Path.
A field of burdock opens to the south.
Six feet of yellow gravel cover you.
The artificial red sage does not stir
In the basket of plastic evergreens they put
At the headstone next to yours, nor does it rot,
Although the rains dissolve a bloody dye:
The ersatz petals drip, and they drip red.[18]

As in the novel, the grave site is disappointing. Here it is not the
neglect, but the tackiness of artificial plants that offends the
daughter. The implicit accusation is, once again, fraud. The grave
should be a monument, but it is only one more headstone in a
crowded "charity ward, this poorhouse," and the daughter is
cheated of her heroic father.

The dream she wakens from is a hibernation in which she believed for twenty years that she was immaculately conceived as by a
god.

As if you had never existed, as if I came
God-fathered into the world from my mother's belly:
Her wide bed wore the stain of divinity.
I had nothing to do with guilt or anything
When I wormed back under my mother's breast.
Small as a doll in my dress of innocence
I lay dreaming your epic, image by image.
Nobody died or withered on that stage.
Everything took place in a durable whiteness.[19]

The "durable whiteness" represents a purity and divinity now lost to
her. Her initiation into guilt is the result of a disillusionment with

sexuality, like a child who has bitterly come to accept how she was conceived. Her father can no longer endure in her imagination as a god; he dies a second time as a man. As if to deny this new knowledge, she repeats the dream of her father's death in lines that echo the Greek tragedy of Agamemnon. Plath designates dream status through the use of italics and then confesses to the dream's falsity.

> *The day your slack sail drank my sister's breath*
> *The flat sea purpled like that evil cloth*
> *My mother unrolled at your last homecoming.*
> I borrow the stilts of an old tragedy.
> The truth is, one late October, at my birth-cry
> A scorpion stung its head, an ill-starred thing;
> My mother dreamed you face down in the sea.
>
> The stony actors poise and pause for breath.
> I brought my love to bear, and then you died.
> It was the gangrene ate you to the bone
> My mother said; you died like any man.
> How shall I age into that state of mind?
> I am the ghost of an infamous suicide,
> My own blue razor rusting in my throat.
> O pardon the one who knocks for pardon at
> Your gate, father—your hound-bitch, daughter, friend.
> It was my love that did us both to death.[20]

In these lines, Plath both conjures up the Electra myth with Clytemnestra's murder of Agamemnon, and denies its validity: "The truth is" that her father died like any man; that it was not her mother who killed him; and that his death was a kind of suicide and rejection of her (Otto Plath's stubborn decision not to see a doctor until it was too late to save his gangrened leg and then his life is interpreted in this way). There is also a suggestion in her final begging for pardon that she was the one responsible for her father's death, but that it was her love that killed him: she may have had her mother to herself after her father's death, and so satisfied a guilty desire to have him out of the way, but she is also innocent in the sense that she exculpated her crime by lifting him into a "durable whiteness," a stage borrowed from Greek tragedy, where "nobody died or withered." On this fantasy stage, her father lived on as a mythic being or god, as if, she says, he never existed, as if he were never a man. She pays for her child's wish to have him dead by endowing him with immortality. As in "Daddy," he lives on in her imagination as a powerful god, dominating her psyche. According to Judith Kroll, "Electra on Azalea Path" is Plath's record of a "split into false and true selves: the true self is the child she was before things went wrong; that part, as 'Electra on Azalea Path' makes plain, lies buried with her father. The part which has continued to live after her father's death is, then, incomplete, a kind of false self; and the life lived by it is, to that extent, unreal."[21] The problem with this interpretation is that it ignores the daughter's bitter confrontation with an admittedly false myth about her origins and her father's death. The whole poem is a fall from the child's fantasy of divinity to the emotionally unacceptable truth of her father's ugly death. "How shall I age into that state of mind?" she asks, acknowledging the truth while also disparaging it and the maturity it requires. The Electra myth is a sham and her father's immortality is a sham. Even more important, the daughter's worship of her father as a god is a sham. The truth is . . . she wanted him dead.

The recognition in this poem, I believe, has a bearing on our interpretation of Esther Greenwood's (and Plath's) attempted suicide. It tells us a good deal more about Esther's feeling of fraudulence: she thought she was perfect, divine, and now she discovers all of her imperfections, just as the daughter in the poem discovers her father's reality as a man. It is as Esther says: "The person you thought all your life was your father is a sham." The suicide attempt, so often seen as an act of father-worship by a girl with an Electra complex, is more complicated. It is and it is not an attempt to unite with her dead father. It is, in the sense that Esther would like to cling to her fantasy of a father-god, to her own divinity, and to a view of her mother as the guilty Clytemnestra; and it is not, because Esther also tries to kill herself as an act of expiation for wanting her father dead, and as an act of revenge against both parents—against her father for dying and deserting her, when, as she says earlier in the novel, she was his favorite, and, as I hope to show, against her mother for being born a woman.

The Electra complex is finally insufficient to explain Esther's anxiety over her sexual identity, shown in her abortive attempts to imitate other women who are regarded as "normal." It also does not explain her vendetta against Buddy, nor her preoccupation with her virginity, nor her indecision about what kind of woman she wants to be. There are Betsy and Doreen, and later in the novel, she turns to the memory of her grandmother and to Dodo Conway, a serene neighbor in Wellesley who is always pregnant.

> I would be simple Elly Higginbottom, the orphan. People would love me for my sweet, quiet nature. They wouldn't be after me to read books and write long papers on the twins in James Joyce. And one day I might just marry a virile, but tender, garage mechanic and have a big cowy family, like Dodo Conway. (P. 108)

> I was thinking that if I'd had the sense to go on living in that old town I might have met this prison guard in school and married him and had a parcel of little kids by now. It would be nice, living by the sea with piles of little kids and pigs and chickens, wearing what my grandmother called wash dresses, and sitting about in some kitchen with bright linoleum and fat arms, drinking pots of coffee. (P. 123)

This longing for simplicity—even simple-mindedness—jars with her equal desire for power over men and shows an ambivalence toward her femininity that is not explained by an Electra complex. The visit to her father's grave, after all, is a rather belated recognition of an old loss. But what initiates this recognition and why is normal grief impossible for Esther?

There is, I have suggested, another "crime" that is also a source of guilt and confusion about her sexual identity and explains Esther's delayed grief over her father. Esther Greenwood, alter ego for Sylvia Plath, also wished her father dead as a rival for her mother's affection, and has managed, we shall see, to project this wish on to her mother.

A Merciful Death

We must go back a few steps in female development to understand the origin of this wish before showing how it is portrayed in *The Bell Jar*. According to Freud, children—both male and female—are jealous of the father, because he is a rival for the mother's affection. Like the little boy, the little girl's primary choice of love object is the mother, not the father. Freud objects to the Electra complex (this is, in fact, Jung's revision of Freud) as a description of female development because it "seeks to insist that the situation of the two sexes is analogous."[22] The symmetry of Oedipal complex for boys, Electra complex for girls, assumes that the female child is capable of sexual discrimination at an extraordinarily early age and that she is naturally disposed toward being "feminine" and loving the opposite sex, despite the primacy of the mother-infant relationship. Freud does not, contrary to popular notions of his thought, regard masculinity or femininity as a biological given, but as the result of a complicated set of psychological developments, any of which may go awry.

In the female child, sexual maturation is complicated by two deprivations: she must give up what was originally her leading genital zone (the clitoris) in favor of a new zone (the vagina) and submit to an exchange of her original object—her mother—for her father.[23] The male child neither gives up his leading genital zone, the penis, nor exchanges his mother for a new love object. The residue of the Oedipal complex in the boy is castration anxiety, and with this development he is initiated into manhood.[24] The girl, however, rr acknowledge her actual lack of a penis. Unlike the little boy, who may one day find a substitute gratification for the loss of his mother in the choice of a woman like his mother, the little girl must shift from mother love to father love, from desire for a woman as a sexual object to desire for a man. This shift completes the "normal" heterosexual pattern of psychological development in women, but as Juliet Mitchell points out in her useful summary in *Psychoanalysis and Feminism*, she makes this shift under the duress of familial sexual arrangements, and

> only because she has to, and then with pain and protest. She has to, because she is without a phallus. No phallus, no

power—except those winning ways of getting one. Recognition of her "castration" is the female infant's entry to girlhood, just as acceptance of the threat and deference to the father expressed in castration anxiety is the boy's debt to his future manhood. The girl's entry into her feminine "destiny" is characterized by hostility to the mother for her failure to make her a boy; it is an entrance marked by penis-envy, that in its turn must be repressed or transformed.[25]

There are alternative paths of repression and transformation. The girl may turn away from women altogether, despising in them her own castration. She may remain in the pre-Oedipal "masculine" phase, regarding herself sexually as a little man and establishing lesbian attachments. In this way, she maintains her identification with the father. Or she can—and this is Freud's description of "normal" female development—transfer her sexual attentions from her mother to her father, wanting first his phallus, then his baby, a substitute for the phallus, and then the man again, to give her this baby. In this way, she transforms the active aims of her sexual instincts into passive aims that are socially acceptable.[26] She is usually rewarded by the father for playing the flattering and seductive little girl.[27]

In *The Bell Jar*, there is much to suggest that Esther's illness is a result of a repressed desire to be a male, and that she is belatedly attempting to transfer affection from her mother to her father and to assume this "normal" female sexual identity. In a passage that Plath finally deleted from the novel, the "bell jar" that cuts Esther off from life is, like a hysterical symptom, an expression of her identification with her father. She is in analysis with her psychiatrist, who is a man in this earlier version.

"I feel so cut off," I finished.

"No, no! It is not *you* who are cut off!" The doctor pointed to me dramatically. "It is your father's *leg* that was cut off!" And, with his right hand, he made a rapid, amputating gesture on his left thigh.

I was glad it was my father's leg, and not me, that had been cut off, and I was just about to ask, the way I always wanted to

ask, what practical suggestions the doctor could give me to feel
joined back again, when somebody tapped on the door.[28]

We can only speculate on why this episode was left out, but perhaps
it is because it says too much about the nature of Plath's own psychic wound. Esther feels "cut off" like her father's leg, but she also
feels castrated as a woman. Plath plants enough other clues—the
lobotomized Valerie, Esther's deflowering, which is as bloody as a
castration, her reaction to Buddy's exhibition—so that we do not
need this additional passage to decipher Esther's problems. But
Plath is reticent. It is only later, in a poem like "Cut," where a
kitchen accident—a Freudian slip of the knife ("What a thrill— / My
thumb instead of an onion.")—leads to an outpouring of her feelings of castration as a woman: "Dirty girl, / Thumb stump."[29]

The bell jar is an overdetermined symbol. Its general meanings
are (1) that Esther feels sealed off from the rest of the world because
of her illness, and (2) that all women tend to be sealed off from
experience because of social inequities. The symbol is used with
greater precision to represent the feeling of (3) being a dead fetus
preserved in a jar, and (4) being physically amputated. These meanings come together neatly to imply that women are by their physical
natures doomed to a severely constricted social and mental development. If we pursue the psychological meaning of the symbol, we
also discover that it represents the female child's feeling of being
"cut off" from the mother.

Esther grieves as much for the loss of her mother as her father
when she weeps over his grave. This may seem paradoxical and out
of character with the scorn she expresses toward her mother
throughout the novel, but such hostility is also typical of the female
child, who eventually becomes angry with her mother for not being
born a man. True to Freudian form, Esther unreasonably blames her
mother for her own inadequacies: "My own mother wasn't much
help. My mother had taught shorthand and typing to support us
ever since my father died, and secretly she hated it and hated him
for dying and leaving no money because he didn't trust life insur-
ance salesmen" (p. 32). Esther can deny her own guilt by projecting
her complaints on to her mother. It is *Esther* who envies the soft life
of the rich girls at the Amazon and worries about money throughout

the novel; *Esther* who hates shorthand and typing and wants to be like "up and coming young men" and compose her own "thrilling letters"; and *Esther* who both wished her father dead and has a grudge against him for dying and deserting her. In psychoanalytic translation, her complaints should read: "It is my mother's fault that I was born a woman; I don't wish to be like her, but like my father; and ultimately, my mother is responsible for his death because she was happy when he died." The contradictory complaint at the root of all these others is that Esther is forever separated from her mother, her first love, because of a new recognition of her femininity. This self-contradiction is evident in the form of her suicide. She does not hang herself or commit hara-kiri; she does not drown herself or slash her wrists. None of these strategies is quite right. Instead she encloses herself in a dark crawl space and falls asleep.

> A few old, rotting fireplace logs blocked the hole mouth. I shoved them back a bit. Then I set the glass of water and the pills side by side on the flat surface of one of the logs and started to heave myself up.
>
> It took me a good while to heft my body into the gap, but at last, after many tries, I managed it, and crouched at the mouth of the darkness, like a troll.
>
> The earth seemed friendly under my bare feet, but cold. I wondered how long it had been since this particular square of soil had seen the sun.
>
> Then, one after the other, I lugged the heavy, dust-covered logs across the hole mouth. The dark felt thick as velvet. I reached for the glass and bottle, and carefully, on my knees, with bent head, crawled to the farthest wall.
>
> Cobwebs touched my face with the softness of moths. Wrapping my black coat round me like my own sweet shadow, I unscrewed the bottle of pills and started taking them swiftly, between gulps of water, one by one by one. (P. 138)

The suicide is a protest against maternal loss. She retreats into a womb and returns to a fetal state. Her recovery is a painful rebirth: "Then the chisel struck again, and the light leapt into my head, and through the thick, warm, furry dark, a voice cried,

'Mother!' " (p. 139). Esther betrays her longing in this cry; it is only after she realizes that she has been brought back to the living, before she is ready, that she turns away from her mother and refuses to see her.

The suicide attempt, then, is directed at both parents, and is both a symbolic act of union and an act of aggression. Against her mother, Esther has one major complaint: she instills guilt in her daughter by playing the role of martyr. Once again, however, it is Esther who sees suicide as a sweet martyrdom. She envisions herself as otherwise steadily declining into insanity and using up her mother's small means on private psychiatric care. There will eventually be no recourse, she thinks, but to put her in a state institution, where presumably her mother can then forget her. To save her mother and brother from ignominy and bankruptcy on her account, Esther reasons, would be a splendid sacrifice. To be sure, Mrs. Greenwood does not like to think of her daughter as "like that"—a "crazy"—and she does worry about money; but Plath gives no evidence for the assumption that Mrs. Greenwood would like to forget her daughter or would feel herself saved from a terrible burden by her daughter's death.

No, what Esther wants to do is prove her mother's responsibility for her father's death. In this way, she escapes her own unconscious sense of guilt. This becomes clear in the indictment of her mother's callousness. Esther is upset by the neglect of her father's grave and regards it as proof of her mother's lack of feeling. Esther also twists her mother's conventional comfort and wisdom into a positive satisfaction.

> I thought it odd that in all the time my father had been buried in this graveyard, none of us had ever visited him. My mother hadn't let us come to his funeral because we were only children then. I had always been my father's favorite and it seemed fitting I should take on a mourning my mother had never bothered with.
>
> Then I remembered that I had never cried for my father's death.
>
> My mother hadn't cried either. She had just smiled and said what a merciful thing it was for him he had died. (Pp. 136–37)

Psychologically, what Esther does is to move from "my mother was happy when my father died" to "my mother would be happy if I died." Esther's suicide, like her father's death, would be a "merciful thing" in her mother's words. And, in this way, Esther will make her mother responsible, guilty, for both their deaths. It is her mother who wished her father dead, not Esther.

The chapter in which this tortured logic comes to the foreground begins, "Of course his mother killed him" (p. 126). We break into a conversation between Esther and a blind date on Ibsen's *Ghosts* (the title is never revealed, but the plot fits Ibsen's play). The play ends with the mother's mercy killing of her son. He is dying of syphilis inherited from the father, who, in Esther's words, fooled "around with unclean women, and in the end [the son's] brain, which has been softening all along, snaps completely, and his mother is debating whether to kill him or not" (p. 126). All of Esther's motives for suicide are reflected in distorted fashion in this description of *Ghosts:* her disillusionment with sex as "unclean"; the father's guilt for her insanity; her mother's responsibility for her suicide—a mercy killing; her need for vengeance; and her desire to be a son, like the budding artist Oswald in the play, and not a daughter.

Father-Seduction and a Feminine Destiny

It may seem that we have exhausted the possible unconscious motives for Esther's depression and suicide attempt. But there is still another, and it explains her persistent, but unsuccessful, efforts to lose her virginity before she attempts suicide and why this is the first task she takes on in her return to normal life. When Irwin seduces her, Esther feels as though she becomes a part of a "great tradition," and she does. In psychoanalytic terms,

> the girl only acquires her secondary feminine identity within the law of patriarchy in her positive Oedipus complex when she is seduced / raped by, and/or seduces the father [in fantasy]. As the boy becomes heir to the law with his acceptance of symbolic castration from the father, the girl learns her feminine destiny

with this symbolic seduction. But it is less important than the boy's "castration," because she has to some extent perceived her situation before it is thus confirmed by the father's intervention. She has already acquired the information that as she is not heir to the phallus she does not need to accept symbolic castration (she is already "castrated"). But without the father's role in her positive Oedipus complex she could remain locked in pre-Oedipal dilemmas (and hence would become psychotic), for the Oedipus complex is her entry into her human heritage of femininity. Freud always said that a woman was "more bisexual" than a man. By this he seems to have been hinting at the fact that within patriarchy her desire to take the father's place and be the phallus for the mother is as strong as is the boy's ultimate right to do so.[30]

This probably sounds more difficult than it actually is. As it applies to Esther, it explains her desire for union with a dead father in explicitly sexual terms. Her decision to take on a mourning her mother "never bothered with" is an attempt to take the mother's place. Where before she took her father's place when he died and gained exclusive possession of her mother, she is now, belatedly, acknowledging the fraudulence and illegitimacy of this possession and trying to take on a feminine role instead. This incestuous marriage with her father is only hinted at in *The Bell Jar*, but in "The Beekeeper's Daughter," the fantasy is fulfilled. The father, "maestro of the bees," moves "among the many-breasted hives" and the daughter waits for him as a queen bee: "Here is a queenship no mother can contest—." At the end of the poem, there is a consummation.

> Father, bridegroom, in this Easter egg
> Under the coronal of sugar roses
>
> The queen bee marries the winter of your year.[31]

Despite the rivalry with the mother, this should not be taken as evidence for a Electra complex, as an act of father worship, but as evidence for a frustrated desire to assume a feminine sexual identity.

For in both *The Bell Jar* and this poem, the daughter is trying to "kill" the father permanently, to resolve her relationship with him. Esther's mourning is an acknowledgment of her father's death, and in the poem, if the analogy to bees is consistent (as it is in other poems by Plath), then we can assume the death of the father as a drone. As the daughter explains in "Daddy," "Daddy, I have had to kill you. / You died before I had time—."[32] The father is conjured up one more time for his seduction and death.

The role of the father-seduction fantasy in the initiation of a woman into her femininity also helps us to explain Esther's worries over her virginity both before and after the suicide attempt. In the first part of the novel, she is "locked in pre-Oedipal dilemmas" and a rival to every man she meets. As Mitchell describes the problem, "her desire to take the father's place and be the phallus for the mother is as strong as is the boy's ultimate right to do so," and Esther persistently asserts her right to what she believes and what her culture continually reminds her are male privileges. The initiating factor for Esther's depression is the date with Buddy, which begins with the birth episode and is closely followed by the revelation of his affair with the waitress and his "exhibition": "After that something in me just froze up." This is a triple blow to Esther's ego: giving birth is presented as a female weakness rather than strength because men control the process; men have sexual freedom because they need not fear pregnancy; and finally, despite Esther's comparison of Buddy's genitals to a "turkey neck and turkey gizzards," her response is a mixture of fascination, repulsion, and embarrassment—of envy and denial.[33] For the first time, Esther regards her body as inferior, and her reactions closely follow those attributed to penis envy by Freud. There is, first a

> general revulsion from sexuality. The little girl, frightened by the comparison with boys, grows dissatisfied with the clitoris, and gives up her phallic activity and with it her sexuality in general as well as a good part of her masculinity in other fields. The second line leads her to cling with defiant self-assertiveness to her threatened masculinity. To an incredibly late age she clings to the hope of getting a penis some time. That hope becomes her life's aim; and the phantasy of being a man in spite

of everything often persists as a formative factor over long periods.[34]

Esther is, at first, alternately attracted to the rebelliousness of Doreen and the passivity of Betsy; she gives up her desire to achieve and begins to dream of the simple-minded contentment of an always impregnated Dodo Conway or her imaginary alias, Elly Higginbottom. But ultimately she balks and clings to what her culture defines as male prerogatives. Her desire to get an edge on Buddy is an instance of this tenacity. An even more extreme instance is Esther's battle with the woman-hater, Marco. Esther is fixated on his diamond stickpin, which she is determined to possess. She gapes at it with the same compulsion to look that she displayed in staring at Buddy when he exhibited himself, and Marco is portrayed in other ways to suggest Esther's penis envy. His smile reminds Esther of a snake she teased in the Bronx zoo: "When I tapped my finger on the stout cage glass the snake had opened its clockwork jaws and seemed to smile. Then it struck and struck at the invisible pane till I moved off" (p. 86). Woman-haters like Marco are also "gods: invulnerable and chock-full of power. They descended, and then they disappeared. You could never catch one" (p. 88). The description recalls Greek mythology and Zeus's various descents to rape a mortal woman—humiliating her, proving his dominance, and retreating to leave her pregnant and alone to bear and nurture his progeny. Marco would be an adequate father substitute (notice his similarity to the Agamemnon-father in "Electra on Azalea Path"), except that Esther is not ready for seduction, not ready to give up her "father's place."

Self-Murder and Choosing a Woman's Role

In *Of Woman Born: Motherhood as Experience and Institution*, Adrienne Rich affirms the Freudian pattern of development—but in more consciously critical terms than Plath's.

The first knowledge any woman has of warmth, nourishment, tenderness, security, sensuality, mutuality, comes from her mother. That earliest enwrapment of one female body with another can sooner or later be denied or rejected, felt as choking possessiveness, as rejection, trap, or taboo; but it is, at the beginning, the whole world. Of course the male infant also first knows tenderness, nourishment, mutuality from the female body. But institutionalized heterosexuality and institutionalized motherhood demand that the girl-child transfer those first feelings of dependence, eroticism, mutuality, from her first woman to a man, if she is to become what is defined as a "normal" woman—that is, a woman whose most intense psychic and physical energies are directed toward men.[35]

And she describes her own vaguely remembered "loss" of her mother and initiation into femininity.

My father's tense, narrow body did not seize my imagination, though authority and control ran through it like electric filaments. I used to glimpse his penis dangling behind a loosely tied bathrobe. But I had understood very early that he and my mother were different. It was his voice, presence, style, that seemed to pervade the household. I don't remember when it was that my mother's sensuousness, the reality of her body, began to give way for me to the charisma of my father's assertive mind and temperament; perhaps when my sister was just born, and he began teaching me to read.[36]

What Rich describes here is her own shift of erotic allegiance from mother to father, from a pre-Oedipal attachment to the mother to a new position of femininity in relationship to her father. There is also an attraction to the father's "assertive mind and temperament," an identification with his intellectual activity, and as Rich describes this experience elsewhere, an attraction to the father's library, filled with books by men and images of women.

My own luck was being born white and middle-class into a house full of books, with a father who encouraged me to read and write. So for about twenty years I wrote for a particular man, who criticized and praised me and made me feel I was indeed "special." The obverse side of this, of course, was that I tried for a long time to please him, or rather, not to displease him. And then of course there were other men—writers, teachers—the Man, who was not a terror or a dream but a literary master and a master in other ways less easy to acknowledge. And there were all those poems about women, written by men: it seemed to be a given that men wrote poems and women frequently inhabited them. These women were almost always beautiful, but threatened with the loss of beauty, the loss of youth—the fate worse than death. Or, they were beautiful and died young, like Lucy and Lenore. Or the woman was like Maud Gonne, cruel and disastrously mistaken, and the poem reproached her because she had refused to become a luxury for the poet.[37]

In Rich's words, femininity is not "a human experience freely chosen and lived,"[38] but a consciousness created out of the pressure of relationships within the family, repeated on a larger scale in the social order, and culturally projected by the male imagination; this pressure on the child's sense of sexual difference determines its consciousness of what is male and what is female, both physically and in terms of activity.

For Esther Greenwood, these differences, these boundaries, are very confused, and for the daughter in Plath's work as a whole, the father "died before I had time"—either for this seduction to a female role in relation to men or an identification, however tenuous as it is described by Rich, with male creative activity. At the end of *The Bell Jar*, Plath gives us a sense of Esther Greenwood choosing femininity, and trying to do it as her "own woman." In their sourness, however, the final episodes tell us a good deal about the "pain and protest" of accepting a "feminine destiny." There is a sense of bitter self-betrayal in the final form of Esther's choice. Esther's recovery is an uneasy compromise at best. In the mental asylum, she is, like Marco, a woman-hater. Esther's solution to her problems is neither to accept her own feminine "castration" nor to continue to assert her masculinity. This latter development is allegorized in Esther's relationship to Joan Gilling.

Her thoughts were not my thoughts, nor her feelings my feelings, but we were close enough so that her thoughts and feelings seemed a wry, black image of my own.

Sometimes I wondered if I had made Joan up. Other times I wondered if she would continue to pop in at every crisis of my life to remind me of what I had been, and what I had been through, and carry on her own separate but similar crisis under my nose. (P. 179)

Joan is a double, like the other female characters, for some part of Esther's personality. Doreen's cynicism, Betsy's naive enthusiasm, Jay Cee's ambition, Hilda's dybbuk voice, and Dodo's Madonnalike serenity are all qualities Esther looks for or fears in herself. But according to Esther, Joan's likeness to her is only external. She goes to the same college; she is a former girlfriend of Buddy Willard; she is inspired by newspaper accounts of Esther to attempt her own suicide. Yet Joan loves Mrs. Willard while Esther hates her; Joan is a horsey, athletic type while Esther is an intellectual and aspiring poet; and Joan is a lesbian while Esther cannot "see what women see in other women" (p. 179). If the preceding analysis of Esther has been accurate, however, Joan's lesbianism doubles for Esther's repressed masculinity and Esther's response to Joan is a vigorous denial of her desire to be like a man. After Esther's inadvertent interruption of Joan's dalliance with another inmate, Joan tells her that she likes her better than Buddy. Esther does not want any closeness with Joan. She replies, " 'That's tough, Joan, . . . because I don't like you. You make me puke, if you want to know' "(p. 180).

Joan is the most important double in *The Bell Jar:* she sees Esther through the hemorrhage that follows her loss of virginity, and her death is concurrent with Esther's final recovery. Allegorically, these events represent Esther's ostensible surrender of her masculinity. Irwin, as a professor and scientist, is a substitute father, and Esther's defloration is like a bloody castration, a full acknowledgment of her wound in real rather than "hysterical" terms (i.e., being "cut off" in a bell jar). This event is closely followed by Joan's suicide and funeral, which is, as Esther describes it, a burial of a shadow-self. It is, indeed, as if Esther has made Joan up as a secret sharer, only to destroy her finally as the diseased part of her mind which must be amputated in order for her to get well and to live successfully under the bell jar that encloses all women in this allegory.

> All during the simple funeral service I wondered what I thought I was burying.
> At the altar the coffin loomed in its snow pallor of flowers— the black shadow of something that wasn't there. (P. 198)

Joan's burial is equivalent to the healing of the wounds in Esther's identity. At the end of the funeral, she is as whole and pure again as the snow over Joan's grave.

> There would be a black, six-foot-deep gap hacked in the hard ground. That shadow would marry this shadow, and the peculiar, yellowish soil of our locality seal the wound in the whiteness, and yet another snowfall erase the traces of newness in Joan's grave.
> I took a deep breath and listened to the old brag of my heart. I am, I am, I am. (Pp. 198–99)

A part of Esther will be sealed off from light, submerged like an alternative self.

It is difficult, however, to decide how conscious Plath is in her use of Joan on the basis of *The Bell Jar* alone. Joan's crucial role in Esther's recovery is coupled with a vigorous repudiation of her significance and likeness to Esther, and this muddles the resolution of the novel. But there is strong evidence in Plath's senior thesis on "doubles" in Dostoevsky that she was aware of what she was doing. She wrote to her mother that she was fascinated with this topic.

> In connection with this [thesis] topic, I'm reading several stories by E.T.A. Hoffmann; *Dorian Gray*, by Oscar Wilde; *Dr. Jekyll and Mr. Hyde*; Poe's *William Wilson*; Freud, Frazier, Jung, and others—all fascinating stuff about the ego as symbolized in reflections (mirror and water), shadows, twins—dividing off and becoming an enemy, or omen of death, or a warning con-

science, or a means by which one denies the power of death
(e.g., by creating the idea of the soul as the deathless double of
the mortal body).[39]

The last part of Plath's description is almost a paraphrase of part of
Freud's essay on "The Uncanny."

> For the "double" was originally an insurance against destruction
> of the ego, an "energetic denial of the power of death," as Rank
> says; and probably the "immortal" soul was the first "double" of
> the body. This invention of doubling as a preservation against
> extinction . . . [springs] from the soil of unbounded self-love,
> from the primary narcissism which holds sway in the mind of the
> child . . . and when this stage has been left behind the double
> takes on a different aspect. From having been an assurance of
> immortality, he becomes the ghastly harbinger of death.
>
> The idea of the "double" does not necessarily disappear with
> the passing of the primary narcissism, for it can receive fresh
> meaning from the later stages of development of the ego. A
> special faculty is slowly formed there, able to oppose the rest of
> the ego, with the function of observing and criticizing the self
> and exercising a censorship within the mind, and this we be-
> come aware of as our "conscience". . . . [This] renders it possi-
> ble to invest the old idea of a "double" with a new meaning and
> to ascribe many things to it, above all, those things which seem
> to the new faculty of self-criticism to belong to the old sur-
> mounted narcissism of the earliest period of all.[40]

Joan is, in those terms, the most infantile of the doubles in *The Bell
Jar*, the one who hearkens back to the "primary narcissism which
holds sway in the mind of the child." Joan loves Mrs. Willard and in
this she represents the old attachment to the mother. Even the form
of her suicide, by hanging, is a denial of maternal loss, a symbolic
reattachment of the umbilical cord. Esther's earlier consideration of
hanging herself with her mother's bathrobe cord, by the rafters in
her grandmother's house, tends to confirm this maternal association. Joan's death is finally a substitution for Esther's.

Plath uses the other doubles mechanically to explore Esther's character—"doubling, dividing, and interchanging the self"—and, as with Hilda ("I'm so glad they're going to die") and Jay Cee ("You'll never get anywhere like that") to signify the severity of her conscience, her ego-criticizing faculties. With Joan, however, she regresses to the primary wound to Esther's self-love: the realization that being born female separates her forever from her mother. By destroying Joan, she releases her anger at this revelation and preserves her self while repressing the most dangerous impulse, her wish to be male. Joan completes a movement in *The Bell Jar* that Plath describes in her thesis, "The Magic Mirror": "In essence, the appearance of the Double is an aspect of man's eternal desire to solve the enigma of his own identity."[41] In *The Bell Jar*, however, it is the enigma of woman's identity.

This psychoanalytic interpretation of *The Bell Jar* has established functions for characters and links between episodes that are not fully developed by Plath. There is a jerky discontinuity to the movement from incident to incident, particularly in the final chapters. Esther's date with Cal and the discussion of *Ghosts*—the title never revealed—followed by the visit to her father's grave and her final decision to commit suicide are presented without transitions. These actions have no apparent inexorability, until a psychoanalysis supplies the causative chain in Esther's behavior. The lack of structural clarity is not so much a result of Plath being a novice in fiction. Although this is her only novel, she had been writing short stories and starting novels for many years. If anything, the formal inadequacies of *The Bell Jar* are symptomatic of Plath's inability, I believe, to master feelings of guilt and hostility and to see herself as a whole person. This is even more apparent in the resolution of the novel, which is no resolution at all in some respects. In spite of Esther's new confidence, her rebirth, there are many instabilities. She may have, in Joan's funeral, symbolically buried her masculinity, but she has not wholeheartedly embraced femininity either. Her special satisfaction at forcing Irwin to pay for her virginity and her sarcastic response to his desire to know when he will see her again—

> "Do you really want to know?"
> "Very much."

"Never," I said, and hung up with a resolute click— (P. 197)

is too much like her old antagonism toward Buddy, her need for vengeance, and her desire to beat Marco by hanging on to his diamond stickpin. She has only managed to compensate for her own sense of inferiority by making men feel inferior. When she feels threatened, she will turn the tables and become threatening herself.

There is much about this conclusion that suggests another outbreak of self-destructive impulses when Esther feels powerless—when she cannot triumph over and punish men.

What we have seen of Plath in her correspondence (chap. 2) tends to confirm this psychoanalysis of her alter ego Esther, while at the same time we can see Plath revising her past, instilling it with this new anger against men. This is evident in the social and artistic allegories of *The Bell Jar*, in their protest against male privilege, but also in the differences between Esther and Plath after they return to their lives from an emotional breakdown. Even though, like Esther, Plath immediately becomes more sexually aggressive to assert her independence from her mother, there is nothing in the correspondence to suggest that she has adopted Esther's vengeful attitude toward men. Instead, she continues her search for the perfect mate and expresses intense relief to her mother and friends when she at last finds and marries her "giant," Ted Hughes. Her marriage, like so many of Plath's "achievements" is testimony to her inordinate compulsion to be "normal," to be like other women. Jane Kopp, her friend at Cambridge, reports that Plath told her,

> "Jane, you can't imagine what a relief it is to be free of that dreadful social pressure." This was said in so earnest a way that I was struck by it; she seemed exceptionally present. I understood that she referred to the pressure to "date," to pretend this and that, to seek to marry, etc. She did not mean that the "dreadful social pressure" was *why* she had married Hughes, but that the relief from all of that was a very blessed thing for her. I believe that in saying what she did to me she also meant to allude tacitly to the naïveté of all her earlier babbling about men and sex.[42]

If Esther were in fact an accurate mirror image of Plath at the age of twenty, a reader might understand the isolated reference to marriage and babies at the beginning of *The Bell Jar* as consistent with her character, because Plath, as we have seen, after her return from McLean's continues to need a "strong" man, not simply to assure her sense of a feminine identity, but as absolute confirmation of her womanliness. She desperately wants marriage and babies. Esther, a character created ten years later, reflects a different consciousness in Plath; she is much more her "own woman"—less passive, less dependent on male strength for reassurance. She is, in novel form, the same voice we confront in "Lady Lazarus" and in Plath's angry letters about Ted Hughes.

I do not wish to extoll the virtues of Esther's anger against men, because it is no more a "cure" for her sense of inadequacy than Plath's earlier tendency to overidealize men, to play the role of admiring daughter to the colossus-father. In one of the most astute analyses of Plath's fury at men, George Stade argues that the rage is, in fact, an inverted form of the admiration and awe.

> The attitudes toward men most persistently expressed in her writing, rather than comprising a spinsterish resentment or a feminist demand for justice, add up to something more like the female equivalent of misogyny, which is not male chauvinism, but the outcome of a need and a longing so urgent and so fantastic that no living woman can satisfy it. The size of the misogynist's hatred of women is equal to the distance between the compliant creatures of his fantasies, who exist only to gratify him, and actual women, who exist in their own right. And yet living women remind him of his fantasies more than anything else. So it seems to me with Sylvia Plath's misandry. For one thing, no living man could measure up to the colossus that bestrode the fantasy world of her childhood, dripping salt water. And yet it was only living men who partook of his quality, no matter how far they fell short.[43]

Although Stade does not venture farther with his analysis, he points to the lack of emotional compromise we sense in Plath's work: the size of her hatred of men is equal to the distance between the divinity she assigned to her father when he died and the disappointing grave of an ordinary man in "Electra on Azalea Path." If Herr God in "Lady Lazarus" does not have powers over life and death, then he is nothing but a sideshow illusionist and fraud—a trickster of the lowest sort.

Despite these qualifications to the virtue of Esther's anger, we must also see this as a sign of Plath's new attempt at artistic independence in the final months of her life. Unburdening herself of a male god also frees her from restraints on her imagination. She need no longer see herself in his image because it was she herself who created that image. In speculating on the "psyche of the woman-writer," Adrienne Rich ponders this issue in

> the work of . . . Sylvia Plath and Diane Wakoski. It strikes me that in the work of both Man appears as, if not a dream, a fascination and a terror; and that the source of fascination and terror is, simply, Man's power—to dominate, tyrannize, choose, or reject the woman. The charisma of Man seems to come purely from his power over her and his control of the world by force, not from anything fertile or life-giving in him. And, in the work of both these poets, it is finally the woman's sense of *herself*—embattled, possessed—that gives the poetry its dynamic charge, its rhythms of struggle, need, will, and female energy. Until recently this female anger and this furious awareness of the Man's power over her were not available materials to the female poet, who tended to write of Love as the source of her suffering, and to view that victimization by Love as an almost inevitable fate. Or, like Marianne Moore and Elizabeth Bishop, she kept sexuality at a measured and chiseled distance in her poems.[44]

If we complement Stade's commentary with Rich's, what we see is that Plath's anger may be the direct result of her experience with men in her life, but that in its expression, she found a new awareness of her distinctively feminine—"fertile" and "life-giving"—creative energies. In this context, too, *The Bell Jar*, with its often comical puncturing of "Man's power" as an illusion, may be seen as at least a partial portrait of the artist as a young woman. Plath's attempt "to free myself from the past" is also the depiction of a young woman who will not be dominated by images of femininity other than her own.

Four. Plath's Imaginative World:
Caught in the Net of Obscure Design

It is always what is under pressure in us, especially under pressure of concealment—
that explodes in poetry.—Adrienne Rich, "Vesuvius at Home: The Powers of Emily
Dickinson"

There is a whole region of human experience which the male deliberately chooses to
ignore because he fails to *think* it: this experience woman *lives*. . . . The experience of
the man is intelligible but interrupted by blanks; that of the woman is, within its own
limits, mysterious and obscure but complete. This obscurity makes her weighty; in his
relations with her, the male seems light: he has the lightness of dictators, generals,
judges, bureaucrats, codes of law, and abstract principles. . . . To the myth of the
praying mantis, women contrast the symbol of the frivolous and obtrusive drone bee.
Simone de Beauvoir, "Women's Situation and Character," *The Second Sex*

$\mathcal{I}$N 1962, Plath wrote a brief essay entitled "Context" that describes her stance toward the world and defines the relevant
context for a consideration of her poems.

> The issues of our time which preoccupy me at the moment are
> the incalculable genetic effects of fallout and a documentary arti-
> cle on the terrifying, mad, omnipotent marriage of big business
> and the military in America—"Juggernaut, the Warfare State,"
> by Fred J. Cook in a recent *Nation*. Does this influence the kind of
> poetry I write? Yes, but in a sidelong fashion. I am not gifted with
> the tongue of Jeremiah, though I may be sleepless enough before
> my vision of the apocalypse. My poems do not turn out to be
> about Hiroshima, but about a child forming itself finger by finger
> in the dark. They are not about the terrors of mass extinction, but
> about the bleakness of the moon over a yew in a neighboring

graveyard. Not about the testaments of tortured Algerians, but about the night thoughts of a tired surgeon.

In a sense these poems are deflections. I do not think they are an escape. For me, the real issues of our time are the issues of every time—the hurt and wonder of loving; making in all its forms, children, loaves of bread, paintings, buildings; and the conservation of all people in all places, the jeopardizing of which no abstract doubletalk of "peace" or "implacable foes" can excuse.

I do not think a "headline poetry" would interest more people any more profoundly than the headlines. And unless the up-to-the-minute poem grows out of something closer to the bone than a general, shifting philanthropy and is, indeed, that unicorn thing—a real poem—it is in danger of being screwed up as rapidly as the news sheet itself.[1]

For the many critics who have evaluated Plath's world and found it wanting in breadth and vitality or in a concern for anything beyond her "self," narrowly conceived, and her immediate problems, this statement may come as a surprise. Plath's imaginative vision is generally perceived as limited and her power and coherence dependent on a narrow range of themes that are expressed in their most succinct, lyrically intense form in a handful of poems found in *Ariel*. If one mentions her name or recommends her poems, the response is frequently immediate and decisive: "minor confessional poet of the 1960s"; "suicidal"; "schizophrenic" or "paranoid"; "pessimistic" and "depressing." Her relation to contemporary history is regarded by many as self-serving, a sign of what Joyce Carol Oates calls a "solipsistic and ironic and self-pitying art" that threatens to subvert a reader's mature judgment into an "emotional cul-de-sac" where the poet "circles endlessly inside the bell jar" of her private, deranged view of reality.[2] The cited virtues of reading a Plath poem are often its "madness and ecstasy"[3] or a "kind of elegant 'dreaming-back,' a cathartic experience" of regression to infantile fears and fantasies. Such a retreat only "explains by way of its deadly accuracy what was wrong with such desires."[4]

Indeed, it is as if critics want Plath mad, and the madder the better. For these are the "virtues" of excess and extremity, of the

mind under duress, and not the Wordsworthian virtues Plath aspires to and claims to follow. If we take her statement seriously,
then she wishes to address herself to universals—"the issues of
every time"—and to speak to the common world of humanity—to
"all people in all places."

Why do the poet and her critics differ so sharply on the appropriate context for understanding her art? One answer to this question is Plath's suicide. As I have already noted in chapter 1, the
circumstances of her death have been crucial in shaping response to
her work and in contributing to the overall estimate of her imagination as morbidly attracted to death. There are, however, other
causes for this view of Plath. One possible source of critical mispri-
sion is Plath's determination to speak of larger issues through the
particulars of experience. Her poems are, she says, "deflections"
from the vacuous generalities of the public realm—the "abstract
doubletalk of newspaper headlines." While this is a common predi-
lection of modern poets, to imply larger signification from specific
dramatic situations and to eschew forthright, all-embracing assertions of meaning, with Plath, it is often assumed that she has only a
private grievance to utter. "Daddy," for instance, is read on a confessional level as an intricate psychomachia drawn from childhood
memories of her father, Otto Plath. We would, in fact, be negligent
as readers if we did not detect the many references in the poem to
details from Plath's biography. I would argue that she is reaching for
the broader statement as well, that "Daddy" is a deflection, but not
an escape from the poet's responsibilities to "all people in all
places." The poem should also be read as an allegory about the way
in which the father-daughter relationship dominates the female
psyche in our culture. Father and daughter are exaggerated figures
of authority and obedience—exaggerated, not in order to magnify
Otto Plath's villainy or Sylvia Plath's personal suffering, but in order
to explode the tragic glory of father worship in the Electra myth.
Plath does not say, "I adore a Fascist," in "Daddy." She says,
"Every woman adores a Fascist." It is easy to ignore this attack on
male-female relationships, once we diminish "Daddy" to a personal
confession of masochism. Plath often expresses a very harsh view of
love between men and women and she should be engaged on the
same level of generality where she makes her assertions. Instead,

she is assumed to be creating a grievance world solely from personal resentments and affronts.

There is, too, a common tendency in Plath criticism to argue that "less is more." Commentators justly concentrate on the stunning *Ariel* volume as Plath's most distinctive work, but then base judgments of her imaginative strengths and weaknesses solely on these poems. Pamela Smith, for example, dismisses *The Colossus,* an earlier collection, as emotionally "straitjacketed" by too much control. In these poems, Plath is "so careful, so conscious as to be self-conscious," and there is "too much . . . 'technique' and too little 'life.' " These early poems should be studied as an apprenticeship to her craft, but Smith turns impatiently from Plath's finicky experiments with form to the real stuff in *Ariel.*[5]

Similarly, Marjorie G. Perloff comes close to arguing that we might well do without the poems in *Crossing the Water* and *Winter Trees.* She argues that the "transitional" poetry of *Crossing the Water,* written in the period immediately prior to *Ariel,* is marred by "gratuitous description, overingenious metaphor, mannered sound patterning often unrelated to meaning, and occasional tonal and structural irresolution"; and though the poems in *Winter Trees* belong to the later "great period" of *Ariel,* Perloff questions whether their posthumous publication provides any "greater depth and variety" to Plath's world or simply emphasizes by repetition her narrowness of vision.[6] Perhaps the most condemnatory comment in the "less is more" vein comes from Oates, who exclaims, "How quickly these six-inch masterpieces, predicated upon ruthless self-examination, demand a repeating of their skills even when the original psychological dramas have been outgrown or exhausted, since the lyric poet is instructed to look into his heart and write, and by tradition, he has only his self to write about."[7] Ultimately, the "less is more" argument is a complaint that poems so exclusively concerned with Plath's fragile psyche—the "solitary ego in its prison cell"—have a limited interest and value, and that the more poems we read by her, the less likely we are to be swayed by their effects.[8]

Such commentary encourages the reader to believe that she or he can comprehend the full scope of Plath's imagination on the basis of her final work, and even then, apparently, from a handful of these poems. All else, it is claimed, is apprenticeship or unworthy repetition. Plath herself probably encourages this view by telling an interviewer four months before her death that the poems of *The Colossus* "quite privately, bore me." They are stillborn literary exercises, meant to be read, not spoken. In her new work, she says, she has found a voice.[9]

This new voice, as I have already argued in chapter 1, is a distinctly female one, and it may be that Plath's imaginative world is also perceived as limited by its feminine decor and perspective. Frequently her poems begin in a heavily domestic, womanly sphere—the nursery, the kitchen, the boudoir, the garden. They are peopled with pregnant women and babies, snoopy neighbors and catty women confidantes, with unfaithful or impotent husbands and interfering parents and relatives. Plath has the power to defamiliarize these all-too-familiar places and beings, but it is still the woman's place she takes as her departure point. Equally often, she will center her poems in woman's body and its functions—the rhythm of the months and menstrual flow; the cycle of each pregnancy, each flowering; the woman's feelings at the loss of a child or the effects of age on her beauty. In "Context," Plath says that she prefers to write about a child forming in the womb to writing about Hiroshima and its effects—a genetic fallout that horrifies her. In this, it seems to me, she chooses to write about the world and history through its effects on woman's body. Then, too, the tone of many poems, as we shall see, is one of female scorn or the powerless victim's fear of the male world, with its generals, dictators, and heavenly fathers, all putting the world in its proper order and creating the historical flow of event and consequence.

In Simone de Beauvoir's words, "Women's fate is bound up with that of perishable things,"[10] where "the sole effect of time is a slow deterioration: it wears out furniture and clothes as it ruins the face; the reproductive powers are gradually destroyed by the passing of years. Thus woman puts no trust in this relentless force for destruction"—in a human history that offers no novelty but a gradual dissolution of her fertility.[11] Woman's fertility, de Beauvoir argues, has been her only sure source of creativity in our culture, and it is, in fact, passive, demanding patience rather than activity.

For this reason, "immanence" is woman's lot; for her the "future and the universe are denied" in "the stunning triumph of the immediate." Hence, she remains inside her subjective experience of life rather than a free, active "existent."[12] For Plath, too, passively waiting for her destiny to be revealed in "A Birthday Present," time's triumph or defeat is not in the world, but in the bedroom: "It breathes from my sheets, the cold dead centre / Where spilt lives congeal and stiffen to history."[13] According to de Beauvoir, unlike man, woman

> lacks the technical training that would permit her to dominate matter. As for her, it is not the matter she comes to grips with, but life; and life cannot be mastered through the use of tools: one can only submit to its secret laws. . . . This mystery of a bloody strawberry that inside the mother is transformed into a human being is one no mathematics can express in an equation, no machine can hasten or delay; she feels the strength of a continuity that the most ingenious instruments are unable to divide and multiply; she feels it in her body, swayed by the lunar rhythm and first ripened, then corrupted by the years. Each day the kitchen also teaches her patience and passivity; here is alchemy; one must obey the fire, the water, wait for the sugar to melt, for the dough to rise, and also for the wash to dry, for the fruits to ripen on the shelf.[14]

De Beauvoir's pronouncements on woman's character and situation in the world are more than compatible with Plath's perspective; they are the very conditions of consciousness in her poetry. Her often-cited paralysis and egotism seem to be the effects of a female bondage, in which she acknowledges her complicity, to an obscure design. Her body, her sexuality, in de Beauvoir's words, "is not for her a pure instrument for getting a grip on the world," but a burdensome sign—"bleeding each month, proliferating passively"— of her subjection to agencies under the control of men and a male deity.[15] The critical evaluation of Plath's vision as too subjective, too private, for larger meanings to be derived, may, then, be the result of this female submission to mystery, to "secret laws" that are, in de Beauvoir's estimate, central to woman's psyche as it has been formed under patriarchal domination. This limitation to her imaginative world, however, is also a virtue. Plath explores and defines the limits of this female consciousness and frequently breaks its hold on her in a free surge of liberty—in the startling effect of emotional release in many of her best poems. For a moment, she becomes, through her art, a free "existent" in de Beauvoir's terms.

The argument of this chapter will confront these assumed limitations to Plath's world and is threefold in its extensions. Throughout, I will try to show that Plath's biography provides only a partial context for her work by reading her poems on a public level, where I believe we may see a stronger and more generous engagement with the world outside the self than has been conceded. My second premise is that the *Ariel* volume is best understood in relation to what went before, since the journey to the final poems is as important as the destination. In the early poems, too, we discover a rich lode of metaphors, image clusters, symbols, and tonalities that find a more dramatic expression in *Ariel*. Third, I hope to illustrate that Plath speaks to "all people in all places" from a distinctly feminine and frequently critical perspective.

I would like, too, to invite the reader gradually into Plath's poetic universe, because these are all issues of development. Despite her own sense of discovery in the final poems, there is a strong continuity between the early and late work in terms of content, and the new choices she makes in *Ariel* are primarily those of style and presentation. The prevalent shades of feeling; the particular color, light, and texture of Plath's landscapes; the presiding human and natural figures remain essentially the same throughout her development. These elements gather force and intensity in the evolution of a dramatic speaking style, in her choice of a personal woman's voice and the discovery of specific situations to govern that voice. The prolix description and metaphorical precocity of her early poems give way to precise poetic statement in the final work by virtue of this grounding in a recognizable persona. It is from a gradual inspection of smaller brushstrokes, too, that a reader may see a slowly expanding set of concerns and themes that in the final poems harden into a definite poetic stance toward the world.

Immanence and the Mind's Eye of the Woman Poet

Simone de Beauvoir provides us with the best term for order in Plath's imaginative world: immanence. This is not the Romantic notion, found in Wordsworth's poetry, of a benevolent force that rolls through all natural, human, and material entities, but a distinction de Beauvoir makes between men, who create their existence by acting upon nature, and women, who passively submit to what they regard as the mysterious laws of their nature and view the world created by men as partaking in these laws. They live as subjects to this order rather than as existents, with control and understanding of how the world works.[16]

Throughout Plath's poetry, early and late, she is preoccupied with just such an "indwelling" design to nature and human societies and with its duplication on an individual level as a principle of consciousness. For Plath, this order is not benevolent, but rigid and paralyzing. It is objectively perceptible in compositions of color, light, and texture in the world, and felt by the subject in a numb "complexion of the mind" that reiterates those designs on a psychological level. It is through her mind's eye that Plath shares in this immanence, and in its most oppressive form, she envisions a world lacking color, light, and texture. I would like to begin then with an examination of Plath's visual imagery as an access point to her imagination.

Light and color are so important in Plath's world that in "Little Fugue," a late poem that announces itself as a musical arrangement, it is not sound but color that controls its form. At one point, the ear is confounded with the eye: she sees her father's "voice / Black and leafy" (*Ariel*, p. 70). Despite a fascination with sound effects, evident in her love for the esoteric word culled from the ever-present thesaurus she worked with ("the verdigris of the condor") and the profusion of experiments with rhyme, rhythm, and stanzaic patterns,[17] the eye overshadows the ear as a creative faculty in Plath's imagination. In "Black Rook in Rainy Weather," for example, poetic inspiration is second sight, when "A certain minor light may still / Leap incandescent / Out of kitchen table or chair"; she waits for "spasmodic / Tricks of radiance" to jolt her from a grey ordinariness.

> . . . a rook
> Ordering its black feathers can so shine
> As to seize my senses, haul
> My eyelids up, and grant
>
> A brief respite from fear
> Of total neutrality.[18]

At times, the eye is omnipotent; it creates and destroys: "I shut my eyes and all the world drops dead. / I lift my lids and all is born again."[19] Without light, things do not exist: "One match scratch makes you real."[20] The instant of light hitting an object is a revelation, and some of Plath's most striking visual images occur at dawn. "Five o'clock in the morning" is a "no-color void,"[21] but then "the outline / Of the world comes clear and fills with color" ("The Thin People," *The Colossus and Other Poems* [*TC*], pp. 33–34); and in "Ariel," a much later instance of this power of light, there is only duration—"Stasis in darkness"—before sunrise: "Then the substanceless blue / Pour of tor and distances" (*Ariel*, p. 26). As an active force in Plath's world, light has a variety of textures, as in "By Candlelight," where a candle's glow is "the fluid in which we meet each other" amidst the darkness of a winter night—"A sort of black horsehair / A rough, dumb country stuff" (*Winter Trees* [*WT*], p. 29). Light has a cutting edge to create surfaces, as in the moonlight that "pares white flesh to the white bone" ("Moonrise," *TC*, p. 65), and in "Mussel-Hunter at Rock Harbor," where a bright sun

> . . . scours
> Sandgrit to sided crystal
> And buffs and sleeks the blunt hulls
> Of the three fishing smacks.
>
> (*TC*, p. 69)

She arrives before the "water-colorists" to get the "good of the Cape light," implying that the softer, muted effects of diffused light, loved by watercolor painters, are less pleasing to her eye than the blinding reflection of a low sun on sand and water.

The preference for harshness and severity in lighting is equally true of Plath's colors. Her world is predominantly black, white, and grey with bold splashes of color—electric or watery blues, the "blooming" reds and purples of flowers, or flamelike yellows and glints of silver, mercury, gold. These bright, pure colors, especially shades of red, as in "Poppies in July" and "Tulips," are unruly, emotionally disturbing, and associated with individuality and self-assertion. Before the tulips arrive in her hospital room, the woman of that poem is "nobody," "swabbed . . . clear of loving associations" in a "snowed-in" whiteness. The tulips are "too excitable," "too red" and

> Before they came the air was calm enough,
> Coming and going, breath by breath, without any fuss.
> Then the tulips filled it up like a loud noise.
> Now the air snags and eddies round them the way a river
> Snags and eddies round a sunken rust-red engine.
> They concentrate my attention, that was happy
> Playing and resting without committing itself.
>
> (*Ariel*, p.11)

"Half in love with easeful death," she erases her features, her dimensions, her identity, in compliance with hospital routine. The vivid tulips draw her, resisting, back to "a country far away as health" and back to an identity associated with the photos of her children and husband on the night table.

Like light, then, a burst of color may seize the senses and "grant / A brief respite from fear / Of total neutrality." The neutrals—black, white, and grey (as in the hospital decor of "Tulips")—are orderly as Plath's pen-and-ink drawings: "a rook / Ordering its black feathers" or the opening image of "Winter Trees."

> The wet dawn inks are doing their blue dissolve.
> On their blotter of fog the trees
> Seem a botanical drawing.
> Memories growing, ring on ring,
> A series of weddings.
>
> (*WT*, p. 43)

Patterns of black and white are aesthetically pleasing in this rigid way, but often, and with increasing regularity in the late poems, they are linked with emotional paralysis and a fearful depression where everything seems flat, thin, two-dimensional.

This disturbing vision of the world originates in Plath's early experiments with color and no-color in *The Colossus*. In "Spinster" and "Man in Black," contrasts of black and white unify the imagery. Plath's prim sense of beauty dominates, but we can also sense the underlying anxiety that will eventually control her mind's eye. While on a walk with a suitor, the young woman in "Spinster" is suddenly "afflicted" by the slovenliness of spring—"By the birds' irregular babel / And the leaves' litter." She begins to long for winter.

> Scrupulously austere in its order
> Of white and black
> Ice and rock, each sentiment within border,
> And heart's frosty discipline
> Exact as a snowflake.
>
> (*TC*, p. 66)

The spinster erects a prickly defense—"a barricade of barb and check"—to protect her maidenhood against "bedlam spring," "mere insurgent man," and finally, against love. Overall, there is a negative charge to the spinster's prudish self-discipline, and something pathetic about her preference for the classic symmetries of winter over the "burgeoning" spring vegetation: "She judged petals in disarray." The black and white sterility of winter is associated with her squeamishness, sexual inhibition, with a repression of impulse. As usual, however, Plath is simultaneously drawn to the austere discipline of winter and the spinster's admiration for purity of form—"Exact as a snowflake."

The "Man in Black" is exact as a stiff black suit. The first four stanzas are a harshly evocative description of the sea and beach around Deer Island Prison. Even in this early poem, the details suggest an uneasy complicity between man and nature in the urge for order. Man has made his environment tidy with "trim piggeries / Hen huts and cattle green" and the prison is testimony to the need

for law. Nature is equally restrained, frozen in ice and rock. But the
rhythm of the sea pounding insistently against a shoreline that both
borders a prison and holds the sea in abeyance makes one dubious
of this surface calm. An undercurrent of frustrated violence per-
vades the poem.

> Where the three magenta
> Breakwaters take the shove
> And suck of the grey sea
>
> To the left, and the wave
> Unfists against the dun
> Barb-wired headland of
>
> The Deer Island Prison.
>
> (TC, p. 52)

Like a prisoner, the fist of the sea bangs incessantly against an
unyielding wall. The order is oppressive, punishing. The entrance of
the man in black "rivets" these details together. He quite literally
locks up the scene with his compelling presence.

> And you, across those white
>
> Stones, strode out in your dead
> Black coat, black shoes, and your
> Black hair till there you stood,
>
> Fixed vortex on the far
> Tip, riveting stones, air,
> All of it, together.
>
> (TC, pp. 52–53)

The poem's one-sentence structure makes the final phrase ring like a
shutting prison door. Despite the deadness and stiffness of this
landscape, we can once again sense Plath's love for formal austerity.
The appearance of the man in black is satisfying to her eye, like the
last stroke of ink on white paper, stiffening the scene into an unyielding unity.

The latent menace in black and white precision is always a tension in Plath's work, but in these early poems, it is kept under control by her aesthetic detachment. She describes the "Spinster," rather than speaking in her voice, and in "Man in Black" she is an observer, not a participant in the scene. This is also true of two other poems, "Watercolor of Grantchester Meadows" and "Two Views of a Cadaver Room," which seem posed for the observant art student. In "Watercolor," Plath paints a serene, pastoral landscape: "There, spring lambs jam the sheepfold," and "Nothing is big or far." But this is also a naive world, "a country on a nursery plate," and the "benign / Arcadian green" an innocent illusion. Beneath the surface, a more disturbing order exists. "The blood-berried hawthorn hides its spines with white" and "black-gowned" students in a "moony indolence" of love are "unaware / How in such mild air / The owl shall stoop from his turret, the rat cry out" (TC, p. 41). Black and white are specifically linked with deception in this charming miniature that hides a nature red in tooth and claw.

The double perspective is developed even more forcefully in "Two Views of a Cadaver Room." Amid "four men laid out, black as burnt turkey, / Already half unstrung" and "white-smocked boys," a lover hands his lady "the cut-out heart like a cracked heirloom" (TC, p. 5). Plath then offers a second view of the cadaver room as "the panorama of smoke and slaughter" in Brueghel's *The Triumph of Death*. As in the dissection room, Plath focuses our attention on a pair of lovers playing in the lower right-hand corner of the painting. They dally with a leaflet of music, oblivious to the chaos around them and the skeleton above, fiddling a violin over "this little country / Foolish, delicate." Her attitude toward love in this poem is ambivalent. It is at once a fragile, precious value, but also "foolish," a perverse whim of Brueghel that only adds to the grotesque carnage in the rest of the painting. It is as queerly out of place as a young man handing his sweetheart an artificially preserved heart as a love token. Plath implies that the survival of love in the face of death's triumph is an absurd artifice. Even more bizarre than the comparison of the two pairs of lovers is Plath's yoking of the antiseptic, black-and-white modernity of the cadaver room with the imaginative excess of Brueghel. But in Plath's world, black-and-

white patterns are forms of concealment; they dissemble with blandness where a malign purpose may exist.

"Mushrooms" and "The Thin People" are about the menace of
blandness in grey and white. They are two of the first poems where
neutral colors and their associations with featurelessness, blankness,
and mindlessness are linked with the mind of the pack, the mass-
motived hordes that eventually serve as Plath's metaphor for order
in human societies. They look forward to the bee poems and those
where Plath herself seems trapped in a no-color void, behaving with
zombielike automatism. In "Mushrooms," Plath stresses the unob-
trusive blandness of these vegetable minds.

> Overnight, very
> Whitely, discreetly
> Very quietly
>
> Our toes, our noses
> Take hold on the loam,
> Acquire the air.
>
> Nobody sees us
> Stops us, betrays us;
> The small grains make room.
>
> (TC, p. 37)

Who would suspect that earless, eyeless, "perfectly voiceless"
mushrooms could have so much purpose? They are meek and mild;
they ask "little or nothing," implying that they do not mind being
eaten or stepped on. They are little martyrs. But they are also
"nudgers and shovers" in spite of themselves, and their "soft fists"
insistently push the earth aside to make room.

> Our kind multiplies:
>
> We shall by morning
> Inherit the earth.
> Our foot's in the door.
>
> (TC, p. 38).

This is probably only playfully frightening: it is hard to worry too much about mushrooms. But in "The Thin People," the fear is more substantial. The thin people are not clearly identified. They have some resemblance to Plath's more personal horror of "The Disquieting Muses"—"mouthless, eyeless, with stitched bald head"—who stand vigil at her bedside with "Faces blank as the day I was born" (TC, p. 58); and to "All the Dead Dears," museum mummies who threaten to "suck / Blood and whistle my marrow clean" (TC, p. 30). The emphasis in all these poems is on featurelessness—the bald darning egg heads of the muses, the skeletal dears. Likewise, the threat of the thin people is "Not guns, not abuses / But a thin silence" that deprives the world of color and dimension. The thin people "persevere" in bad dreams, old newsreels, and headlines about the victims of war. They belong to the greyness before dawn. The sun obliterates them as the "world comes clear and fills with color." But like the meek mushrooms, one morning the thin people "persist" and the "wall-paper pales," the "tree-holes flatten / And lose their good browns." Effortlessly, they will make "the world go thin as a wasp's nest / And greyer; not even moving their bones." Although never explicitly stated, the thin people seem to be the speaker's memories and nightmares that threaten to overwhelm her everyday reality. They may resemble photographs of Nazi death camps, but ultimately they belong to the "contracted country of the head." Their martyrdom—"The insufferable nimbus of the lot-drawn scapegoat"—makes them haunting figures of guilt, on an individual as well as historical level. This is why they need no more than "simply stand in the forest" with their "thin-lipped smiles" to wither the world of its delights (TC, pp. 32–34).

The Father's Design: Master and Slave

Gradually, Plath expands and deepens the thematic significance of color in her poetry. Her love of patterns in black and white may originate in her perfectionism, her fussy need for sharpness of outline. In the late poems, though, these no-colors come to represent a sadomasochistic "complexion of the mind," a mentality shared by master and slave. The slaves are a mindless pack, working together for their own enslavement: bees, Nazis, zombies, mannequins, and robots. Often, too, they are female: the honey-drudging worker bees, the robot-wife of "The Applicant," "The Munich Mannequins" waiting for a pickup. They behave automatically or, like the social insects, on instinct, even if it is suicidal. The master is "the man in black with a Meinkampf look": the Nazi storm trooper, Herr Doktor, or gestapo. He also appears in blander, but no less threatening, guises, as the beekeeper, the scientist, the priest in black cassock, or the husband in a stiff black suit. Finally, he is "Daddy"—the archetypical colossus with a black boot and white eyes who imposed this efficient order of bees, robots, armies, and zombies. He is the Herr God, Herr Lucifer over it all, and it is his need for discipline that flattens the burgeoning forms and colors of the world to a black-and-white monotony.

We should not see this masculine deity as a mere product of Plath's love-hate for the dead Otto Plath. Other poets, too, have shared this bleak view of divinity. Like William Blake's Newtonian deity, Plath's Herr God is completely rational and abstract, a clockmaker who set the world in motion and then withdrew into the "black amnesias of heaven" ("The Night Dances," *Ariel*, p. 17); yet the order he imposed on nature and, it seems, forgot, is insane at its core—red in tooth and claw, or, as Plath describes it in "Totem," "blood-hot and personal." Plath's creator is the author of the "gross eating game," of a world that is above all, an efficient engine of destruction and sacrifice. If he is not the spider, he is the idea of the spider.

> I am mad, calls the spider, waving its many arms
> And in truth it is terrible,
> Multiplied in the eyes of the flies.
> They buzz like blue children
> In nets of the infinite,
>
> Roped in at the end by the one
> Death with many sticks.
>
> (*Ariel*, p. 76)

The irony for Plath is that human beings, and particularly women, believe there is some purpose to death and martyrdom,

that there will be a millennium beyond the "one death with many
sticks." For Plath, there is only blank indifference. The "sky is like a
pig's backside, an utter lack of attention" (WT, p. 33); or it is "a
heaven / Starless and fatherless, a dark water" ("Sheep in Fog,"
Ariel, p. 3). In "Apprehensions,"

> There is this white wall, above which the sky creates itself—
> Infinite, green, utterly untouchable
> Angels swim in it, and the stars, in indifference also.

And at the end of the poem, vultures, predators

> On a black wall, unidentifiable birds
> Swivel their heads and cry.
> There is no talk of immortality among these!
> Cold blanks approach us:
> They move in a hurry.
>   (WT, p. 3)

Beyond death there are only these "cold blanks" like the underwater
eternity of "Lyonesse," a country in Arthurian legend that sinks into
the sea like Atlantis. Plath envisions the Lyonians in their

> . . . clear, green, quite breathable atmosphere
> Cold grits underfoot,
> And the spidery water-dazzle on field and street.
>   (WT, p. 31)

They believe this is heaven, although they "always thought /
Heaven would be something else." What they do not know is

> . . . that they had been forgot,
> That the big God
> Had lazily closed one eye and let them slip

> Over the English cliff and under so much history!
> They did not see him smile,
> Turn, like an animal,

In his cage of ether, his cage of stars.
He'd had so many wars!
The white gape of his mind was the real Tabula Rasa.

(WT, pp. 31–32)

More terrifying than outright malevolence is the "white gape" of
God's mind—the glacial indifference of the "white, high berg on his
forehead" and the "Grey, indeterminate gilt / Sea of his eyes." The
smile hints of purpose and malice, as if he enjoys his irony at the
expense of the Lyonians, but he is anesthetized "in his cage of
ether"; he quietly forgets.

If God's mind is ideally a tabula rasa, he must wipe it clean
from time to time, which explains the abrupt erasure of whole civilizations like Lyonesse and their submergence "under so much history." Like Blake's Urizen ("your reason"), Plath's divinity is at once
the compass-wielding scientist, plotting out the universe, and a
primitive Druid, who demands regular human sacrifice. In another
late poem entitled "Brasília," these two aspects, primitive totem and
rationalist clockmaker, perfectly mesh. Plath envisions the final erasure of humanity from God's mind in an atomic holocaust. In lines
that echo her statement in "Context" about the warfare state, Plath
evokes the "terrors of mass extinction."

Brasília is not only Brazil's capitol city. As one observer describes it, the city is a "symbol of a national urge to conquer the
unknown backlands": "In 1955 no one lived there but a rancher
named Gama. . . . Then, in 1956, bulldozers began to rip open the
green fields, exposing raw, red earth. In four years, some 30,000
workmen erected an architectural fantasy, resembling a gigantic bird
or plane, with a ten-mile wing spread, alighting at the edge of an
artificial lake."[22] Ironically, the bird/plane layout of Brasília also resembles a crucifix, and the raw, red earth ("motherly blood" in
Plath's poem) is the sacrifice made to a god of progress. One native
describes his city in millennial terms that ironically underscore
Plath's frightening vision: "My town is super for clear thinking and
productive work. I care more about where we're going than where
we've been. Like all Brazilians, my sights are set on the year 2000.
That's when we'll become a major power. . . . By then our conquest

of the west will be complete" (Luiz Dietra, age twenty-three; native of Brasília).[23]

Luiz Dietra wants to erase the past in the name of progress, while Plath, speaking in the voice of Mary, can only remember the "old story" of human sacrifice, the story of her son Jesus, and can only see a cruciform in the shape of Brasília.

> And my baby a nail
> Driven in, driven in.
> He shrieks in his grease,
>
> Bones nosing for distances.
> And I nearly extinct,
> His three teeth cutting
> Themselves on my thumb—
> And the star,
> The old story.
>
>   (WT, p.11)

For Plath, the impulse to subdue mother nature that Brasília represents is also a denial of what is human and fleshly. Mary wonders whether this is what God has in mind—a perfection of mechanism that annihilates the necessity for fragile flesh and blood.

> Will they occur,
> These people with torsos of steel
> Winged elbows and eyeholes
>
> Awaiting masses
> Of cloud to give them expression
> These super-people!—
>
>   (WT, p. 11)

Super-peopled by featureless automatons, Brasília is finally Plath's image of civilization after the apocalypse. God will demand the extinction by radiation of ordinary mortals to make way for the perfect society.

Plath ends her poem with a prayer acknowledging God's power

and glory, but its placatory tones seem absurdly human and womanly delivered to a father-deity who has big plans for his son and humanity. Her appeal must be trivial to a god whose millennium comes with the force of an atomic blast.

> O You who eat
>
> People like light rays, leave
> This one
> Mirror safe, unredeemed
>
> By the dove's annihilation,
> The glory
> The power, the glory.
>
> (WT, pp. 11–12)

Perhaps the shape of Brasília, like a "gigantic bird . . . alighting at the edge of an artificial lake" reminds Plath of Milton's dove, brooding over a vast abyss at the original moment of creation. But for Plath, as Mary, Brasília is the "dove's annihilation," a prefiguration of a world moving toward technological destruction—a world *not* without end. Likewise, God's "power" and "glory" (echoes of the Lord's Prayer) are manifest only as destructive "light rays"—the radiation of a nuclear holocaust. Despite the submissive posture of prayer, Mary challenges divinity. She does not want her son to be the chosen one, to play again the role of scapegoat-redeemer. The peculiar phrase, "Mirror safe, unredeemed," is consistent with Plath's view of God's mind as a tabula rasa, a clean slate. Humanity is "redeemed" periodically by total destruction—as if to clear his head of a bad cold. To be "mirror safe" is to escape reflection in the clear glass of God's eye. As in "Lady Lazarus," where Plath speaks as Lazarus, claiming resurrection on her own terms, telling Herr God that she would rather do it herself, so in "Brasília" Plath speaks as Mary, asking to be left alone.

God's blank mind is numb to individual pain and impervious to questioning. In "The Hanging Man," he punishes her—"By the roots of my hair some god got hold of me. / I sizzled in his blue volts like a desert prophet" (*Ariel*, p. 69). Such punishment implies selection; she must be guilty of something or chosen, like Jeremiah, for some special oracular task. Instead of selection, God's smiting is arbitrary, and when the veil between her and God is torn, there is no revelation, but a void. As suddenly as she is seized, she is left with a "vulturous boredom"—"A world of bald white days in a shadeless socket." Such imagery reminds one of Robert Frost's in "Design": a white spider eating a white moth on a white heal-all: "What but design of darkness to appall?" Is it coincidence or design that governs the "gross eating game," the "one death with many sticks"? Is there a divine intelligence in the order of the universe, or just a tabula rasa? Plath's answer, like Frost's or Melville's probing at the whiteness of the whale, is that the uncertainty itself confronts human intelligence with its greatest terror.

The Mind of the Hive

The "black, intractable mind" of the beehive, with its efficient order of queen, workers, and drones, and the rituals of beekeeping, provide Plath with an objective correlative for this terror, on both a personal and historical level. In many ways, the hive is her father's house. She is drawn to bees and beekeeping for their associations with Otto Plath, the entomologist and author of *Bumblebees and Their Ways,* and in her bee poems, she explores many of her attitudes toward her femininity as it has been governed by these associations. At the same time, the mind of the hive is consistent with her view of society as a mass-motived pack.

In this aspect, Plath's fascination with bees is very similar to Lewis Thomas's description of the widespread human discomfort with the "mind" of social insects in *The Lives of a Cell.*

What makes us most uncomfortable is that they [i.e., ants, bees, termites, and social wasps] seem to live two kinds of lives: they are individuals, going about the day's business, without much evidence of thought for tomorrow, and they are at the same time component parts, cellular elements, in the huge, writhing, ruminating organism of the Hill, the nest, the hive.

Still, there it is. A solitary ant, afield, cannot be considered to

have a mind at all, much less a thought. Four ants together, or
ten, encircling a dead moth on a path, begin to look more like
an idea. They fumble and shove, gradually moving the food
toward the Hill, but as though by blind chance. It is only when
you watch the dense mass of thousands of ants, crowded together around the Hill, blackening the ground, that you begin
to see the whole beast, and now you observe it thinking, plan-
ning, calculating. It is an intelligence, a kind of live computer,
with crawling bits for wits.[24]

This combination of individual mindlessness with overall design and
intelligence is precisely what frightens Plath. There must be a mas-
termind or rather, master mindlessness, behind it all. "The Swarm"
is first about the springtime formation of new honeybee colonies
around a queen, but the allegory throughout is to Napoleon's forg-
ing of an empire, his Grand Army overrunning Europe and Russia.
The slave mentality of the bees is like the slave mentality of Napoleon's soldiers. They are willing to kill and die for the emperor, but
also for the questionable opportunity of giving up their individual
freedom. The bees entering a new hive are like soldiers sacrificing
their lives for France's glory. They are the anonymous sacrifice to
Napoleon and

> The white busts of marshals, admirals, generals
> Worming themselves into niches.
>
> How instructive this is!
> The dumb, banded bodies
> Walking the plank draped with Mother France's upholstery
> Into a new mausoleum,
> An ivory palace, a crotch pine.
>
> (Ariel, p. 65)

When the swarm momentarily gets out of control, like Napoleon's
army deserting its emperor after the Russian debacle,

> It must be shot down. Pom! Pom!
> So dumb it thinks bullets are thunder.

It thinks they are the voice of God
Condoning the beak, the claw, the grin of the dog
Yellow-haunched, a pack-dog,
Grinning over its bone of ivory
Like the pack, the pack, like everybody.

(Ariel, p. 64)

The mass-motived horde is "dumb," submissive to regular blood-shed, but also dangerous in its stupidity. Its "black, intractable mind" can be manipulated to serve the beekeeper-Napoleon, but this mindless force might as easily turn on him: "Pom! Pom! They would have killed *me*." God, emperor, beekeeper—he is the idea behind the pack, the one who knows that the swarm must be encouraged in its violence with a cause like the glory of empire to justify individual enslavement.

The man with grey stands under the honeycomb
Of their dream, the hived station
Where trains, faithful to their steel arcs,
Leave and arrive, and there is no end to the country.

(Ariel, p. 65)

And he also knows with the "intense practicality" of the "man of business" that he must occasionally punish the pack to prove that he is fittest to rule.

In beekeeping, however, it is almost impossible to determine who rules whom, who owns whom. Do the queen and keeper rule, or are they "lot-drawn scapegoats" for the hive? In "Daddy," "every woman adores a Fascist," because the master cannot exist without a slave and the slave without a master. There is a psychological symbiosis and economy at work in sadomasochism. In "The Arrival of the Bee Box," the Roman mob of bees, the box of maniacs, governs the speaker, despite her protestations of control: "They can die, I need feed them nothing, I am the owner" (*Ariel*, p. 59). Likewise, in "Wintering," she is the head of a prison camp of bees, "all women, / Maids and the long royal lady," but "It is they who own me" (*Ariel*, p. 67). She feeds them on Tate and Lyle, sugar syrup, "to make up for the honey I've taken," and "They take it," accepting mere survival from their keeper. But the mind of the hive is a "black asinin-ity" in which she participates as owner.

> Now they ball in a mass,
> Black
> Mind against all that white.
> The smile of the snow is white.
> It spreads itself out, a mile-long body of Meissen,
>
> Into which, on warm days,
> They can only carry their dead.
>
> (*Ariel*, p. 68)

They are sluggish in movement, more docile than the angry bees in "The Arrival of the Bee Box," but in this state, her degree of control over them is even more tenuous.

> Possession.
> It is they who own me.
> Neither cruel or indifferent,
>
> Only ignorant.
> This is the time of hanging on for the bees—the bees
> So slow I hardly know them,
> Filing like soldiers
> To the syrup tin.
>
> (*Ariel*, p. 67)

The "hanging on" of the bees is an allegory for her own hibernation and withdrawal. There is some satisfaction in the eviction of the drones and the imposition of female orderliness—"They have got rid of the men, / The blunt, clumsy stumblers, the boors"—but also a frightening numbness and blankness.

> Winter is for women—
> The woman, still at her knitting,
> At the cradle of Spanish walnut,
> Her body a bulb in the cold and too dumb to think.
>
> (*Ariel*, p. 68)

The black and white stillness and armylike discipline are a form of mental subsistence; the speaker, like the mind of the hive, is barely alive.

Despite the overall bleakness of the poem, Edward Butscher sees "Wintering" as a poem about the strength of women in the face of depression and desertion, as a poem about Plath's emotional resilience after Ted Hughes left her. For Butscher, the final line of "Wintering," "The bees are flying. They taste the spring," is an affirmation: "Like the gladioli, the hive and its female occupants will endure beyond winter."[25] But this is an answer to the previous line: "What will they taste of, the Christmas roses?"—a line, I suspect, that Plath means to be delivered with ironic intonation. If Christmas roses are poinsettias, then they are poisonous. They harbinger spring and are a symbol for the "old story" of Christ's crucifixion and resurrection. These connotations seriously complicate, if not cancel out altogether, any affirmation in the final line. The bees, "too dumb to think," behaving automatically, believe the poinsettias announce spring when it is still winter. Their flying is then a certain death.

In "The Bee Meeting" and "Stings," Plath explores the triumphant side of her femininity through an identification with the queen rather than the "honey-drudgers," the female worker bees. Her identification is not without ambivalence, because the queen, although she rules the hive, is also owned by it, subject to its laws. She is a murderess and scapegoat for her society, just as the worker bees are little housewives. When she grows too old, she must pay for her creative powers—her tenure on the throne as the only fertile female in the hive—by killing the virgin queens or being killed by one of them. In "The Bee Meeting," this natural drama is ceremonial, ritualized, and again, the imagery is black and white. The speaker joins her neighbors in their white smocks, led by a man in black, in a "white straw Italian hat / And a black veil that moulds to my face, they are making me one of them" (Ariel, p. 56). She is drawn into a ritual of beekeeping, paying obeisance to "the mind of the hive" that "thinks this is the end of everything." Even more, the human society seems mystically joined with the mental process of the hive. The human community is uniformed and gathered to move the virgins who threaten to kill the old queen.

> She is old, old, old, she must live another year and she knows
>   it.
> While in their fingerjoint cells the new virgins
>
> Dream of a duel they will win inevitably,
> A curtain of wax dividing them from the bride flight,
> The upflight of the murderess into a heaven that loves her.
>
> (Ariel, p. 57)

The old queen may be "ungrateful" for the reprieve given to her by her human owners. She may not want to live another year and defend her throne from the virgins or go through the "bride flight" and the inevitable death of another male drone.

The fertility ritual of the hive is so mingled with bloodletting that the speaker, in confusion, mistakes the lushness of the spring vegetation around her with death: "Is it blood clots the tendrils are dragging up that string? / No, no, it is scarlet flowers that will one day be edible." The hawthorn smells sickly sweet, like ether, and the removal of the queen is analogous to an operation, with a surgeon dressed in a "green helmet, / Shining gloves and white suits."

The final stanza is ambiguous: is it the queen or the poet who speaks?

> I am exhausted, I am exhausted—
> Pillar of white in a blackout of knives.
> I am the magician's girl who does not flinch.
> The villagers are untying their disguises, they are shaking
>   hands.
> Whose is that long white box in the grove, what have they
>   accomplished, why am I cold?
>
> (Ariel, p. 58)

The surgery is successful, the queen is saved, but the white box resembles a coffin. For the tired queen and the magician's girl who speaks for her, the risk of death has become commonplace. Like Lady Lazarus before the "peanut-crunching crowd," the queen and the girl are exhausted by the ceremonial exhibition of their fertility. While they "come back" with death-defying powers, they are also scapegoats to the mind of the hive—"a pillar of white in a blackout of knives."

The question of the queen's destiny and the final outcome of the ceremony—"Is she dead, is she sleeping?"—is posed again in "Stings." This poem, however, comes to a more triumphant conclusion. Together with a man in white, a bee seller, the speaker is transferring combs to make her own hive, her own "honey machine." The success of the operation depends, once again, on the elusive queen; if she is in the new hive,

> . . . she is old,
> Her wings torn shawls, her long body
> Rubbed of its plush—
> Poor and bare and unqueenly and even shameful.
> (*Ariel*, p. 61)

The tie between the speaker and the old queen is reiterated. This time, the speaker is not a magician's girl in a knife-throwing act, but a woman who has stood "in a column / Of winged, unmiraculous women, / Honey-drudgers." She refuses this identity with the infertile worker bees, the little housewives for the hive.

> I am no drudge
> Though for years I have eaten dust
> And dried plates with my dense hair
> And seen my strangeness evaporate.
> (*Ariel*, p. 61)

With such analogies between the female society of the hive and her own position as a woman, the beekeeping ritual becomes an allegory of female identity. Is the speaker one of the workers, "These women who only scurry," who "will work without thinking, / Opening in spring like an industrious virgin"? Or is she the queen?

The answer comes with the arrival of a male intruder—"a great scapegoat." The "honey-drudgers" launch a full-scale assault on the man, who is sacrificed, it is suggested, because of his deception. The bees find him out and transform his mouth into lies.

He was sweet,

The sweat of his efforts a rain
Tugging the world to fruit.
The bees found him out,
Moulding onto his lips like lies,
Complicating his features.

(Ariel, p. 62)

I take these lines to mean that although the man was necessary for
the fertility of the hive, that he was also untrue, and the honey-
drudging housewives "found him out." The speaker refuses an
identity as a vengeance-seeking housewife; for unlike the female
workers, who must die by stinging the man to death, she, and the
queen, will not commit suicide for the sake of revenge. Instead, the
discovery of the man's infidelity releases both the speaker and the
queen from being honey-drudgers for the hive. Suddenly she wakens, a sleeping beauty, and flies in her original color and splendor.

They thought death was worth it, but I
Have a self to recover, a queen.
Is she dead, is she sleeping?
Where has she been,
With her lion-red body, her wings of glass?

Now she is flying
More terrible than she ever was, red
Scar in the sky, red comet
Over the engine that killed her—
The mausoleum, the wax house.

(Ariel, pp. 62–63)

"They" are the worker bees. They have no personality, but are the
collective mind of the hive. Their sacrifice in righting the man's
wrong "was worth it" because they operate solely for the benefit of
the society. For a queen, though, the "honey-machine" is an engine
of destruction—a "mausoleum" and "wax house" threatening her
individuality and transforming her into an unmiraculous housewife.

At the end of the poem, her "strangeness" is restored and she is reborn with a mind and purpose of her own, distinct from the slave mentality of the hive, the bees who "work without thinking." The queen and the speaker bear the mark of the man's betrayal—a "red scar"—but it is also a sign of healing. Like the intrusion of strong color in other poems, the redness is a sign of individuality and of violent release from the "black asininity" that is the mind of the hive.

By using color and light as an access point to Plath's imagination, one may see a gradual hardening of these finite brushstrokes into theme and allegory. In her early poems, like "Spinster" or "Man in Black," color patterns are formal, aesthetic principles of construction, and Plath seems very self-conscious in their imposition. What begins, perhaps, as a personal visual asceticism—Plath's particular love for the borders and limitations of black on white—grows into an all-embracing vision. Such habitual image clusters come to stand for God's mind and a master-slave principle of order in nature and history; and she finds in the beehive a symbol for the master mindlessness—a "live computer with crawling bits for wits"—at work in human societies. In the bee poems, too, the minds of the hive and the speaker blend, so that we see Plath dealing with personal themes simultaneously with her larger statements about God, history, society—"nets of the infinite." In "Wintering" and "Stings," particularly, there are inevitable analogies to her private situation. Plath, like the woman in these poems, found herself "hibernating" in Devon without Hughes, having "got rid of the men" and wondering whether she would "have a self to recover, a queen," or whether she would remain a "drudge." Plath's sense of betrayal and desire for vengeance also find their way into these poems, and they may easily be read as psychological defenses by reversal of the actual situation. It is not she who is deserted, but the neglible drones who are expelled from the hive in "Wintering"; and the deceiving man of "Stings" is found out and sacrificed in a ceremony to release the queen, and release Plath herself from her identity as the wife of Ted Hughes.

Despite the confessional dimension to the bee poems, they are accessible allegories about the tension between the individual and an oppressive social order immanent in nature and the mind of a malignant creator. The personal warp to the bee poems does not detract from their representative qualities. Instead, this confessional impulse shows a deepening of Plath's themes, in that the female structure of the hive permits her to explore the master-slave mentality as it applies specifically to women. The bee colony offers a double image of femininity—the queen creator-destroyer and the dust-eating worker—adequate to Plath's conflicted feelings toward her womanhood and her own creative powers as an artist.

The Daughter and the Colossus

Even in poems that seem to be solely about her personal history, Plath's relationship with her father Otto, we can discern the female "mind of the hive" as a controlling principle of consciousness. The "mind of the hive" is, as we have seen, a "black asininity"—a mindless automatism that fulfills some order imposed from without. Plath creates a sense of secret laws at work in the homely rituals of beekeeping and of a female society with tremendous energies kept under lock and key by these laws.

In an early poem, "The Colossus," and the late "Little Fugue," Plath explores this state of consciousness on a more personal level. Both poems depict a daughter struggling unsuccessfully to recover a dead father, to retrieve his voice and persuade him to speak to her. In both poems, too, Plath evokes a mood of futility. Even if the father could speak, it is implied that he would have nothing to say; and the daughter meanwhile wastes her energies in this obsessive activity directed at giving him life. As in "Daddy," the daughter sacrifices her own vitality to the task of revivifying a dead father.

While both poems are clearly confessional, I would argue that they also illuminate woman's psyche as it is shaped by a patriarchal culture. In "The Colossus," the action takes place under "A blue sky out of the Oresteia," implying that the daughter's personal drama partakes of a tragic and universal lawfulness. In "Little Fugue," the black-and-white order of the world is the father's "Grosse Fuge," and it is duplicated in the daughter's psyche as a little fugue, giving her life a rigid order but no meaning. There is, then, as in the bee poems, a symbiosis between the individual and a larger, oppressive design. Both poems are exemplary expressions, too, of Simone de Beauvoir's description of women's submission to laws they do not understand.

> "Men make gods," says Frazer, "women worship them". . . . In particular they like to have Order and Right embodied in a leader. In every Olympus there is a supreme god; the magic male essence must be concentrated in an archetype of which father, husband, lovers, are only faint reflections. . . . The general, the dictator—eagle-eyed, square-jawed—is the heavenly father demanded by all serious right-thinkers, the absolute guarantor of all values.[26]

The daughter in Plath's poems is looking for an oracle, a father who will be the "guarantor of all values" and absolute measure of meaning in her life. At the same time, Plath is critically aware of the fact that her father is nothing but a dead man, a mere mortal. She illuminates the complicity de Beauvoir describes between woman and the man who creates her gods, her laws.

The effect of this double perspective—devoted and critical—in "The Colossus" is confusing. The archaeologist-daughter displays contradictory emotions toward the huge statue she is restoring. At first, she seems totally exasperated with the father and his godlike proportions and pretensions.

> I shall never get you put together entirely,
> Pieced, glued, and properly jointed.
> Mule-bray, pig-grunt and bawdy cackles
> Proceed from your great lips.
> It's worse than a barnyard.
>
> Perhaps you consider yourself an oracle,
> Mouthpiece of the dead, or of some god or other.
> Thirty years now I have labored
> To dredge the silt from your throat.
> I am none the wiser.
>
> > (TC, p. 20)

In these lines, she appears to be challenging the colossus-father to give her wisdom and comically implies that he has nothing oracular, only animal sounds to utter. She quickly reverses her ironic stance to that of a worshipful suppliant.

> I crawl like an ant in mourning
> Over the weedy acres of your brow
> To mend the immense skull plates and clear
> The bald, white tumuli of your eyes.
>
> A blue sky out of the Oresteia
> Arches above us. O father, all by yourself
> You are pithy and historical as the Roman Forum.
>
> (TC, pp. 20–21)

Like the blank mind of God in "Lyonesse," the colossus is a cipher, his eyes expressionlessly "bald" as the clouds in the sky. Even in this state, however, he is a "pithy" god and she is a pygmy living in his colossal body, squatting in his "left ear, out of the wind." While he does not speak, "the sun rises under the pillar of your tongue." It is enough for the daughter to be totally married to her mourning and the task of giving him life.

This disparity between what the daughter knows and what she does with her life is an inconsistency in "The Colossus." It deprives the daughter of any motive other than self-punishment for her devotion, and it appears to be entirely conscious. We may well wonder why she does not release herself from a predicament that she thoroughly understands as self-destructive. Plath's only clue to such behavior is the reference to the Oresteia, implying that the daughter is compelled by blood-guilt and revenge to persist in her work.

Plath overcomes this inconsistency in "Little Fugue" with a devotion presented as mindless and motiveless. It is a thoroughly unconscious compulsion. The daughter in this poem is not actively engaged in restoring a dead father, but "surviving" in a terrible void, a stillness and absence of meaning that is the aftermath of his death. Because "Little Fugue" is a more subtle exploration than "The Colossus" of the daughter's state of mental subsistence, and also one of Plath's most elaborate designs in black and white, we will look at it in greater detail.

> The yew's black fingers wag;
> Cold clouds go over.
> So the deaf and dumb
> Signal the blind, and are ignored.
>
> I like black statements.
> The featurelessness of that cloud, now!
> White as an eye all over!
> The eye of the blind pianist
>
> At my table on the ship.
> He felt for his food.
> His fingers had the noses of weasels.
> I couldn't stop looking.
>
> He could hear Beethoven:
> Black yew, white cloud,
> The horrific complications.
> Fingertraps—a tumult of keys.
>
> Empty and silly as plates,
> So the blind smile.
> I envy the big noises,
> The yew hedge of the Grosse Fuge.
>
> Deafness is something else.
> Such a dark funnel, my father!
> I see your voice
> Black and leafy, as in my childhood,
>
> A yew hedge of orders,
> Gothic and barbarous, pure German.
> Dead men cry from it.
> I am guilty of nothing.

The yew my Christ, then.
Is it not as tortured?
And you, during the Great War
In the California delicatessen

Lopping the sausages!
They colour my sleep,
Red, mottled, like cut necks.
There was a silence!

Great silence of another order.
I was seven, I knew nothing.
The world occurred,
You had one leg, and a Prussian mind.

Now similar clouds
Are spreading their vacuous sheets.
Do you say nothing?
I am lame in the memory.

I remember a blue eye,
A briefcase of tangerines.
This was a man, then!
Death opened, like a black tree, blackly.

I survive the while,
Arranging my morning.
These are my fingers, this my baby.
The clouds are a marriage dress, of that pallor.

                              (*Ariel*, pp. 70–71)

The title, "Little Fugue," refers to a contrapuntal formal arrangement of two "melodic" themes in the poem: first, the blankness in expression of black and white, and second, the psychological
blankness in memory of her father. The poem combines two meanings for fugue that in a dictionary appear to have nothing to do with
each other. A fugue is both a tightly controlled musical composition
and a form of amnesia—a flight of the mind. The deranged individ-

ual suffers a loss in memory, assumes a false identity, and seems to perform rationally, even while the mind wanders from its true course. The two meanings of fugue come naturally together in Plath's world to represent the master mindlessness, the numb and passive psychological state of Plath's victims. Here it is a wife and mother in her going-through-the-motions life. The line, "These are my fingers, this my baby," captures the stillness and detachment of this mind, incapable of distinguishing a fragment from a whole, and listing the human elements of her world as mere things. Like the mourning ant she compares herself to in "The Colossus," instinctively going about its business of putting the father together again, the woman in "Little Fugue" arranges her morning, a pun on the unconscious mourning that determines her empty existence. As we might expect, the dead father, in his "utter lack of attention"—so much like the indifference of Plath's deity in other poems—is more hurtful in his absence than he might be if she could hear, see, or talk to him.

In terms of meaning, the black-and-white design is purposely frustrating for the reader, so that we might share the void experienced by the speaker of the poem. The "horrific complications" of variations on "Black yew, white cloud," a stark color contrast, dissolve into a disturbing harmony of colorlessness and featurelessness. Through design, Plath creates a blank slate, a tabula rasa that stands for her mind, washed clean of memory and feeling. During the first part of the poem, she "plays" black and white images as a virtuoso pianist plays the black and white keys on a piano, but her skill is a snare—"Finger-traps—a tumult of keys." The ultimate emptiness of her playing is established in the opening stanza: "So the deaf and dumb / Signal the blind and are ignored." The signal is unseen, unspoken, unheard, as if a deaf-mute were attempting to communicate with a blind person. Such ironies make the black and white visual clarity of the opening stanza into a dreadful joke: "I like black statements. / The featurelessness of that cloud, now!" So the pianist cannot see her, while she stares at him fascinated and undetected. The pianist's fingers are not those of a sensitive artist when he is eating, but unattractive weasels rooting for food, and therefore mock his skill. The pianist can play and hear Beethoven's music, even though Beethoven's Grosse Fuge is the composition of a deaf man. This series of ironic "jokes" climaxes in an awful grin as the piano keys metamorphose into the teeth of the blind man who smiles at nothing—a smile "Empty and silly as plates."

These images are minor chords that lead directly into the "big noises" of Beethoven's Grosse Fuge. The deafness, blindness, and muteness introduced as themes in the little fugue resolve into a "great silence": "I cannot hear you, I cannot see you, and I cannot speak to you" are the daughter's complaints to the dead father. After the blankness of black and white, there is a momentary recovery of the colors of memory. First, the nightmarish color red jars the monotony of her no-color void, in the memory of her father as a butcher and amputee. As in *The Bell Jar*, a gap in the mind is associated with bodily affliction—being a woman is to be psychologically amputated, lame, handicapped. Here she is "lame in the memory," cut off from her past, and this is an inheritance from her father, who "had one leg, and a Prussian mind." All her memory can afford her are two more glimpses of color—"blue eyes" and a "briefcase of tangerines"—which do not tell her anything and are only fragments, quickly swallowed by blackness again: "Death opened, like a black tree, blackly." She "survives" the death of her father, but she does not really live, except as a kind of zombie, in a black-and-white monotony.

In a paradoxical way, this "black asininity" she lives is a fulfillment of a "Gothic and barbarous" order imposed by the father. Though she can only see his voice, not hear it, it forms a border of accusatory "you's," a "yew hedge of orders" around her life. And she arranges her life to complete an unconscious pattern of guilt— "The yew my Christ then"—though she may consciously perceive herself as "guilty of nothing." Even though he is dead, she lives in her father's house, doing what she is supposed to do, but without knowing why.

A Double World

My survey of Plath's poems in black and white might be seen as an attempt to codify her world, to assign specific meanings to this recurring image cluster. While there is a certain amount of stable signification from poem to poem, it should also be noted that Plath's primary "complexion of the mind," as she calls it in the early poem, "Moonrise," is one of ambivalence: we enter a double, hypocritical, dissembling world, with at least two kinds, two faces, two aspects to everything. Instead of a landscape of familiar and stable signification, we confront a mirrory variety, with frequent paradoxes and reversals and inversions of meaning. If we glance briefly at the poems I have just examined, we discover a polarity always at work. Plath is both drawn to and repelled by the austerity of the "Spinster" and "Man in Black." "Mushrooms" and "The Thin People" are at once mindless and purposeful. The scenes in "Watercolor of Grantchester Meadows" and "Two Views of a Cadaver Room" are both bland and innocent and bloodcurdling. On a grand scale, God's mind is at once a tabula rasa and a slate on which he writes and erases whole civilizations. He is both a primitive totem and a rationalist clockmaker. The beehive organizes sterile workers and a fertile queen, and the queen is both a creator and a murderess, a ruler and a scapegoat for the hive. The father in Plath's poems is both dead and absent and at the same time an oppressive ruler over his daughter, who is both guilty of his death and "guilty of nothing." This pervasive tension creates depth, variety, and complexity to Plath's world, since it reflects an imagination that offers no easy answers, no easy meanings for dealing with the uncertainties of life.

This doubleness is equally true of Plath's recurring symbols. When Eileen Aird investigates Plath's ubiquitous "moons," for example, she ends with a peculiar and by no means exhaustive assortment of meanings and associations: "hospitals and illness . . . sterility, madness, grief, the sea, fertility, despair, and blood." Hospitals and the sea? Sterility *and* fertility? Oddly, these inventories of Plath's world that aim to specify and codify also seem to collapse into unconvincing generalization: "Ultimately," Aird argues, "the moon represents death."[27]

Aird is right in her list, but not her conclusion. The moon is sometimes associated with all of these meanings, but the association is governed by Plath's "complexion of the mind." The moon is a symbol of fertility or sterility, depending on its phase. The roundness of a new moon is like a woman with child, a sign of something

ripening within her; but in "Parliament Hill Fields," the waning
moon, like a "crook," or the "skin seaming a scar," reminds the
woman speaker of her recent miscarriage and feelings of sterility,
dryness: "I'm a stone, a stick" (*Crossing the Water* [*CTW*], pp. 7–8).
Plath evinces a similar ambivalence toward the menses; the "blood
bag" dragged by the moon each month is evidence of woman's
fertility, but also of something dying in her: "The tree of life and the
tree of life / Unloosing their moons, month after month, to no purpose" ("The Munich Mannequins," *Ariel*, p. 73), or "It is she that
drags the blood-black sea around / Month after month, with its
voices of failure" (*Three Women: A Poem for Three Voices*, *WT*, p. 55).

In "Moonrise," an early poem about woman's feelings toward
pregnancy, this ambivalence is the governing principle of the
poem's structure and meaning. The goddess of childbirth, Lucina, is
described paradoxically as a deathlike presence.

> bony mother, laboring
> Among the socketed white stars, your face
> Of candor pares white flesh to the white bone.
>
> (*TC*, p. 65)

She is linked with the white light of the moon that both ripens and
rots.

> Berries redden. A body of whiteness
> rots, and smells of rot under its headstone
> Though the body walk out in clean linen.
>
> (*TC*, p. 64)

For every image of growth in "Moonrise," Plath offers another of
death and dissolution: the white berries are turning red, but the
white catalpa flowers are dying; grubs and ant eggs mature under
rocks, while simultaneously white bodies rot under headstones.
Plath so confounds the process of ripening with rotting—"Death
whitens in the egg and out of it"—that her reader is unsure whether
the woman who goes out to "sit in white" succumbs to decay or to
the promise of fruition in her womb: "The berries purple / And

bleed. The white stomach may ripen yet" (*TC*, p. 65). The whole poem reflects a state of consciousness that is peculiarly disturbing because of its polarities. Is this a woman waiting for fulfillment or death? Is the pregnancy a sign of life or decay? The power of "Moonrise" depends on Plath's ability to provoke these questions in a reader, to defamiliarize pregnancy as a solely "fruitful" event for the woman.

Typical of the early poems, Plath does not speak in the woman's voice in "Moonrise." As a result, much of the dramatic tension of these double responses to pregnancy is submerged in purely descriptive imagery. In the late poems, Plath is more likely to enhance the psychological state of ambivalence that is, I would argue, her actual subject, with a speaker who is pulled in two directions at once. She describes "Death & Co.," for example, as "about the double or schizophrenic nature of death—the marmoreal coldness of Blake's death mask, say, hand in glove with the fearful softness of worms, water, and other catabolisms," and then immediately creates a situation for exploring the horrific way they work together on a victim: "Imagine these two aspects of death as two men, two business friends, who have come to call."[28] The first is the stiff death mask—"The one who never looks up, whose eyes are lidded / And balled, like Blake's"—and he is a perfectionist, a kind of artist who brags about his accomplishments.

> He tells me how sweet
> The babies look in their hospital
> Icebox, a simple
>
> Frill at the neck,
> Then the flutings of their Ionian
> Death-gowns,
> Then two little feet.
>
> (*Ariel*, p. 28)

He is also the more overtly threatening of the two, a "condor" whose beak / Claps sidewise," snatching his victim when she is inattentive. In contrast, the second is oily, sociable, and fawning.

While the first wishes to be respected and admired, the second "wants to be loved." Yet they operate together: "The frost makes a flower. / The dew makes a star" (*Ariel*, p. 29). The momentary and frozen perfection of frost blooming into a floral shape and the moist drops of dew that look hard like stars—these are the contrary signs that "Somebody's done for."

Contradictions of this kind are a source of energy and dialectical movement in many of Plath's poems. She creates destinations—poems about "getting there"—out of her divided impulses. In "Edge," the dead woman is perfected in rigor mortis. As in "Death & Co.," so in "Edge" Plath counterpoints the marmoreal coldness of the woman's statuelike accomplishment with the soft, moist description of the garden she lies in, and the tension vivifies a scene that on the surface seems cold and lifeless. In "Lady Lazarus," too, images of hardness and softness are combined. The Lady is brought back from death and worms are picked off her like "sticky pearls," an image that recalls the transmutations of death by water in *The Tempest*: "Those are pearls that were his eyes."

States of being—softness and hardness, stasis and process—play an important role in shifts of mood from paralysis to release. Although there are exceptions, a good rule is that when substance seems immutable, when images have a stiff, iconic finish to them, as if carved in stone, they correspond to feelings of impotence and despair, of oppression and imprisonment. In turn, when substance is mutable, and images quickly give way to others by rapid displacement, there is a corresponding sense of "getting there," of omnipotence and triumph over physical weight. In the first instance, emotional paralysis is matched by constriction, and in the second, emotional freedom is represented by processes—of sublimation, transubstantiation, disintegration, and new syntheses of matter. Melting, burning, blurring of the vision, motion that destroys what has been left behind (e.g., "The engine is eating the track")—all of these changes in form indicate that revelation of some kind is at hand, as if the doubleness or hypocrisy of surfaces has been penetrated.

"Fever 103°" and "The Moon and the Yew Tree" are good illustrations of these opposing tendencies in Plath's world. Plath describes "Fever 103°" as a poem about "two kinds of fire—the fires of hell which merely agonize, and the fires of heaven, which purify. During the poem, the first sort of fire suffers into the second."[29] This is a somewhat euphemistic description for the sexual transformation the woman undergoes in the poem. In the course of "Fever 103°," a woman, heavy and sick with sexual desire, dissolves into a paradise of fulfillment. Her lust is finally and paradoxically sublimated into a virginal fire.

The poem opens with a question—"Pure? What does it mean?"—and with an answer that tells her reader what purity is not.

> The tongues of hell
> Are dull, dull as the triple
>
> Tongues of dull, fat Cerberus
> Who wheezes at the gate. Incapable
> Of licking clean
>
> The aguey tendon, the sin, the sin.
> (*Ariel*, p. 53)

Cerberus licking himself is an image of self-arousal and of fires that merely agonize, raising the passions higher. Hell is an eternity of sexual desire without consummation and completion in another. Cerberus is triple-headed, triple-tongued, but onanistic in his delight. The ugliness of his pleasure is captured in "the indelible smell / Of a snuffed candle," like a life snuffed out. In the speaker's feverish state, one image rapidly consumes another and the candle's "yellow sullen smokes" become Isadora Duncan's scarves. The poetic logic of this displacement is in Isadora's reputation as a voluptuary and free spirit and the circumstances of her bizarre death. Her scarves were the pathetic display of an old woman's passion, and they caught in the spokes of her youthful lover's car, strangling her. The speaker associates this old woman's lust, one of the fires of hell, to the artificial heat of a hothouse, producing unnatural blooms.

Love, love, the low smokes roll
From me like Isadora's scarves, I'm in a fright

One scarf will catch and anchor in the wheel.
Such yellow sullen smokes
Make their own element. They will not rise,

But trundle round the globe
Choking the aged and the meek,
The weak

Hothouse baby in its crib,
The ghastly orchid
Hanging its hanging garden in the air.

(*Ariel*, p. 53)

The orchid metamorphoses into a "Devilish leopard," a symbol of sinful fire that eats, like burning sulphur, marring the flower with spots that can only be cleansed with a greater fire—the radiation of an atomic blast: "Radiation turned it white / And killed it in an hour." This heat, too, is a false fire because it does not purge; it only greases "the bodies of adulterers / Like the Hiroshima ash and eating in."

Although these opening stanzas imitate the disjointed impressions of a delirious woman, they take shape as a meditation by free association on self-destructive passion, on the fires that consume without purgation. The second part of the poem turns inward, to the mutations of the speaker's body while it burns. She is in hell, too, physically ill with unconsummated desire.

Darling, all night
I have been flickering off, on, off, on.
The sheets grow heavy as a lecher's kiss.

(*Ariel*, p. 54)

Nothing reduces the fever: "Lemon water, chicken / Water, water makes me retch." But after three days and nights, the heat performs its own alchemy. Her head turns to a

> . . . moon
> Of Japanese paper, my gold beaten skin
> Infinitely delicate and infinitely expensive.
>
> Does not my heat astound you. And my light.
>
> (Ariel, p. 54)

Self-arousal and orgasm, like a "huge camellia / Glowing and coming and going, flush on flush" finally purify her body with an astounding and intense heat and light.

> I think I am going up,
> I think I may rise—
> The beads of hot metal fly, and I, love, I
>
> Am a pure acetylene
> Virgin.
>
> (Ariel, p. 54)

In an ironic inversion, perhaps of "Ash Wednesday," the way to spiritual purity is not by sexual abstinence, but by complete immersion in the fires of lust. She emerges from this suffering as an infinitely desirable but untouchable virgin—too hot for any man to enjoy. Self-arousal and consummation lead to apotheosis. She begins in desperate need for a man to fulfill her sexual desire and ends by turning all men away from her unquenchable fire.

> Not you, nor him
>
> Not him, nor him
> (My selves dissolving, old whore petticoats)—
> To Paradise.
>
> (Ariel, p. 55)

To understand fully Plath's wit in "Fever 103°," I believe the reader must visualize Plath's Virgin as a parody of Renaissance paintings of Mary—a Raphael Madonna perhaps, surrounded by her icons.

Attended by roses,

By kisses, by cherubim,
By whatever these pink things mean.

(Ariel, p. 54)

Framed and haloed in gold leaf ("Infinitely delicate and infinitely expensive"), accompanied by adoring aerial *putti*, and enthroned on her own heavenborne cloud, the Renaissance Madonna is the ultimate symbol in Western culture of female purity. She is not a real woman, but an object of adoration. Plath's Virgin is likewise an idol, but it is her body itself that is gold leaf—"my gold beaten skin"—an image that recalls the "pure gold baby" resurrected by Herr God in "Lady Lazarus." She, like Mary, is on a pedestal, "holy" and taboo, but ironically because of her orgasmic heat. To touch an icon of Mary with unholy thoughts is an act of desecration; to touch the acetylene virgin would be suicidal, for it would release the consuming fires of her body. What Plath implies in such ironic inversions of conventional signification is that Mary was originally enthroned on her pedestal out of dread for female sexuality. As in "Lady Lazarus," where Plath gives Lazarus a rebellious feminine voice to mock the myth of divine creation and resurrection, so in "Fever 103°" she endows the Virgin with a "purity" that mocks the myth of immaculate conception.

The two kinds of fire in "Fever 103°," sexual and spiritual, like the concepts of impurity and purity, fuse by the end of the poem; or in Plath's words, "the first sort of fire suffers into the second." The woman's body is the "suffering" vehicle for this movement, as she moves in her ordeal by fire from sexual frustration to sexual triumph. Plath employs the opposite poetic strategy in "The Moon and the Yew Tree," where elements seem eternally fixed in an emotional gridlock. There are two pairs of parental figures in this poem: the mother and father as the moon and yew tree, who punish and are indifferent to her pain; and the icons of the church, Mary and the saints, who offer forgiveness and holiness. Because of her despair, the speaker cannot believe in the church as a refuge. The poem opens, "This is the light of the mind, cold and planetary. / The trees of the mind are black. The light is blue" (*Ariel*, p. 41). The radiance of the moon, the threatening shadows of the yew tree, and the bruiselike combination of black and blue are composed into a mental landscape of "complete despair." In contrast to "Fever 103°," where one image quickly dissolves into another, in "The Moon and the Yew Tree" everything is static, unchanging, a formula for hopelessness. In this emotional state, there is no place for comfort, no place to get to. The house, graveyard, and church that organize the scene are all closed to her.

> Fumy, spiritous mists inhabit this place
> Separated from my house by a row of headstones.
> I simply cannot see where there is to get to.
>
> (*Ariel*, p. 41)

Like an unquiet spirit, she has no resting place; she resides in a permanent limbo.

As the poem develops, it is this mood of quiet melancholy which dominates, rather than any revelation of its causes in the life of the poem's speaker. Plath herself describes the poem as having no story, no history behind the voice.

> It was not a yew tree by a church on a road past a house in a town where a certain woman lived . . . and so on, as it might have been in a novel. Oh, no. It stood squarely in the middle of my poem, manipulating its dark shades, the voices in the churchyard, the clouds, the birds, the tender melancholy with which I contemplated it—everything! I couldn't subdue it. And, in the end, my poem was a poem about a yew tree.[30]

There is the suggestion that the "dark crime" the moon drags with it is the speaker's own—"I have fallen a long way"—and we may speculate on the exclusion of suicides from religious burial as the reason for her ghostlike presence on the periphery of the churchyard. But Plath is chiefly concerned with creating an oppressive formal arrangement of colors and objects that are in some mysterious way the very conditions of spiritual immobility. Moon and yew tree preside over her consciousness as punishment and oblivion. They are set against the promises of the church for those who are

believers: resurrection, tenderness, and holiness. One state of consciousness—hope—is set against guilty despair. The yew tree,
with its message of "blackness—blackness and silence" is an
answer to the message of the church bells: "Eight great tongues
affirming the Resurrection." And the moon and Mary are explicit
antagonists.

> The moon is my mother. She is not sweet like Mary.
> Her blue garments unloose small bats and owls.
> How I would like to believe in tenderness—
> The face of the effigy, gentled by candles,
> Bending, on me in particular, its mild eyes.
>
> (*Ariel*, p. 41)

Momentarily, she recognizes maternal solace in the church. Mary's
mildness might lead to forgiveness and the sweet, protective mother
guard her against the cruelties of the moon, a mother who is "bald
and wild" and "white as a knuckle," like a clenched fist.

At this point, however, Plath introduces a less inviting image of
the church as smug, holier-than-thou, unforgiving.

> Inside the church, the saints will be all blue,
> Floating on their delicate feet over the cold pews,
> Their hands and faces stiff with holiness.
>
> (*Ariel*, p. 41)

With a characteristically divided perspective, she presents the
church as unyielding, demanding a martyrdom as harsh as the one
already inflicted on her by the moon and the yew tree. The woman's
despair dominates her vision, so that salvation becomes impossible.

Unlike "Fever 103°," where the two kinds of fire become one,
and the woman moves from sinful lust to a virginal flame, the only
movement in "The Moon and the Yew Tree" is circular, from a state
of despair back to a state of despair; and the color blue is the major
link in this movement. The blue "light of the mind," "cold and
planetary," that opens the poem returns at the end in the blue saints
and the image of clouds "flowering / Blue and mystical over the face
of the stars." At the beginning, blue is combined with black to give

the sense of mental injury. By the end, it is also associated with a moral chill that condemns the speaker to the yew tree's "blackness and silence." "Fever 103°" and "The Moon and the Yew Tree" are strategies, typical symbolic actions by Plath in dealing with an ambivalent state of consciousness. In the first, she achieves release by a process of transubstantiation. She succumbs to her sexual fever and permits herself to be immolated. Contrarily, there is no progression in "The Moon and the Yew Tree." It is the brute fact of her despair, captured in plain statements such as "The moon is no door" and "I live here" that Plath attempts to convey. In "Fever 103°," images melt one into another, while in "The Moon and the Yew Tree," the images are static, unchanging icons to match the permanence of her position, caught between two views of her condition—forgiveness and punishment.

It is not particularly useful, then, to codify symbols in either poem (i.e., fire means this, the moon means that). In "Fever 103°," it is the displacement of one meaning for fire by another, the emotional suffering that matters. "The Moon and the Yew Tree," too, is in one sense contentless, because the questions it raises—"Why is she stuck here? What are the causes for her despair? What do the moon and yew tree represent for her?"—are never answered. If there is a specific meaning to either poem, it is in the complexion of the mind, the emotions of the speaker, and Plath's deft transference of these feelings to her reader.

Elsewhere in Plath's poetry, the stasis and emotional paralysis of "The Moon and the Yew Tree" create an expectation of sudden violence, of repressed energy and concealed meaning that will eventually explode. While nothing finally happens in many of these poems, there is a breathless urgency to their dramatic situations that upsets the reader's own emotional equilibrium. We expect something awful to happen even after the poem's closure. The tension in "The Arrival of the Bee Box," for instance, is the result of the speaker's alternating feelings of being the powerful owner of the hive—"They can die, I need feed them nothing, I am the owner"— and her powerlessness—"I am not a Caesar"—in face of a "Roman mob," "a box of maniacs" (Ariel, p. 59). She asks herself in horror, "How can I let them out?" but then reassures herself, "Tomorrow I will be sweet God, I will set them free." The vacillation between

feelings of Godlike control and total helplessness before a slave re-
volt ("Black on black, angrily clambering") is matched by a combination of fear and fascination.

> The box is locked, it is dangerous.
> I have to live with it overnight
> And I can't keep away from it.
>
> (*Ariel*, p. 59)

In fantasy, she imagines herself free of the bees if she lets them out
and then stands back still as a tree.

> I wonder if they would forget me
> If I just undid the locks and stood back and turned into a tree.
> There is the laburnum, its blonde colonnades,
> And the petticoats of the cherry.
>
> (*Ariel*, p. 60)

This is purposely naive: the cascading flowers of the laburnum and
the cherry blossoms would attract a full-scale assault by the hive.
The speaker's wish for escape disguises the equal desire for passive
submission to the bees, with their "swarmy feeling of African
hands." The poem ends with the statement, "The box is only temporary." By itself, this sounds sane, official, in control, like an official announcement from the Pentagon, but in the emotionally
charged situation of the poem, it is ominous.

In "Poppies in July" as well, the speaker rocks between extremes, drawn both to the redness of the flowers like "little hell
flames" or a "mouth just bloodied" and to their "colourless"
"fumes" and "liquors." The dual nature of the poppies matches her
own ambivalent desire for violence or oblivion, for intense pain or
numbness.

> If I could bleed or sleep!
> If my mouth could marry a hurt like that!
> Or your liquors seep to me, in this glass capsule,
> Dulling and stilling.
>
> (*Ariel*, p. 81)

What is intolerable is the state of limbo, a paradoxical form of suffering in that there is an intense visual sensation of redness, yet she cannot feel: "You flicker. I cannot touch you. / I put my hands among the flames. Nothing burns." In Plath's world, the ultimate suffering is not death, but a psychological blankness induced by extremes of feeling cancelling each other out. This is true of Plath's "Widow," paralyzed by anger and tenderness for her dead husband. She is like a spider caught in its own web.

> The bitter spider sits
> And sits in the center of her loveless spokes.
> Death is the dress she wears, her hat and collar.
> The moth-face of her husband, moonwhite and ill,
> Circles her like a prey she'd love to kill.
>
> (CTW, p. 22)

The widow would, paradoxically, like to kill her husband for dying and leaving her. The bitterness of her loss makes her vengeful and longing at the same time, like a black widow spider who kills her mate in the act of love and then regrets her loneliness.

Ambivalence and Femininity

The ambivalence that I see as the dominant mood of Plath's poetry is also, I have suggested in a previous chapter, a peculiarly feminine attribute, part of what Nancy Chodorow calls woman's relational capacities and psychological adaptation to the world.[31] According to Simone de Beauvoir as well, an ambiguity of feeling—toward man, nature, law, and her own body—is at the heart of a female sensibility.

> The domain in which she is confined is surrounded by the masculine universe, but it is haunted by obscure forces of which men are themselves the playthings; if she allies herself with these magical forces, she will come to power in her turn. Society enslaves Nature; but Nature dominates it. The Spirit flames out beyond life; but it ceases to burn when Life no longer supports it. Woman is justified by this equivocation in finding more ver-

ity in a garden than in a city, in a malady than in an idea, in a
birth than in a revolution; she endeavors to re-establish that
reign of the earth, of the Mother . . . in order to become again
the essential in face of the inessential. . . . This ambivalence is
evident in the way woman regards her body. . . . Her body
displays reactions for which the woman denies responsibility; in
sobs, vomiting, convulsions, it escapes her control, it betrays
her; it is her most intimate verity, but it is a shameful verity that
she keeps hidden. And yet it is also her glorious double; she is
dazzled in beholding it in the mirror; it is promised happiness,
work of art, living statue; she shapes it, adorns it, puts it on
show. When she smiles at herself in the glass, she forgets her
carnal contingence; in the embrace of love, in maternity, her
image is destroyed. But often as she muses on herself, she is
astonished to be at one and the same time that heroine and that
flesh. . . . Nature similarly presents a double face to her, sup-
plying the soup kettle and stimulating mystical effusions.[32]

De Beauvoir's irony in dealing with woman's world of contraries—
soup kettles and mystical effusions—is both crushingly critical and
eloquent. As we shall see, Plath too is capable of this irony. She
affirms and participates in many of the stereotypes about woman's
dreamy, intuitive nature and also achieves a critical view of this
female sensibility. What emerges from her poetry is a sense that
woman's ambivalent nature is culturally determined. The individual
woman duplicates in her own self-image a larger ambivalence toward femininity. As Adrienne Rich describes this double view of
woman in *Of Woman Born,*

throughout patriarchal mythology, dream-symbolism, theology,
language, two ideas flow side by side: one, that the female body
is impure, corrupt, the site of discharges, bleedings, dangerous
to masculinity, a source of moral and physical contamination,
"the devil's gateway." On the other hand, as mother the
woman is beneficent, sacred, pure, asexual, nourishing; and
the physical potential for motherhood—that same body with its
bleedings and mysteries—is her single destiny and justification
in life. These two ideas have become deeply internalized in

women, even in the most independent of us, those who seem to lead the freest lives.[33]

Archetypes of motherhood are particularly oppressive, since this seems to be at once woman's great creative power and a biological destination of her body over which her mind may exert little or no control.

The vast majority of literary and visual images of motherhood comes to us filtered through a collective or individual male consciousness. As soon as a woman knows that a child is growing in her body, she falls under the power of theories, ideals, archetypes, descriptions of her new existence, almost none of which have come from other women (though other women may transmit them) and all of which have floated invisibly about her since she first perceived herself to be female and therefore potentially a mother.[34]

Always the good student, Plath imbibed these stereotypes. Where in her personal life she often seems totally in conformity with cultural norms for womanhood, in her poetry she is capable of exploring and playing with clichés about femininity. Her "Heavy Women," for example, are treated with loving mockery, their condition a stereotype of the pregnant, waiting woman.

Irrefutable, beautifully smug
As Venus, pedestalled on a half-shell,
Shawled in blond hair and the salt
Scrim of a sea breeze, the women
Settle in their belling dresses.
Over each weighty stomach a face
Floats calm as a moon or a cloud.

Smiling to themselves, they meditate
Devoutly as the Dutch bulb
Forming its twenty petals,
The dark still nurses its secret.
On the green hill, under the thorn trees,

They listen for the millennium,
The knock of the small, new heart.

Pink-buttocked infants attend them.
Looping wool, doing nothing in particular,
They step among the archetypes.
Dusk hoods them in Mary-blue
While far off, the axle of winter
Grinds round, bearing down with the straw,
The star, the wise grey men.

(CTW, p. 9)

Plath both affirms some of the clichés about women's feelings during pregnancy and adroitly prevents a stock, sentimental response from her reader with irony. In their self-absorbed vanity, the heavy women believe they are all Madonnas, with *putti*-flocks flying about, and they "listen for the millennium," as if every child born were destined for the greatness of Christ. Despite the comic absurdity of lines like "Venus . . . on a half-shell" and "They step among the archetypes," there is something serious, weighty about these blue-hooded women that Plath is unwilling to explode with ridicule. Instead, she qualifies their irrefutability with a serious reversal at the end of the poem, once again provoking an ambivalent response from her reader toward pregnancy. Birth is, yes, a portentous event, but not in the way that the pregnant woman hopes. In the last three lines, it is not the future triumph but the machinelike certainty of the child's sacrificial fate, and not the joy, but the pain of childbirth that is revealed. Every child is the "chosen" one, but chosen for mortality, and the smugness of the heavy women who lovingly nurse a "dark secret" in their wombs looks, in retrospect, like pathetic gullibility. This is, too, why de Beauvoir criticizes women. They equivocate, these heavy women, asserting the truth of birth over a revolution, the garden of their bodies over the cities created by men, and their physical maladies over ideas—even though "inessential" revolutions, cities, ideas will determine the ultimate fate of their babies.

In an essay on feminist criticism, Annette Kolodny argues that much of contemporary women's writing employs a device similar to the one we see at work in "Heavy Women."

I have labelled [it] for want of a better term, "inversion"—and it
works in a number of complex ways. On the one hand, the
stereotyped, traditional literary images of women—as, for example, the loving "Mom," the "bitch," the Sex Goddess—are
being turned around in women's fiction, to explore their inherent absurdity, or, in other instances, to reveal their hidden reality, though in new ways, not previously apprehended. . . . We
seem to discover almost a conspiracy to overthrow all the nice,
comfortable patterns and associations of a previous . . . literary
tradition.[35]

Plath both inverts many of the "traditional literary images of
women" and contributes new areas of feeling to the literary domain.
There are few poems, I would guess, about miscarriage. "Parliament
Hill Fields" takes this as its subject. It is also, in some ways, a
typical Plath poem—another mental landscape of depression like
"The Moon and the Yew Tree." Everywhere the speaker looks,
there is total neutrality, and the dominant image in these "nature"
poems is a lonely figure facing an unresponsive universe. In "Parliament Hill Fields," the woman speaker strolls aimlessly through an
open field; as she walks, each object that comes into view provides a
reflection of what happens internally. Throughout the poem, emotional pain is numbed and endured rather than released. There are
no cathartic cries from the heart, no breast beating. Nor is the mood
one of stoic calm, an intellectual acceptance of the infant's death.
The indifference of the natural and human world is an affront, but
the woman seems incapable of rousing herself to anger.

> The round sky goes on minding its business.
> Your absence is inconspicuous;
> Nobody can tell what I lack.
>
> (CTW, p. 7)

A cluster of hospital images dominates the first half of the poem, as
if she were reliving the miscarriage on her solitary walk. Time passing is like a surgeon, efficiently cutting away even the memory of
the lost child: "On the bald hill the new year hones its edge." Gulls
settle and stir like "the hands of an invalid"; "The wind stops my

breath like a bandage"; and "an ashen smudge / Swaddles roof and tree," like a stillborn child, bundled, buried, and forgotten:

> I suppose it's pointless to think of you at all.
> Already your doll grip lets go.

> The tumulus, even at noon, guards its shadow.
>   (CTW, pp. 7–8)

The ironic flinch of the language—the offhand "suppose" and "pointless"—only underscores the bitterness of the loss. As in many of Plath's landscapes, the moon is associated with female fertility. Instead of the promise in a new moon, she sees an old, whitening crook, "Thin as the skin seaming a scar," an apt image for a pregnancy that miscarries.

The second half of the poem is concerned with the aftermath, the emotional healing process. The presiding emotion is a reluctant but inexorable letting go of the dead child: "I lose sight of you on your blind journey." The dissolving relationship between mother and child is reflected in images of disintegration in the landscape: "the city melts like sugar" when her eyes "wince and brim" in the sun; she is briefly swallowed by a passing "crocodile of small girls" and walks on while "Their shrill, gravelly gossip's funneled off"; the baby's cry fades like the cry of a gnat; water rivulets "unspool, and spend themselves" and her "mind runs with them." Finally, the whole day "empties its images / Like a cup or a room." What is striking about this unravelling process is its lack of release. She absorbs the loss, making it a permanent part of herself, so that the healing process of forgetfulness does not leave her completely whole again. The emptiness lingers as a reproach to her infertility: "I'm a stone, a stick." She contrasts herself with "faithful dark-boughed cypresses," asserting that she is "less constant," and "too happy."

The poem ends with her return to a living child. As in other poems, bright colors interrupt her thought, previously blended with the grey neutrality of the fields.

> Now, on the nursery wall,
> The blue night plants, the little pale blue hill

In your sister's birthday picture starts to glow.
The orange pompons, the Egyptian papyrus
Light up. Each rabbit-eared
Blue shrub behind the glass
Exhales an indigo nimbus

A sort of cellophane balloon.
The old dregs, the old difficulties take me to wife.
Gulls stiffen to their chill vigil in the drafty half-light;
I enter the lit house.

(CTW, p. 8)

The reminder of the living daughter waiting for her asserts itself
in blue and orange, jolting her from the dull ache; but the return
home is not enough to console her for the baby's loss. The concluding lines are neither overly optimistic nor pessimistic. A "lit
house" is a warm, inviting image after the harshness of the landscape, but there is also a sense of guilt in the refuge it offers from
grief. While the gulls stand vigil and the somber cypresses watch
over the grave mound, she cannot give herself over to the mourning she desires. She must return to the nursery, another child,
and the business of getting on with life—"the old dregs, the old
difficulties."

Marjorie Perloff argues that the theme of "Parliament Hill
Fields" is a "tension between the desire to blend into the scenery,
thus becoming invisible and beyond attack, and the opposite urge to
maintain one's autonomy as a person." The poem "is above all a
poem of absence, absence not only of others but oneself." She attributes the emptiness to the fragile identity of a schizophrenic ego.[36]
This interpretation of the speaker seems both descriptively precise
and thematically abstract. The poem is, quite simply, a record of
how a woman who has just lost a baby might feel. The tension in
the poem is between the desire to mourn, to preserve the dead
baby's presence by suffering and effacing herself, and the growing
realization of numbness to the pain of loss. She would like to be as
contorted as the "writhen trees," to bear witness to her sorrow, but,
she says guiltily, "I am too happy." If the poem is schizophrenic, it
may be that the mourning process itself is a schizophrenic emotional

state, a state of being torn between anger and tenderness at the death of a loved one that leaves the survivor emotionally paralyzed.

Like Adrienne Rich, Plath is "haunted by the stereotype of the mother whose love is unconditional; and by the visual and literary images of motherhood as a single-minded identity."[37] The woman in "Parliament Hill Fields" seems to know that she should be mad with grief to fulfill conventional expectations about women who lose their babies. But like Rich, too, Plath is aware of parts of herself "that would never cohere to those images."[38] In *Three Women: A Poem for Three Voices*, Plath explores a wide range of conventional and unconventional attitudes toward motherhood in the characters of a "perfect" mother, a secretary who miscarries, and an unmarried student who does not want to be pregnant. For the first woman, the ripeness of her body is all: "I do not have to think, or even rehearse. / What happens in me will happen without attention" (*WT*, p. 47). During this waiting time, her body is a passive instrument of natural process—a "seed about to break" (*WT*, p. 51) and "drummed into use" (*WT*, p. 53) by forces outside herself. The delivery itself is a cruel miracle that arouses questions: "I am the center of an atrocity. / What pains, what sorrows must I be mothering?" (*WT*, p. 53). But almost immediately she is "reassured" and "simple again," a woman who papers her new son's room "with big roses" and paints "little hearts on everything" (*WT*, p. 62). She is so much the stereotypical earth mother that she fights off intuitions of future sorrow and blindly turns away from the real world, with its thalidomide babies.

> I do not believe in those terrible children
> Who injure my sleep with their white eyes, their finger-
>   less hands.
> They are not mine. They do not belong to me.
>   (*WT*, p. 61)

She rejects any deeper thoughts than "normality": "I do not will him to be exceptional." "I will him to be common" (*WT*, p. 62).

There is a sentimental banality to this portrait, but the secretary and student provide ironic counterpoint to the earth mother's confidence and complacency. To the same degree that the earth mother feels herself a "great event" of fertility, the secretary feels herself the center of sterility: "The sun is down, I die. I make a death" (WT, p. 54). Like the earth mother, she has tried to be normal—"tried not to think too hard. I have tried to be natural. / I have tried to be blind in love, like other women" (WT, p. 50), but she is elected to be "Neither a woman, happy to be like a man, nor a man / Blunt and flat enough to feel no lack" (WT, p. 55). Because she does not fulfill the process her body was presumably created for, she feels guilty: "I am found wanting" (WT, p. 48). And she feels unworthy of her husband's affection. Her statement that he "will love me through the blur of my deformity" sounds as though he is doing her a favor, forgiving her for an all-too-obvious deficiency as a woman (WT, p. 58).

With the student, we hear a woman who has "no reverence" for the new life growing uncontrolled in her body: "It was too late, and the face / Went on shaping itself with love, as if I was ready" (WT, p. 49). The whole notion of the naturalness of feminine, motherly feeling is called into question: "I wasn't ready for anything to happen. / I should have murdered this, that murders me" (WT, p. 52). For the earth mother, the "one cry" of her baby "is the hook I hang on" (WT, p. 57), an irresistible link with the baby. For the student, her baby's "cries are hooks that catch and grate like cats" (WT, p. 56), and she leaves her girl behind, because "It is so beautiful to have no attachments!" (WT, p. 62). With such parallel but opposite images, Plath confirms the individuality of female response to their bodies. There is no biological destiny to women's emotions.

The intuition of the earth mother that new life might be new grief—"What pains, what sorrows must I be mothering?" (WT, p. 53)—is confirmed by the secretary. For her, the "dark earth" is not solely life-giving, not only a nurse, but "the vampire of us all." The "old time bomb" mortality means that giving birth is to participate in death as well, the "gross eating game."

> So she supports us,
> Fattens us, in kind. Her mouth is red.
> I know her. I know her intimately—
> Old winter-face, old barren one, old time bomb.
> Men have used her meanly. She will eat them.
> Eat them, eat them, eat them in the end.
>
> (WT, p. 54)

The woman who miscarries also knows, "I, too, create corpses" (*WT*, p. 55).

The balance of the poem, despite these reservations, is in favor of the smug, irrefutable wisdom of the mother. The student, happy to return to her freedom, ends with the question, "What is it I miss?" (*WT*, p. 62), from which we must infer regret at the daughter left behind for adoption. And the secretary is healed by the knowledge that she may still bear a child. She will "wait and ache" for yet another annunciation. Only the mother is content, even though her possession of the infant male is fleeting: "He does not walk. He does not speak a word. / He is still swaddled in white bands" (*WT*, p. 62). The lines hint at a future when the mother will not be so completely in control, when the boy walks and speaks, freed from his infant swaddling and of the mother's protection.

One of the surprising aspects to the mother's triumph is the exclusion of any mention of a father in the waiting, delivery, or homecoming. Not so for the secretary and student, who see men as powerful victimizers.

> Second Voice: It is these men I mind:
> [Secretary]   They are so jealous of anything that is not flat!
>   They are jealous gods
>   That would have the whole world flat because
>   they are.
>   I see the Father conversing with the Son.
>   Such flatness cannot but be holy.
>   "Let us make a heaven," they say.
>   "Let us flatten and launder the grossness from
>   these souls."
>
>   (*WT*, pp. 50–51)

> Third Voice: The Doctors move among us as if our bigness
> [Student]   Frightened the mind. They smile like fools.
>   They are to blame for what I am, and they know it.
>   They hug their flatness like a kind of health.
>
>   (*WT*, p. 52)

The secretary and student believe a male deity has usurped the woman's body to manifest his ideas, his powers. Men do not live in

their bodies as women do in Plath's poetry. The woman who miscarries blames a masculine principle for her emptiness—man's

> . . . flat, flat flatness from which ideas, destructions,
> Bulldozers, guillotines, white chambers of shrieks proceed,
> Endlessly proceed—and the cold angels, the abstractions.
>
> (*WT*, p. 47)

The antagonism between mind and body is between man and
woman, God and nature. The man thinks and acts, the woman
bears the consequences. His are the ends; she is but the means.
Hence the student sees herself as Leda, Danae, or as the shapeless
matter for God's word, the *logos*, to incarnate itself.

> And all I could see was dangers: doves and words,
> Stars and showers of gold—conceptions, conceptions!
> I remember a white, cold wing
>
> And the great swan, with its terrible look,
> Coming at me, like a castle, from the top of the river.
> There is a snake in swans.
> He glided by; his eye had a black meaning.
> I saw the world in it—small, mean, and black,
> Every little word hooked to every little word, and act to act.
>
> (*WT*, p. 49)

The woman's womb is an empty space to be filled by the man, a
world to be filled with manifestations of divine potency, but then
flattened out of jealousy.

In contrast, the earth mother feels confident of her power and
that she might prevent this deity from assuming authority over her
son's fate.

> I do not will him to be exceptional.
> It is the exception that interests the devil.
> It is the exception that climbs the sorrowful hill.
> Or sits in the desert and hurts his mother's heart.
>
> (*WT*, p. 62)

It does not matter whether it is God or Lucifer to the earth mother, since they appear as a united force in the temptation and martyrdom of Christ. For her the baby is valuable for his vitality and warmth— "he is pink and perfect. He smiles so frequently"—not for what he will achieve in the future, what he will eventually be in the world. To use de Beauvoir's distinction, she asserts an "essential" nature and fleshiness against the "inessential" enterprise of history.

Plath's earth mother does not mention a father and she alludes only briefly to the malignant deity who haunts the secretary and student, perhaps because the nursery, in Plath's view, is one place where woman exerts absolute authority.

> The helplessness of the child confers a certain narrow kind of power on the mother everywhere—a power she may not desire, but also often a power which may compensate to her for her powerlessness everywhere else. The power of the mother is . . . to give or withhold nourishment and warmth, to give or withhold survival itself. Nowhere else . . . does a woman possess such literal power over life and death.[39]

This is the "unilateral parental power" Dorothy Dinnerstein speaks of as the mother's peculiar privilege in the nursery. Balancing this is the father's complete domination of the child's future—his civilization building. This division of responsibility and female-male sensibility is what Dinnerstein means by the title of one of her chapters in *The Mermaid and the Minotaur*, "Mama and the Mad Megamachine." The female is a spectator to history-making men, what Plath's secretary calls "The faces of nations, / Governments, parliaments, societies, / The faceless faces of important men" (*WT*, p. 50). The woman's nursery is, contrarily, the realm of the body—"a garden of black and red agonies"—opposed to a male realm of mind and spirit. This is why, when the secretary first sees the signs of her miscarriage—"the small red seep"—she feels that she has caught a male disease.

> I watched the men walk about me in the office. They were so flat!

> There was something about them like cardboard, and now I
>   had caught it.
>
> (WT, p. 47)

If she is not "Mama," then she must belong to the male world of the
"Megamachine."

> And the man I work for laughed: "Have you seen
>   something awful?
> You are so white, suddenly." And I said nothing.
> I saw death in the bare trees, a deprivation.
> I could not believe it. Is it so difficult
> For the spirit to conceive a face, a mouth?
> The letters proceed from these black keys, and these black
>   keys proceed
> From my alphabetical fingers, ordering parts,
>
> Parts, bits, cogs, the shining multiples.
>
> (WT, p. 48)

In the secretary's work, she merges with the machine, ordering
parts, while her body gives itself over to a natural process—death.
The man's misunderstanding of what is happening is the result of
his " 'de-natured' environment 'fit only for machines to live in'."[40] It
is also a world of spirit laundered of the "grossness" of the female
body, which may explain the woman's anguished response, "Is it so
difficult / For the spirit to conceive a face, a mouth?" in response to
her boss's bewilderment.

In *Three Women*, Plath links her ambivalence—conflicting feelings of women toward their femininity—to her larger view of the
world as ruled by a male deity struggling to embody his spirit in a
"megamachine." Indeed, if we look at the poem's imagery—the
student's "small, mean, black" world and the secretary's flat, cold,
abstract world—it should remind us of all the poems where Plath is
not explicitly speaking in a woman's voice, but simply confronting
the "black, intractable mind" of nature, history, society. "Three
Women" makes this vision a clearly feminine one.

Woman as Nietzsche's Mirror

Let woman be a plaything, pure and simple as a priceless gem reflecting the virtues

of a world which is not yet here.—Nietzsche, *Thus Spake Zarathustra*

The opposition of Mama to the Megamachine, of the female body to the male spirit and civilization building, is the central issue in the poem "Brasília" (discussed earlier in this chapter). Brasília is the "dove's annihilation"—the father-God's "conception" and "abstraction" of a perfect world. It is the apocalypse, too, of male enterprise and history making—Lewis Mumford's "world of light and space, disinfected of the human presence."[41] Plath speaks in the opposing voice of Mary, clinging to the "red earth, motherly blood," to a world of "sheep and wagons" more primitive than the robot-peopled millennium God has in mind for mankind. I would like to return to the image, "Mirror safe, unredeemed," in "Brasília," which I described earlier as a plea to escape reflection in the clear glass, the tabula rasa of God's mind. For Plath, the image of mirror reflection is at the heart of destructive relationships, not only between God and humanity, but between man and woman, mother and child, and woman with herself. It is yet another image cluster, like her black-and-white designs, her moons, her beehive societies, where we may see her imaginative vision taking shape. Plath's mirrors, perhaps more than any other of these favored figurative structures, also reflect her concern with human relationships.

The mirror reflection is "The Other" that both obstructs a direct, vital link between human beings and prevents them from being at one with themselves: "Cold glass, how you insert yourself / Between myself and myself!" (*WT*, p. 22). The "Childless Woman" who aborts time and again says she is

> Spider like, I spin mirrors,
> Loyal to my image,
>
> Uttering nothing but blood—
>
> (*WT*, p. 34)

and "The Gigolo" is a modern Narcissus who prefers "A palace of velvet / With windows of mirrors" because he wants no family, no attachments.

> There one is safe,
> There are no family photographs
>
> No rings through the nose, no cries.
>
> > (WT, p. 6)

He desires only his own garish reflection in the hotel mirrors of Miami where he plies his trade.

> . . . and I
> Glitter like Fontainebleau.
>
> Gratified,
> All the fall of water an eye
> Over whose pool I tenderly
> Lean and see me.
>
> > (WT, p. 7)

Like Narcissus, he drowns in an illusory image of himself. He is not real, but a sacrifice to the women who see only his mirror reflection and want only his sex.

> Bright fish hooks, the smiles of women
> Gulp at my bulk
> And I, in my snazzy blacks,
>
> Mill a litter of breasts like jellyfish.
> To nourish
> The cellos of moans I eat eggs—
> Eggs and fish, the essentials,
>
> The aphrodisiac squid.
> My mouth sags,

The mouth of Christ
When my engine reaches the end of it.

(*WT*, p. 6)

The male whore is a sex machine and a two-dimensional mirror for female vanity, a martyr to old women's sterility.

More often in Plath's poetry it is the wife who is the victim of such mirror relations. The harem wife of "Purdah" is Nietzsche's "priceless gem"—a piece of jade carved from the side of Adam. The Spanish root for jade, *ijada*, in fact means "loin stone," implying that the woman is the priceless sex of man.[42] As a male possession, the harem wife is ironically also the guardian-possessor of his sexual being. She is little different from Plath's gigolo, except that she will finally reveal her true self, a "lioness," and murder her husband, the supreme "Lord of the mirrors!" He has no idea that the "small jeweled / Doll he guards like a heart" reflects anything more than his own image, that she is a conscious being in her own right. Her female fertility—imaged here in the moon that drags the menses each month—disguises her to the lord.

And should
The moon, my
Indefatigable cousin

Rise with her cancerous pallors,
Dragging trees—
Little bushy polyps,

Little nets,
My visibilities hide.
I gleam like a mirror.

(*WT*, p. 40)

The purdah, a sign of female modesty and humility, is, in this context, a male invention that hides the fearful female genitals from male eyes. He does not wish to see the woman or to confront her sexually. He wishes to see himself as an autonomous sexual being, to see only himself; so woman's face and sexual being must be screened, sheathed.

It is himself he guides

In among these silk
Screens, these rustling appurtenances.
I breathe, and the mouth

Veil stirs its curtain
My eye
Veil is

A concatenation of rainbows.
I am his
Even in his

Absence, I
Revolve in my
Sheath of impossibles

Priceless and quiet.

                                    (WT, pp. 40–41)

The husband is an "I" and the harem wife an object, an "it"—a two-dimensional reflector and spectator to the man's performance in the bedroom. She hides her "I" like a multifaceted gem—a little jade Buddha.

Jade—
Stone of the side,
The agonized

Side of a green Adam, I
Smile, cross-legged,
Enigmatical,

Shifting my clarities.
So valuable!
How the sun polishes this shoulder!
                                        (*WT*, p. 40)

In these mirror images, one may see what Dinnerstein (borrowing from de Beauvoir) calls the " 'I's stance toward the non-'I'—the stance that sets the direction of the world-making thrust."

> Man's monopoly of history-making follows from the double sexual standard. As the unpossessed possessor of woman he is freer than she is to come and go—geographically or psychologically—from the place where they are intimate: It is he, not she, who can leave what belongs to him—to go to war or a laboratory, to spend all night writing or painting—without violating the terms of ownership.[43]

What man does not know is that woman as precious "loin-stone" is also the "unpossessed possessor" of the power to destroy his freedom if she chooses to destroy his illusion. This complementarity between male-female is also the relation in Plath's world between creator-creature, man and Mother Nature, between male enterprise in the world and the female, intimate "place" of the boudoir, harem, and nursery. In "Purdah," the existential tie between husband and wife is like that described by de Beauvoir. Man

> aspires in contradictory fashion both to life and repose, to existence and to merely being; he knows full well that "trouble of spirit" is the price of development, that his distance from the object is the price of nearness to himself; but he dreams of quiet in disquiet and of an opaque plenitude that nevertheless would be endowed with consciousness. This dream incarnated is precisely woman; she is the wished-for intermediary between nature, the stranger to man, and the fellow being who is too closely identical.[44]

The harem wife's enigma is the "deep reality under the appearance of things"[45]—what Plath calls the "rustling appurtenances" of the harem-boudoir where man may find his ease. The purdah itself is the veil between man's consciousness and Mother Nature—femaleness. Dinnerstein, expanding on de Beauvoir's notion of the male "existent" and the female as the "quasi-sentient living stuff from which their [i.e., men's] 'I'-ness has carved itself out," explains the woman as man's mirror.

> He needs her as a mirror "because the inwardness of the existent" (that is, of the self-aware, purposeful creator of human reality, the history-maker) "is only nothingness and because he must project himself into an object in order to reach himself." So "what he really asks of her is to be, outside of him, all that which he cannot grasp inside himself." Woman's "whole situation destines her" to act as the "concerned spectator" in his life. And she can do and be all this only by remaining "outside the fray." It is through her embodiment of this—to him precious—otherness, as well as through her work as his practical servant, that woman acts to maintain life while man extends its range through his activities.[46]

The woman, as long as she sees herself as man's "other," as his mirror and spectator, as a nature and body to be filled with meaning by the male, cannot be either a sentient being or creator in her own right. She will be only a "rustling appurtenance" to man.

Plath asserts the evils of this relationship poetically and struggles against it. The woman of "Purdah" is the angry mother Clytemnestra behind the veil, seeking revenge on Agamemnon for sacrificing their daughter Iphigenia to history, to the favor of the gods in the war against Troy. She is the mother versus the megamachine of male history making. At the end of the poem, she screams and shatters the lord's mirrors into a million slivers—"a million ignorants" because they reflect only male blindness to the woman behind the veil.

> I shall unloose
> One note

Shattering
The chandelier
Of air that all day plies

Its crystals,
A million ignorants

(WT, p. 41)

And later, she will unloose

The lioness,
The shriek in the bath,
The cloak of holes.

(WT, p. 41)

In these few lines, Plath captures Clytemnestra's fury, the mother's rage at this violation of nature, and asserts in mythic form woman's right to take back the self she has been denied.

This may seem like burdening Plath's images with an intellectual freight they cannot carry, yet everywhere in her poetry, the mirror reflection is the haunting "other" who reminds woman of what she should and cannot be. Dame Kindness, the stereotypically sweet Mama who prevents her from writing poetry by reminding her of her children's needs, is a pervasive image.

Kindness glides about my house.
Dame Kindness, she is so nice!
The blue and red jewels of her rings smoke
In the windows, the mirrors
Are filling with smiles.

(Ariel, p. 82)

Such passages remind one of Adrienne Rich's frustration at the news of a new child and consequently, "the crumbling to death of that scarcely-born physiognomy which my whole life has been a battle to give birth to—a recognizable, autonomous self, a creation in poetry and in life."[47] For Plath, as for Rich, there does not seem time enough to be the perfect mother and the created self of one's art: "For me, poetry was where I lived as no one's mother, where I existed as myself."[48] Rich remembers moments like those in "Kindness," torn between tending her children and the project of creating an "I" in her work.

> From the fifties and early sixties, I remember a cycle. It began when I had picked up a book or began trying to write a letter, or even found myself on the telephone with someone toward whom my voice betrayed eagerness, a rush of sympathetic energy. The child (or children) might be absorbed in busyness, in his own dream world; but as soon as he felt me gliding into a world which did not include him, he would come to pull at my hand, ask for help, punch at the typewriter keys. And I would feel his wants at such a moment as fraudulent, as an attempt moreover to defraud me of living even for fifteen minutes as myself. . . . It was as if an invisible thread would pull taut between us and break, to the child's sense of inconsolable abandonment, if I moved—not even physically, but in spirit—into a realm beyond our tightly circumscribed life together. It was as if my placenta had begun to refuse him oxygen. . . . The emotion-charged, tradition-heavy form in which I found myself cast as the Mother seemed, then, as ineluctable as the tides. And, because of this form—this microcosm in which my children and I formed a tiny, emotional cluster, and in which (in bad weather or when someone was ill) we sometimes passed days at a time without seeing another adult except for their father—there *was* authentic need.[49]

Like Plath, Rich does not deny the authenticity of the mother-child relationship—"What is so real as the cry of a child?" It is the image of woman as Dame Kindness she refutes, the mother who "can cure everything, so Kindness says," but only at the cost of losing herself.

Plath explores the narcissism of women with her mirror images as well, and inevitably discovers that it is skin-deep; that it is not self-love at all, but self-doubt—a worry that they may not exist—that urges women constantly to check their mirror reflections. So the "most chaste" eyes of the woman in the early "Strumpet Song" look in a "black tarn, ditch, and cup," and see the "rank grimace" of a "foul slut"—a "mouth / Made to do violence on" (TC, p. 51). Self-loathing is also the motive of the woman in "Face Lift" who grows "backward" and destroys "the dewlapped lady / I watched settle, line by line in my mirror" (*CTW*, p. 6). The face lift creates only the cosmetic illusion of a new identity—"Pink and smooth as a baby." "Old sock-face" does not simply disappear; instead she is hidden away, withering in a laboratory jar. In this way, "Face Lift" becomes a metaphor for self-murder. This is also true of the woman in "Mirror." The mirror compares the aging process to murder: "In me she has drowned a young girl, and in me an old woman / Rises toward her day after day like a terrible fish" (*CTW*, p. 34). Her pathetic dependence on a beautiful surface is captured in the mirror's knowledge that it is "important to her," that to the woman, the mirror reflects "what she really is." The woman in "The Courage of Shutting Up" is equally two-dimensional, herself a mirror who reflects only the emptiness of a husband who has deserted her. Her tongue may no longer chide the absent husband,

> But how about the eyes, the eyes, the eyes!
> Mirrors can kill and talk, they are terrible rooms
> In which a torture goes on one can only watch.
> The face that lived in this mirror is the face of
>   a dead man.
>
>   (*WT*, p. 9)

Similarly, in "The Couriers," "A disturbance in mirrors / The sea shattering its grey one" is one of the messengers of failed marriage, as though a surface deception had been broken: "A ring of gold with the sun in it? Lies, lies and a grief" (*Ariel*, p. 2). The mirror symbolizes the amputated self-image of the wife in "The Applicant." Marriage means the wife must be a robot, an automaton to a man in a stiff black suit. She must be what ever her husband wants her to be—an image in the husband's eye. The applicant is promised a glittery reflector of his comforts.

> But in twenty-five years she'll be silver.
> In fifty, gold.
> A living doll, everywhere you look
> It can sew, it can cook,
> It can talk, talk, talk.

It works, there is nothing wrong with it.
You have a hole, it's a poultice.
You have an eye, it's an image.

(Ariel, p. 5)

Like the husband in "Purdah," a lord of the mirrors, the husband in "The Applicant" wants another quasi-sentient being, not another conscious self. All of these mirror relationships between woman and her archetypes of feminine perfection—the youthful beauty, the virgin, the ideal housekeeper, the sexually prized harem wife, and the all-good, all-giving mother—are brutally mocked and tested by Plath to discover what truths about female psychology they might convey.

Only in the relationship between mother and child, another creator-creature link, does Plath find a positive "mirroring." When the mirror is used to express joy in the dependence of her children, there is also a realization that a child in her own image must eventually be its own independent self. In "Morning Song," once the child is born, it "shadows our safety." It is a reminder of mortality.

I'm no more your mother
Than the cloud that distills a mirror to reflect its own slow
Effacement at the wind's hand.

(Ariel, p. 1)

This is the ideal mirror relationship and all others are ironic parodies. What Plath seems to be saying here is, "I am no more you than you are I. I am but a cloud, a vaporous distillation from a reflecting pool of water. You who carry my living image now also mirror my dissolution with the wind and time." Or, in another paraphrase: "I am like the creator, breathing life into a being in my own image. But this is breath on a mirror, eventually rubbed clean, effaced, to leave a new reflection." This is a complex and yes, healthy, kind of mirror dialogue between creator-creature that we find nowhere else in Plath's world except between mother and child. Once again, it is akin to Rich's description of the mother-infant relationship.

From the beginning the mother caring for her child is involved in a continually changing dialogue, crystallized in such moments when, hearing her child's cry, she feels milk rush into her breasts; when, as the child first suckles, the uterus begins contracting and returning to its normal size. . . . The child gains her first sense of her own existence from the mother's responsive gestures and expressions. It's as if, in the mother's eyes, her smile, her stroking touch, the child first reads the message: *You are there!* And the mother, too, is discovering her own existence newly. She is connected with this other being, by the most mundane and the most invisible strands, in a way she can be connected with no one else except in the deep past of her infant connection with her own mother. And she, too, needs to struggle from that one-to-one intensity into new realization, or reaffirmation, of her being-unto-herself.[50]

This is, I believe, the drama and the meaning of Plath's "Morning Song." In the course of the poem, the baby evolves for her from a hoarded valuable, "the fat gold watch" ticking in the womb, to a "bald cry"—"bald" because the emotion expressed in the cry is too elemental for adult understanding. They, adults, can only "stand round blankly as walls" in response to this new being, or else ooh and aah, "magnifying your arrival." At first, the baby is one more "new statue," a new work of the mother's art, in the "drafty museum" of the sterile hospital nursery. It may be looked at through glass, from a distance, but not touched. Plath's images capture this new strangeness—how odd it must seem for the mother who carried the baby in her body for nine months. The mother must reestablish closeness to a being who is finally not her possession, though "love set you going" in her womb. She reconstructs the relationship between herself and the baby in the image of the cloud and mirror and then through the dramatic situation of suckling the baby. At the end of the poem, both the independence of the baby and its dependence on the mother are portrayed in its morning song.

> Your mouth opens clean as a cat's. The window square
>
> Whitens and swallows its dull stars. And now you try
> Your handful of notes;
> The clear vowels rise like balloons.
>
> (*Ariel*, p. 1)

The final lines achieve a "mirroring" that is a reciprocal glow for both mother and child, seen as independent entities. The baby's cooing is very different from its "bald cry" at birth. The baby's dependence on the mother for sustenance is combined with its first independent efforts to answer, to sing to her, its contentment.

In "For a Fatherless Son," this loving reciprocity lasts only in the nursery.

> But right now you are dumb
> And I love your stupidity.
> The blind mirror of it. I look in
> And find no face but my own, and you think that's funny.
>
> (WT, p. 33)

A "blind mirror" has no self yet; it is only pleased by what it reflects and sees no blemishes, no faults. This innocence will not last. Inevitably, the baby's face will reflect the father's absence and "a sky like a pig's backside, an utter lack of attention." For awhile, the baby's smiles are "found money," but "One day, you may touch what's wrong / The small skulls, the smashed blue hills, the godawful hush." The self-reflective joy of mother in son, son in mother, face to face like doubles for one another, will finally be replaced by mutual self-reproach. The baby's face will mirror her failed marriage, as the son both feels and reminds her of the father's, the husband's absence. In "Child," too, Plath tells the baby, "Your clear eye is the one absolutely beautiful thing" and a

> Pool in which images
> Should be grand and classical
>
> Not this troublous
> Wringing of hands, this dark
> Ceiling without a star.
>
> (WT, p. 18)

Because a baby is a kind of tabula rasa, "A clean slate with your own face on," it will be vulnerable to the emotions in the eyes of its parents. Its "self" will depend initially on what the mother and father "write" on its mirror of consciousness.

Finally mirror images appear as harbingers of death and destiny. The unknown menace of "A Birthday Present" is in its deceptive surface: "the gleam / The glaze, the mirrory variety of it." As the poem develops, the "mirrory variety" of the speaker's existence becomes a tortuous self-consciousness, a self-watching that makes every act compulsive.

> When I am quiet at my cooking I feel it looking, I feel it thinking
>
> "Is this the one I am to appear for,
> Is this the elect one, the one with black eye-pits and a scar?
>
> Measuring the flour, cutting off the surplus.
> Adhering to rules, to rules, to rules.
>
> Is this the one for the annunciation?
> My god, what a laugh!"
>
> (*Ariel*, p. 42)

It is as if she has two selves—a disembodied consciousness that thinks and observes and a two-dimensional figure, a woman who performs her kitchen duties like a robot. Like the illusion-creating veils and mirrors of "Purdah," that disguise the thinking, observing harem wife from her lord, the birthday present shimmers, glitters, and gleams, a dissembling "other" just beyond her reach.

> It stands at my window, big as the sky.
> It breathes from my sheets, the cold dead centre
>
> Where spilt lives congeal and stiffen to history.
> ....
> Only let down the veil, the veil, the veil.
> If it were death
>
> I would admire the deep gravity of it, its timeless eyes.
>
> (*Ariel*, p. 44)

What she wants is something definite, a self-confrontation and truth
to rend the veils "killing my days." As Judith Kroll describes the
speaker, she wants to move from a death-in-life to a death that
might bring a new life. The brutal knife of truth would

> . . . not carve, but enter

> Pure and clean as the cry of a baby,
> And the universe slide from my side.
> > (*Ariel*, p. 44)

This is preferable to the butchery she experiences in a state of uncertainty—"a prolonged mutilation, like an animal inspected, priced,
and butchered alive, piece by piece."[51]

> . . . O adding machine—

> Is it possible for you to let something go and have it go whole?
> Must you stamp each piece in purple,

> Must you kill what you can?
> > (*Ariel*, pp. 43–44)

Although Kroll argues that death is only a metaphor for a cutting
truth that will release her into a new birth, the revelation at the end
seems to be the end of consciousness, of a painful self-observation
that makes her birthday only a celebration of days and years that are
small deaths.

> Sweetly, sweetly I breathe in,
> Filling my veins with invisibles, with the million

> Probable motes that tick the years off my life.
> > (*Ariel*, p. 43)

The only way to end duplicity is in death, and in two of Plath's
final poems, the mirror is a key image of that end. In "Contusion,"

The heart shuts,
The sea slides back,
The mirrors are sheeted.

(Ariel, p. 83)

There is no self to be reflected, no more "others" to haunt her consciousness. And in "Words," "From the bottom of a pool, fixed stars
govern a life." Despite the fluid efficacy of the poet's words in
creating a self worth beholding, the pool mirrors death. A poem's
words are

> . . . like the
> Water striving
> To re-establish its mirror
> Over the rock

> That drops and turns,
> A white skull,
> Eaten by weedy greens.

(Ariel, p. 85)

At the end of the poem, she leaves her "Words dry and riderless,"
as though the task of reestablishing a self through her poetry had
failed.

I hope that the preceding discussion has qualified, perhaps even
recovered Plath's imaginative world from the critical evaluation of it
as narrow and deranged. Even the view of her development—from
the fussy apprenticeship of *The Colossus* to the ecstatic risk taking of
Ariel—seems to be an unnecessary distinction that confines her to a
category of brilliantly mad but minor poets. What I have tried to
illustrate instead is an expanding network of concerns and themes
and a gradual hardening of images, symbols, and metaphors into
precise poetic statements about timeless and universal issues: God
and nature; the individual and society; creator and creature; and in
Plath's words, "love in all its forms." The bleakness of Plath's vision—her love of "black statements"—cannot be denied; but the
pessimism is neither morbid nor peculiar to her. Most important,

this pessimism is poetically earned by the variety and complexity, the ambivalence of its representations. Finally, in Plath's arrival at a distinctively feminine voice and in her exploration of a wide range of women's feelings, there is something new about her work. If the "I" is sometimes fragile, passive, and powerless against outside forces, it is not necessarily a sign of self-willed extinction. Such passivity is often framed in a "feminine" drama (e.g., *Three Women*, "Wintering," "Stings") where woman's body or role in society seems to betray her consciousness—to invite her fertility to be usurped ("drummed into use") rather than self-controlled. These poems are also matched by others where male-female antagonism ends with the woman defiantly asserting power over her body and releasing its energies for her own ends (e.g., "Fever 103°," "Purdah," "Lady Lazarus"). To describe the "I" of these poems as weakly submissive or infantile before hallucinated enemies is to deny Plath one of her imaginative strengths.

Five. The Female Body of Imagination

We need to imagine a world in which every woman is the presiding genius of her own body.—Adrienne Rich, *Of Woman Born*

*I*N the last chapter, I attempted to show the variety and richness of Plath's imagination—to explode the notion that her poetic world is narrow and solely concerned with self. Rather than a confessional stance, we confront in Plath's poetry a world shaped by a principle of malign immanence, complicated by ambivalence, and filtered through a distinctly feminine sensibility. There are some critics, I believe, who might still argue that this world is "decadent"—an extreme declension from the assertiveness of a lyric impulse that originally sought in the Romantic period to create a new heaven and earth wedded to the human imagination. Plath may be a representative woman's voice, but her strategies are those of a Romantic isolationist: she gives us nature, history, society, yes, but as a feminine theater, as if nothing were more important than woman's private dramas. This complaint is part of Denis Donoghue's criticism of poems like "Cut," which takes a simple kitchen accident as its departure point: "The moral claims enforced by these poems now seem exorbitant. It requires an indecently grandiose rhetoric to make a cut finger, in the poem 'Cut,' bleed such global agony."[1] Plath confesses, postures, poses, but with her affinity for numbingly "black statements," she has neither the wit nor self-irony of a Byron, living out, with extemporaneous panache, the myths of his age; nor has she the representatively human, historical, and guilt-ridden consciousness of a Robert Lowell, taking responsibility for the atrocities of his. Instead, her drama is domestic and played out on a stage that is often reduced to a suffocating decor.[2]

One of my arguments in the previous chapter was, indeed, that Plath has a gift for speaking in the voice of the victim, with an amputated consciousness and oppressed imagination. The question

235

for many readers might well be whether this is her solitary virtue. Does Plath ever invent the world in new forms? Does she participate in what Northrop Frye calls the "divine activity" of the poet? Or is she so caught in the nets of a malign design that she can only passively perceive, describe, and impose this pessimistic vision on her reader?

In Plath's work, there is not, to be sure, a Romantic confrontation with nature, of the poet's shaping consciousness with the universe around her. Plath's nature is too much like her own female body—a passive vessel to be filled with a male deity's conceptions. For Plath, nature mirrors woman's subjugation rather than offering any matter for her to work upon. Instead of an imaginative seizure of the external world, Plath seeks to repossess the female body. Her own body is the starting point for imaginative autonomy, and she manipulates it as a psychic and physical space or reinvents it in new forms. It is the medium on which she exercises her divine activity and the vehicle for her imaginative, sometimes apocalyptic, revelations. In this project, the distinctions between inner and outer, subject and object, between the suffering body and the mind that creates, are erased. This is the impulse in many of the poems I have already discussed. Lady Lazarus takes back her mutilated body from Herr God and incarnates herself as a man-eating phoenix woman. In multiple orgasms, the delirious woman of "Fever 103°" sublimates a body sick with desire into an acetylene virgin flame and thereby rids herself of any need for men to complete herself sexually. The dust-eating housewife of "Stings" emerges from the mausoleum of the hive as a queen bee and lioness. And the doll-wife in "Purdah" tears away her veil to reveal another lioness—Clytemnestra. Plath also implies something larger than domestic revenge in these incarnations. The repossession of the female body has historical and social consequences. There cannot be a Nazi victimizer without a Jewess victim; there will be no more pure Mother Marys of the male imagination, if woman makes purity out of her orgasmic heat; and there will be no more human sacrifices to history like Agamemnon's or the god's in "Brasília," if there are no more doll-wives to serve as reflectors of male history making. If this is not a reinvention of the world we live in, it is at least a restructuring of the human relationships on which that world is based.

I would be remiss if I did not note that there are too few of these triumphant poems, or if I did not also qualify these assertions, as I did in my discussion of *The Bell Jar*. In becoming her own woman, Esther Greenwood unleashes her self-destructive energies on those around her, especially men; and in these poems, as well, we can see the victim often transformed into a powerful and vengeful victimizer. The threatening posture Plath assumes may be read as a defensive gesture, a marking off of the legitimate play space of the woman-creator and a fending off of potential enemies; but too often the reader is a priori assumed to be unsympathetic, callous, one of the "peanut-crunching crowd" clamoring for blood.

From a psychoanalytic and speculative perspective, as well, this is a troublesome tendency in Plath's work. I suspect Freud would argue, literary values aside, that this is a release and inversion of a feminine masochism. Plath turns on herself, identifying with her oppressor, and sadistically punishes her body in the process of re-creating it. She may transform herself into a being more vital than the plastic dolls and mannequins, the mechanized robots and zombies, or even the Mary-idols of the male imagination, but she still treats her body as an object, and in this, we may see her self-destructive energies given a poetic license to betray her. Likewise, women might ask why she cannot compromise with her body, enjoy it as it is, rather than submitting it to an art of fire and ice.[3]

These are reservations that I would like to incorporate into my discussion, because at times we may discern Plath's self-hatred at work—an unconscious desire to rid herself of a female body altogether. At the same time, I would like to suggest along with Adrienne Rich that this repossession is an assertion of the poet's divine activity—an exercise of the artist's power to reshape the nature given to her into free forms of energy and desire. A phoenix woman, an acetylene virgin, and a queen bee–lioness are, after all, mythic creatures, and perhaps to be judged only as projections of the woman creator's powers. Repossession also implies an original usurpation of the woman's body and its potentialities. This provides a partial answer to those who want Plath to compromise, simply to revel in her body as it is. As Plath suggests everywhere in her work—in *The Bell Jar* and its depiction of birth, in "Lady Lazarus," in *Three Women*—woman cannot enjoy her body when it has been "drummed into use" that is not her own.

Man and Woman: The Idea and the Garden

I have already discussed *Three Women* as a poem where Plath explores women's varied, conflicting feelings toward pregnancy and
birth through three different dramatic voices. On one issue, the
three women seem to be in agreement: what it feels like to inhabit a
female body and how distinct that is from male experience. Such
unity, I believe, reflects Plath's own view of sexual differences. For
Plath, man lives more outside his body than woman—in abstrac-
tions and concepts, and in mental and spiritual activity. The intellectual sister of "Two Sisters of Persephone," in fact, dies an early
death for actively pursuing a male life of the mind instead of passively giving her body over to procreation.[4]

Man's body is persistently described as stiff and mechanical, flat
and two-dimensional, and as an instrument or tool to work upon
the outside world and other creatures. His relationship to nature
and woman is exploitative: nature and woman are only media for
realizing his ideas, ideas that in turn reflect his desire to cleanse the
world of the body's grossness and replace it with something clean
and manufactured, fresh off an assembly line. As Plath's secretary
complains, man's body is "Blunt and flat enough to feel no lack,"[5]
and the doctor in "The Surgeon at 2 A.M." is a smug Frankenstein,
similar to Herr Doktor in "Lady Lazarus."

> I have perfected it.
> I am left with an arm or a leg.
> A set of teeth, or stones
> To rattle in a bottle and take home,
> And tissues in slices—a pathological salami.
> Tonight the parts are entombed in an icebox.
> Tomorrow they will swim
> In vinegar like saints' relics.
> Tomorrow the patient will have a clean, pink plastic limb.[6]

He seems to prefer his own mechanical wonders, which remind him
of the miracles of Roman plumbing and irrigation, to the human
body, which makes him feel "so small / In comparison to these

organs!" He appeals for sympathy in his efforts to tame the uncivil-
ized world of the human body.

> It is a garden I have to do with—tubers and fruits
> Oozing their jammy substances,
> A mat of roots. My assistants hook them back.
> Stenches and colors assail me.
> This is the lung-tree.
> These orchids are splendid. They spot and coil like snakes.
> The heart is a red bell-bloom, in distress.
> ....
> I work and hack in a purple wilderness.
>
> (*Crossing the Water* [CTW], p. 30)

The doctor's activity—taming this unruly and virgin wilderness into
a clean, pink, plastic perfection—is clearly a way for man to take
command of what he fears. There is also something uncomfortably
female and Evelike in the way the body is depicted, and the surgeon
behaves like a modern Adam, resisting the trees and serpents, ultimately the temptations of this female bodily garden.

As Plath shows in "The Munich Mannequins," however, this
clean, pink, plastic perfection "is terrible, it cannot have children."[7]
"The Munich Mannequins" is a very difficult poem, but I believe
Plath suggests in it that men prefer Barbie dolls, mannequins with
no sexual organs—"Naked and bald in their furs, / Orange lollies on
silver sticks"—to the fearful garden of the woman's body,

> Where the yew trees blow like hydras,
> The tree of life and the tree of life
> Unloosing their moons, month after month, to no purpose.
>
> (*Ariel*, p. 73)

The mannequins seem to be prostitutes, waiting in their "sulphur
loveliness" for assignations with black-booted men in the hotels of
Munich, "morgue between Paris and Rome." Men may release their
passions on such sexless dolls—"Intolerable, without mind"—while
real women, with their hydra-headed genitals, threaten engulfment.

There is a suggestion, too, in lines like "Nobody's about" and images of broad-toed, thick German men, and black phones "digesting / Voicelessness," of something unspeakably obscene taking place behind closed doors, of sexual abuse on women who will say nothing, because they are mindless, voiceless rubber dollies for male pleasure.

The female body, particularly in its procreative functions, is frightening to men in Plath's poetry. A pregnant woman is also weighty, cumbersome, and three-dimensional, an affront to the flat, two-dimensional man. The earth mother of *Three Women* sees herself as a house and world-orb for her son: "I shall be a wall and roof, protecting. / I shall be a sky and a hill of good." When Plath is pregnant, she calls herself a miner and the baby in her cave-womb is "the one / Solid the spaces lean on, envious" (*Ariel*, p. 34). Woman's body is identified with the natural world: a pregnant woman is a "seed about to break" (*Winter Trees* [*WT*], p. 51) and "leaves and petals attend" her (*WT*, p. 47). And this is a passive body, too, worked upon by forces not her own.

> I am breaking apart like the world. There is this blackness,
> This ram of blackness. I fold my hands on a mountain.
> The air is thick. It is thick with this working.
> I am used. I am drummed into use.
>
> (*WT*, p. 53)

The inwardness and openness of the woman's body shape her consciousness. When the mother of *Three Women* gives birth, she is like a wounded flower: "A red lotus opens in its bowl of blood" (*WT*, p. 54), and her dominant feeling is one of vulnerability.

> It is a terrible thing
> To be so open: it is as if my heart
> Put on a face and walked into the world.
>
> (*WT*, p. 60)

Plath's contrary views of male and female extend to her children. She displays very different attitudes toward her daughter Frieda and her son Nicholas. Plath envisions "Magi" hovering over her baby daughter. These are the wise men of Christian myth, but also the Zoroastrian priests who know the mysteries of the universe, who understand the struggle between the forces of light and dark, good and evil. Theoretical spirits, they have nothing to do with mundane existence.

> The abstracts hover like dull angels:
> Nothing so vulgar as a nose or an eye
> Bossing the ethereal blanks of their face-ovals.
>
> Their whiteness bears no relation to laundry,
> Snow, chalk, or such like. They're
> The real thing, all right: the Good the True—
>
> Salutary and pure as boiled water,
> Loveless as the multiplication table.
>
> (CTW, p. 26)

The Magi may know the Good and the True, but not the Beautiful, which Plath saves for more fleshly, human attributes. As it turns out, "these papery godfolk"—like flat paperdoll cutouts—have nothing to do with her daughter, whose idea of Evil is no more substantial than a "bellyache," nor her idea of Good, which is "the mother of milk, no theory." The mother scoffs at their mistake and in her final question implies that a little boy, not a little girl, might fill their requirements.

> They want the crib of some lamp-headed Plato.
> Let them astound his heart with their merit.
> What girl ever flourished in such company?
>
> (CTW, p. 26)

The sex of the child might be arbitrary in "Magi," and the poem may be read as a mother's protest—what baby of either sex ever flourished in the company of priests and theoreticians?—except that Plath shows a much different attitude toward the infant male. In "The Night Dances," she wonders whether Nicholas's "pure leaps and spirals" in the crib will lose themselves "in mathematics." And though his dancelike gestures are at first "warm and human" in their joy, they "flake off," "Bleeding and peeling / Through the black amnesias of heaven" (*Ariel*, p. 17). They "travel / The world forever" like ominous comets and are compared to falling planets and "flakes / Six-sided" (*Ariel*, p. 18).

Such comparisons—as though the baby boy dances to some heavenly music of the spheres that she cannot hear—underscore her feeling of estrangement: "Their flesh bears no relation." The male child somehow belongs to a Pythagorean, theoretically plotted universe, while the little girl is sensually grounded in her bellyaches and need for the mother of milk.

The Passive Female Body

Plath responds in two very different ways to this sensual grounding, to the openness and vulnerability she perceives in the female body. One impulse is complete passivity and self-absorption. She permits woman's body to be transformed completely by forces from without. This is the triumph of the earth mother in "Two Sisters of Persephone" who opens her body to the "sun's blade" and conceives the sun god's child. The long "Poem for a Birthday," which Ted Hughes describes as an "underground, primitive drama . . . where the self, shattered in 1953, suddenly finds itself whole,"[8] is, in many ways, a celebration of passivity. There is no conscious, purposeful activity of the creature or voice in these poems; and "voice" is a better term than "speaker" for these utterances from the womb. She is an "all mouth" in "a mummy's stomach" in "Who" (*CTW*, p. 48). The title of the poem is itself a question about identity, and there is no self, only a mouth, a tongue.

> Mother, you are the one mouth
> I would be a tongue to. Mother of otherness
> Eat me.
>
> (*CTW*, p. 49)

From her mouth-oozings, she makes a protective shell, a "dark house" with "eelish delvings" in "Dark House" (*CTW*, p. 50). She floats with other lunatics in the "moon's vat" of "Maenad" (*CTW*, p. 51). In "The Beast," she is friends with "Fido Littlesoul, the bowel's familiar" (*CTW*, p. 52). She hides in the "cellar's belly" in "Witch Burning" to escape the flames (*CTW*, p. 53). She is a "foetus in a bottle" in "A Life" (*CTW*, p. 55), and "a soft caul of forgetfulness" enfolds her in a fetal state in "Flute Notes from a Reedy Pond."[9] Finally, she is "a still pebble" in "the stones of the belly" in "The Stones" (The Colossus and Other Poems [*TC*], p. 82). Throughout these poems, she is so unformed that we cannot tell whether she is animal, vegetable, or mineral. At times she is only a single human feature, a mouth or a tongue, an eyeball whose life is an "egg-shaped bailiwick, clear as a tear" ("A Life," *CTW*, p. 54). More often, she is not recognizably human or even animal—just a plant stored for the winter in a root cellar, a grain of rice submitted to the explosive torture of boiling water, or a pebble smoothed over by water. Most important, she is acted upon everywhere in "Birthday," in celebration of the "beauty of usage!" ("Who," *CTW*, p. 48), and in "The Stones," by doctors in a "city of spare parts" (*TC*, p. 83), who put her humanity back together again.

One wonders, however, about the vitality of this mechanical enterprise. The tone throughout "Birthday" is cheerfully childlike, filled with wonder, even though there are disturbing moments like, "I am ready to construe the days / I coupled with dust in the shadow of a stone" ("Witch Burning," *CTW*, p. 53). It is as if Plath had made a series of gruesome nursery rhymes from her misery, for when we arrive at "The city of spare parts," the place sounds too much like Santa's workshop.

The grafters are cheerful,

Heating the pincers, hoisting the delicate hammers.
A current agitates the wires
Volt upon volt. Catgut stitches my fissures.

A workman walks by carrying a pink torso.
The storerooms are full of hearts.

(TC, p. 83)

When she finally emerges as "The elusive rose," a figure of fragile feminine beauty, from "The vase, reconstructed" ("The Stones," *TC*, p. 84), it is not the result of her own recuperative powers. As in *The Bell Jar*, this birth-day comes at the end of brutal shock treatments. In "Witch Burning," she tries to ward off this punishment by making herself small, insignificant.

> If I am a little one, I can do no harm.
> If I don't move about, I'll knock nothing over. So I said,
> Sitting under a potlid, tiny and inert as a rice grain.
> They are turning the burners up, ring after ring.
> We are full of starch, my small white fellows. We grow.
> It hurts at first. The red tongues will teach the truth.
>   (*CTW*, p. 53)

This brutalization seems about as healing as the Inquisition's exorcisms, but by the end of "Birthday," the witch burners are Santa's workmen—cheerful little grafters and mechanics. She accepts the shock treatments as a necessary therapy.

Hughes regards "Poem for a Birthday," "the underworld of her worst nightmares," as "the first eruption of the voice that produced *Ariel*."[10] The sensual grounding and dramatic voices of "Birthday" are certainly a departure from the largely descriptive and detached tone of Plath's early work. In *Ariel*, though, Plath is skeptical of "Birthday"'s vegetablelike passivity and vulnerability. In "Elm," where she speaks in the voice of a tree, she explores the anguish of this rootedness. "Elm" is a stoic, but only because she must be.

> I know the bottom, she says. I know it with my great tap root:
> It is what you fear.
> I do not fear it: I have been there.
>   (*Ariel*, p. 15)

Elm's roots shiver with the tremors of galloping horses and her branches endure the "atrocity of sunsets" and the scathing light of the moon. At night, she must listen to the predators who live in her.

> I am inhabited by a cry.
> Nightly it flaps out
> Looking, with its hooks, for something to love.
>
> I am terrified by this dark thing
> That sleeps in me;
> All day I feel its soft, feathery turnings, its malignity.
>
> (*Ariel*, p. 16)

If this is a metaphor for the human need "for something to love," then Plath gives us female dependency as predation. Finally, in a storm, the elm cannot silently abide her suffering.

> Now I break up in pieces that fly about like clubs.
> A wind of such violence
> Will tolerate no bystanding: I must shriek.
>
> (*Ariel*, p. 15)

Unlike the early "Birthday," where the passive submission to electroshock therapy ends with healing and a happy acceptance of being someone else's creature, in "Elm," her inability to act is life-destroying. Like the "red tongues" in "Witch Burning" that "teach the truth," submission makes "Elm" a tree of knowledge, but the knowledge is as corrupting as the snake in the garden.

> What is this face; this face
> So murderous in its strangle of branches?—
>
> Its snaky acids kiss.
> It petrifies the will. These are the slow isolate, faults
> That kill, that kill, that kill.
>
> (*Ariel*, p. 16)

The cost of the elm's passivity, its "bystanding" of violence, is a petrified will.

Plath assumes an even more negative attitude toward passivity in "Tulips" and "Paralytic," both hospital poems where the speaker prefers corpselike serenity to "loving associations" with the world outside the self. In these poems, Plath illuminates the narcissism and self-absorption of this passivity. We may feel some sympathy for the woman of "Tulips," plagued by the vital flowers into a real-ization of her self-hatred.

> And I see myself, flat, ridiculous, a cut-paper shadow.
> Between the eye of the sun and the eye of the tulips,
> And I have no face, I have wanted to efface myself.
>
> (*Ariel*, p. 11)

But this martyrlike self-effacement is also an escape from all guilt and human responsibility.

> I have let things slip, a thirty-year-old cargo boat
> Stubbornly hanging on to my name and address.
> They have swabbed me clear of my loving associations.
> Scared and bare on the green plastic-pillowed trolley
> I watched my tea-set, my bureau of linen, my books
> Sink out of sight, and the water went over my head.
> I am a nun now, I have never been so pure.
>
> (*Ariel*, pp. 10–11)

She begins with self-criticism ("I have let things slip"), but as the anesthesia takes hold, and she watches the "cargo" of her identity sink into an ocean of unconsciousness, she begins to revel in the purity of being "swabbed" clear of all human connections.

In "Paralytic," the patient is, even in his total immobility, self-pleased. The paralysis confers on him a sense of superiority. He is a world unto himself, and he views his "loving associations" as flat photographs, who attend him like the iron lung and "starched, inac-cessible breast" of the nurse.

> Dead egg, I lie
> Whole
> On a whole world I cannot touch,
> At the white, tight

Drum of my sleeping couch
Photographs visit me—
My wife, dead and flat, in 1920 furs,
Mouth full of pearls,

Two girls
As flat as she, who whisper "We're your daughters."
                                    (*Ariel*, p. 77)

Instead of despair, he smugly revels in his paralysis, a flowerlike
exhibit. His complete dependence on an iron lung is, paradoxically,
a spiritual self-sufficiency.

I smile, a buddha, all
Wants, desire
Falling from me like rings
Hugging their lights.

The claw
Of the magnolia,
Drunk on its own scents,
Asks nothing of life.
                                    (*Ariel*, p. 78)

In the grasping image of the "claw of the magnolia," inebriated with
"its own scents," Plath portrays the utter self-absorption, the selfish
pleasure of total passivity and dependence.

From Passive to Active

In "Getting There" and "Cut," Plath's mind and imagination are
active, "insane for the destination," while her body remains passive,
acted upon by the mind's transforming powers. While she does not
reinvent her body in new forms, we can see her exploiting the
female body's victimization to move toward new self-perceptions.

Both poems are also remarkable for their speed. Images and metaphors tumble forth as the imagination struggles to name the shifts in feeling she endures.

In "Cut," her decapitated thumb is the source for this imaginative outpouring. Her mind races from one metaphor to the next, as the thumb becomes a "little pilgrim," a "turkey wattle," a "red carpet" of flowing blood, "a bottle / Of pink fizz" champagne, an army of "redcoats," then a "homunculus," "saboteur," "Kamikaze man," its bandage a "Ku Klux Klan / Babushka," and finally, a

> Trepanned veteran,
> Dirty girl,
> Thumb stump.
>
> (*Ariel*, pp. 14–15)

Similar to "Fever 103°," where a feverish woman free-associates on her "fire" and images rapidly consume one another as her body reaches a state of purity and fulfillment, here a kitchen accident is a Freudian slip of the knife that opens up a whole world of unconscious motives to the woman's imagination. The dramatic immediacy of the situation is captured in the first metaphors, drawn from early American history. We are invited to imagine a woman preparing a Thanksgiving dinner, and the celebration suddenly turns into violent war when she scalps her thumb. With her question to the "redcoats"—"Whose side are they on?"—the images become self-exploratory and she anatomizes her own feelings: Whose side is *she* on, if she is capable of harming herself so easily? The "cut" is evidence for a little "saboteur" and "Kamikaze man" inside her, of insidious self-destructive impulses sabotaging her life or plunging her toward death. The "Ku Klux Klan / Babushka" image conflates the oppressor with the victim and suggests a shared consciousness with the lynch victim or little downtrodden women from Eastern Europe. Ultimately, her thumb is a symbol of female castration. She is a little man, an immature "homunculus," a thumb stump and "dirty girl" with something missing to make her pure and whole. With these final lines, Plath understands her self-amputation as an acting out of her self-hatred as a woman. She is deficient by virtue of her female wound and the kitchen accident is an acknowledgment, against her conscious will, of this sense of inferiority.

In "Getting There," as well, Plath speaks in the voice of the victim. This time she is the Jew in the box car, one of the casualties of war. But she is also the train engine, hurtling toward her own death.

> Pumped ahead by these pistons, this blood
> Into the next mile,
> The next hour—
>
> (*Ariel*, pp. 36–37)

In the progress of the poem, the speaker becomes inextricably mingled with the panorama of smoke and slaughter she passes through—the "black muzzles" of Krupp's war machines, the fire and the mud, the "tent of unending cries," the funeral procession for a woman with "charred skirts and death mask." She identifies with all the wounded and dead.

What gives the speaker this solemn sympathy with the casualties of war is her female body. She knows these atrocities as a part of her very being, her genesis.

> There is mud on my feet,
> Thick, red and slipping. It is Adam's side,
> This earth I rise from, and I in agony.
> I cannot undo myself, and the train is steaming.
>
> (*Ariel*, p. 37)

She cannot extricate herself from the agony of these others because this is what she was meant for, she cannot undo her very nature. The violence around her is as old as woman's creation from Adam's rib.

Instead of submitting to the train engine's inexorable movement in creaturely subjection, however, she makes this movement her own. At the beginning of the poem, she is just a victim—"I am dragging my body / Quietly through the straw of the boxcars" (*Ariel*, p. 36). By the end of the poem,

> The train is dragging itself, it is screaming—
> An animal

> Insane for the destination
> The bloodspot,
> The face at the end of the flare
>
> (*Ariel*, p. 37)

She usurps the destructive force of the train to reach a destination for her body very different from the devastation around her. She assumes responsibility, too, for all the dead and wounded, making her body a vessel for the atrocities committed on them. With her body, she makes a birth out of all this bloodshed.

> I shall bury the wounded like pupas,
> I shall count and bury the dead.
> Let their souls writhe in a dew,
> Incense in my track.
> The carriages rock, they are cradles.
> And I, stepping from this skin
> Of old bandages, boredoms, old faces
>
> Step to you from the black car of Lethe,
> Pure as a baby.
>
> (*Ariel*, pp. 37–38)

Like Lady Lazarus arising from Herr Doktor's ovens as a new being, her own incarnation, the woman in this poem emerges from war's carnage, born again, "pure as a baby." This is an example of what I mentioned earlier as the victim taking on the powers of the victimizer and drumming herself into uses that are her own.

In "Getting There," however, it is not so much an opposition of Mama vs. the Megamachine of male history making, as Mama assuming the Megamachine's energy and assuring that nothing and no one will be lost ("I shall count and bury the dead") in this holocaust. The train's carriages are transformed into the mother's cradles, rocking the dead and wounded toward resurrection, and the blood on her track is sacrificial incense in a ceremony of innocence. While the woman of this poem cannot, as she says, "undo" herself or undo the agony of these mutilated bodies, she can find the "still place / Turning and turning in the middle air / Untouched and untouchable" that provides a release and new birth for their souls. This "destination" is "untouched" in the sense of being holy: a place where those who have been abused may find solace and redemption. This place is female—a nursery for the "pupas" she buries—and in a bodily sense, it is the woman's birth canal—the "bloodspot / The face at the end of the flare"—that all these bodies hurtle down. The woman of the poem is finally a mother-god, raising the dead, her body the divine vehicle for human salvation from history.

The Transformed Female Body

Despite the imaginative energy of "Cut" and "Getting There," the female body in both poems remains bloody, "dirty" and stumplike, or cumbersome, a body that must be dragged toward release. In the earth mother's words of *Three Women*, "It is a terrible thing / To be so open," so vulnerable to suffering. One must prefer the liberty of the woman in "Lady Lazarus" or "Fever 103°," where the female body is a flame, consumed and self-consuming, rather than a wounded victim, a "trepanned veteran" of too many wars.

Plath employs yet other poetic strategies for dealing with the female body in "Edge" and "Ariel." In "Edge," Plath freezes the woman's body into statuary, but instead of the cumbersome and lifeless stone we might expect, this figure is one of defiant transcendence.

> The woman is perfected.
> Her dead
>
> Body wears the smile of accomplishment,
> The illusion of a Greek necessity
>
> Flows in the scrolls of her toga,
> Her bare
>
> Feet seem to be saying:
> We have come so far, it is over.

Each dead child coiled, a white serpent,
One at each little

Pitcher of milk, now empty.
She has folded

Them back into her body as petals
Of a rose close when the garden

Stiffens and odours bleed
From the sweet, deep throats of the night flower.

The moon has nothing to be sad about,
Staring from her hood of bone.

She is used to this sort of thing.
Her blacks crackle and drag.

                              (*Ariel*, p. 84)

The tone of "Edge" is peculiarly detached—similar perhaps to
Yeats's tone in "Lapis Lazuli," evoking the cathartic aftermath of
tragedy. There is "gaiety transfiguring all that dread" in the "smile
of accomplishment" the woman wears. The gaze of the moon, who
"has nothing to be sad about," is as dispassionate as Yeats's china-
men with their glittering eyes: "On all the tragic scene they stare."
The dead woman could, in fact, be several tragic heroines. The
image of "Each dead child coiled, a white serpent, / One at each
little / Pitcher of milk, now empty," echoes the Greek necessity in
Medea's murder of her children after Jason's desertion; or Cleopa-
tra's suicide for Antony, a serpent like a suckling child on her breast;
or Lady Macbeth, who swears, if need be, to tear the nursing babe
from her breast. Plath's intention in "Edge," I believe, is the depiction of the woman's body in a pose that will contain the pity and
fear of tragedy. After the suffering is over, the woman's body assumes an inviolability that transcends the worst that has been done
to her: "We have come so far, it is over."

The repossession of the female body is also the major theme of
"Edge." The woman's statuelike repose is hard, unyielding, as to-

tally self-possessed as the effigy on a tomb. Her babies, too, are part of the statuary, taken back into herself as the fruits of her body. Plath also chooses a vital metaphor—a rose with furled petals—to vivify the woman in death and this contradicts the stony rigor mortis of her body.

In the contrast of the two flowers, however, Plath also "unsexes" her "perfected" woman, so that we understand her "accomplishment," like the man-eating woman of "Lady Lazarus" or the "acetylene virgin" of "Fever 103°," as carnal vengeance. The woman as rose is closed to the pleasures of the night, while the night flower opens her "sweet, deep throats" and like a wound, "odours bleed" from its petals. The erotic night flower I take to be the mandrake, a species of nightshade, with its similarity to the human form and its associations with fertility and conception. It is open, like the female genitals, to the stiffened garden—like an erect phallus—while the rose is closed, impervious to seduction and penetration. This is a vision, then, of sexual sterility, with unyielding breasts and dead children folded back into the womb. The lady moon watches over the chastity of the rose and the incontinence of the night flower, and the tension between the moon as chaste muse and governess of the female sexual cycle in Plath's poetry is resolved. The woman perfected is unsexed, unresponsive to the sexual demands of men because her body is hard, sealed, invulnerable.

The obvious denial of the fertile powers of the female body in this vision of transcendent inviolability is troublesome. Even more haunting is the sense of the poem that woman's sexual passivity can only triumph in death. And this deathly hardness and invulnerability to male penetration is also an "overdetermined" symbol. From a psychoanalytic perspective, one may induce an unconscious wish fulfillment of the desire to be male. The woman is "stiffened" in defiant challenge to the "stiffened" garden. The woman in death, in this aspect, is not transcendently female, but male. As in *The Bell Jar*'s conclusion, where Esther Greenwood "buries" her desire to be male in the funeral of Joan Gilling, so the woman in "Edge" seems to be a symbol of frustrated male power, as if Plath were incapable of compromising with the female body and could only make it potent in death.

What, perhaps, Plath is incapable of compromise on as an artist

is both her own and her culture's perception of the female body as
incapable of divine activity. In "Ariel," the masculine and feminine
components of Plath's personality join triumphantly in the figure of
a divine androgyne. Here Plath is capable of sublimating her sexual
ambivalence into an essentially hermaphroditic vision of released
artistic energy.

> Stasis in darkness.
> Then the substanceless blue
> Pour of tor and distances.
>
> God's lioness,
> How one we grow,
> Pivot of heels and knees!—The furrow
>
> Splits and passes, sister to
> The brown arc
> Of the neck I cannot catch,
>
> Nigger-eye
> Berries cast dark
> Hooks—
>
> Black sweet blood mouthfuls,
> Shadows.
> Something else
>
> Hauls me through air—
> Thighs, hair;
> Flakes from my heels.
>
> White
> Godiva, I unpeel—
> Dead hands, dead stringencies.
>
> And now I
> Foam to wheat, a glitter of seas.
> The child's cry

Melts in the wall.
And I
Am the arrow,

The dew that flies
Suicidal, at one with the drive
Into the red

Eye, the cauldron of morning.
                              (*Ariel*, pp. 26–27)

The poem is one of fulfilled desire, of flying thighs and hair and "Pivot of heels and knees," as in sexual consummation. Her identity merges with her stallion's Ariel. With her horse, she is a "lioness," but wears the male lion's mane of a "white Godiva." She is defiantly female like Godiva, but she assumes the masculine power of her horse. She is both the female "furrow" of earth, ready to be sown with male seed, that "splits and passes" and also "the brown arc / Of the neck I cannot catch." Like Prospero's Ariel, her horse is her muse, a spirit of fire and air, who can translate desire into action with the speed of flight, and in flight, she herself metamorphoses into an arrow of desire.

The evocation of Shakespeare's Ariel is significant, too, for its implicit statement about woman's creative energy. As Shakespeare's Ariel is neither male nor female, so the divine activity of the poet is not a sexual prerogative. It is pure energy, both and neither male nor female, and belonging to no one. In the moments when the woman is given over to the apocalyptic fury of her muse, she is also not subject to her feminine roles. Unlike in "Kindness," where Plath feels compelled by the "child's cry"—"What is so real as the cry of a child?"—to put her poetry aside and respond, here "The child's cry / Melts in the wall," forgotten in the flight that takes her to revelation.

The revelation is of a new world created by this rarefied lyric impulse. As a peal of thunder opens the first seal in God's Book of Revelation and a white horse with a rider armed in bow and arrows rides forth, so in "Ariel" Plath begins her creation with the thunder of a stallion's hooves. The poem is at once about a woman on a

runaway stallion, flying dangerously toward the morning's rising
sun, and about the divine energy that creates worlds and ends
them. The fierceness of "Ariel" is not a surrender to dying, but a
sloughing off of the "Dead hands, dead stringencies"—all obsta-
cles—which prevent her incarnation as a divine androgyne. The
"suicidal dew," like the incense on the track in "Getting There," is a
sacrifice made to the splendor of dawn, to the moment the lyric poet
aspires for, when everything has the freshness and illumination of
the sun's first light. "Ariel" captures this moment dramatically in
the sense of mere duration—"stasis in darkness"—and then the glittering revelation, when everything takes form and perspective from
light.

"Ariel" is Plath's most triumphant assertion of her poetic
powers, because unlike "Lady Lazarus," "Fever 103°," or "Edge,"
the transcendence is achieved at no one's expense. It is not a poem
directed toward vengeance or turning the tables on a male victimizer, nor does it depict woman's body as a burden to be dragged
toward rebirth. She does not simply repossess her body from an old
usurpation, but in "Ariel" she is possessed by and in possession of
that instant when the Word is incarnated, when the world becomes
a vision of energy unfettered by mortal substance, and in Plath's
development as a poet, freed from the carnal sting. She is, in this
moment, the presiding genius of her own body.

Notes

Chapter 1

1. "Lady Lazarus" and "Ariel," *Ariel* (New York: Harper and Row, 1961). pp. 7 and 27. Subsequent page numbers for poems from this work appear in the text.
2. "Sylvia Plath: The Trepanned Veteran," *Centennial Review* 13 (1969):138.
3. " 'Candor Is the Only Wile,' " in *The Art of Sylvia Plath*, ed. Charles Newman (Bloomington: Indiana University Press, 1970), p. 21.
4. "Foreword," *Ariel*, p. viii.
5. "An Informal Check List of Criticism," in *The Art of Sylvia Plath*, p. 290.
6. *Sylvia Plath: Poetry and Existence* (London: Athlone Press, 1976), p. 5.
7. Ibid., p. 179.
8. Ibid., p. 200.
9. "The Plath Celebration: A Partial Dissent," in *Sylvia Plath: The Woman and the Work*, ed. Edward Butscher (New York: Dodd, Mead and Co., 1977), p. 233. Reprinted from *The Critical Point* (New York: Horizon Press, 1973).
10. Ibid., p. 230.
11. Ibid., p. 235.
12. Ibid., p. 233.
13. *Seduction & Betrayal* (New York: Random House, 1970), p. 108.
14. Howe's final judgment, "The Plath Celebration," p. 235.
15. *Sylvia Plath: Method and Madness* (New York: Seabury Press, 1976), p. xi. Butscher singles out "the bitch goddess" as Plath's primary identity from several other more sympathetic Sylvias he encounters in his research: "Like other complex personalities, of course, there were other Sylvias as well: Sylvia the little girl still hurting from the profound wound of her father's rejection and abandonment of her and wanting to crawl back into her mother's cave-safe womb; and Sylvia the ordinary teenager who yearned for a kind husband, children, and a house like her grandmother's by the seashore" (p. 67). Subsequent references to this work appear in the text.
16. *Chapters in a Mythology: The Poetry of Sylvia Plath* (New York: Harper and Row, 1976), p. 1. Subsequent references to this work appear in the text.
17. Box 6: Correspondence, August 1962–1977. This and all other quotations from unpublished letters are in Plath MSS II, Lilly Library, Indiana University. Subsequent references to these manuscripts appear in the text.
18. Interview with Peter Orr, October 30, 1962, on *Plath Reads Plath*, Credo 3 (1975).
19. *Chapters in a Mythology*, pp. 174–211.
20. "On the Road to *Ariel*: The 'Transitional' Poetry of Sylvia Plath," in *Sylvia Plath: The Woman and the Work*, p. 142.

21. *Naked and Fiery Forms: Modern American Poetry by Women, a New Tradition* (New York: Harper and Row, 1976), p. 114.

22. Ibid., p. 3.

23. (New Haven and London: Yale University Press, 1979), p. 66. Subsequent references to this work appear in the text, except where additional material is included in a note.

24. *Naked and Fiery Forms*, p. 87.

25. Gilbert and Gubar's discussions of Elizabeth Barrett Browning, Christina Rossetti, and Emily Dickinson, in chapters entitled "The Aesthetics of Renunciation" and "A Woman—White: Emily Dickinson's Yarn of Pearl," frequently focus on these artists' anxiety over committing themselves to the "quasi-priestly role" of poet: "But in Western culture women cannot be priests. . . . How then—since poets are priests—can women be poets?" (p. 546). Gilbert and Gubar depict Browning and Rossetti dealing with this problem by "a passionate renunciation of the self-assertion lyric poetry demands" (p. 564). They write narrative rather than lyric poems, and create artist-heroines who are either dead by the end of the story, or, as in the case of "Aurora Leigh," give up their writing ambitions for a life of "self-abnegating servitude" (p. 580). Dickinson's strategy for dealing with her anxiety, on the other hand, was to refuse to grow up and play a woman's role; instead she embraced childlikeness and the role of eccentric in "seemingly demure resignation to poetic isolation or obscurity" (p. 564). Both strategies are forms of self-renunciation to compensate for the presumptuousness of being poets.

26. *The Madwoman in the Attic*, p. 603. The quotation is from *The Complete Poems of Emily Dickinson*, ed. Thomas H. Johnson (Boston and Toronto: Little, Brown, and Co., 1960), no. 186, p. 88. In contrast to previous critics, who have tried to identify the Master in Dickinson's poetry and letters with someone in her life, Gilbert and Gubar are concerned with the "mental state" (p. 602) of these poems and with analogous situations in other women writers' situations: "Like [Charlotte] Brontë's, Dickinson's case seems to be hopeless, for both women are suffering from what is for an artist the worst anguish: the psychological constriction of mental slavery" (p. 605).

27. *Complete Poems*, no. 462, p. 222.

28. Sylvia Plath, "Electra on Azalea Path," *Hudson Review* 13 (Autumn, 1960):415.

29. *The Madwoman in the Attic*, pp. 554–58. Gilbert and Gubar conclude their comparison of Dickinson's and Whitman's careers by wondering "what she would have done if she had had Whitman's freedom and 'masculine' self-assurance. . . ," in answer to previous critics' "conclusion that Dickinson's isolation and literary failure were . . . beneficial" to her genius (p. 557).

30. Gilbert and Gubar develop the thesis that what may have been Dickinson's free choice originally—obscurity in her father's house—gradually became a pernicious addiction: "The child mask (or pose or costume) eventually threatened to become a crippling self, a self that in the crisis of her gothic life fiction locked her into her father's house in the way that a little girl is confined to a nursery" (p. 591). In the same way, Whitman's self-assurance may have originally been a poetic mask, but

"prospering, indefatigably self-publicizing despite painful rejections and attack, [he] becomes the 'Unofficial Laureate of America' " (p. 557).

31. *Naked and Fiery Forms*, p 87

32. "A Fine, White Flying Myth: The Life/Work of Sylvia Plath," in *Shakespeare's Sisters: Feminist Essays on Women Poets*, ed. Sandra M. Gilbert and Susan Gubar (Bloomington and London: Indiana University Press, 1979), pp. 247–48. According to Olwyn Hughes, the poems did not appear in *TLS*, but the *Observer*.

33. Ibid., p. 251.

34. Ibid., p. 250.

35. *The Manwoman in the Attic*, p. 188. In the chapter titled "Milton's Bogey: Patriarchal Poetry and Women Readers," Gilbert and Gubar borrow the term "Milton's Bogey" from Virginia Woolf to describe Milton's "cosmology, his vision of 'what *men* thought' and his powerful rendering of the culture myth" of creation (p. 191) that intimidates women writers into seeing themselves as heirs of his version of female invention—his inferior and Satanically inspired Eve.

36. *Shakespeare's Sisters*, p. 259 and p. 260, respectively. Gilbert ends her essay on Plath by asking, "What is the way out of this dilemma? How does a woman reconcile the exigencies of the species—her desire for stasis, her sense of her ancestry, her devotion to the house in which she has lived—with the urgencies of her own self? I don't know the answer. For Sylvia Plath, as for many other women, there was apparently, in real life, no way out" (p. 260). My reading of the poem "Edge" in chapter 5 is, in many ways, an illustration of this dilemma, showing Plath's frightening poetic reconciliation of a deathlike stasis with a perfection of self. Unlike Gilbert, I am unwilling to read this as evidence for the self-destructive impulses in Plath's "real life," which I believe deserve a separate analysis involving factors additional to the struggle to find a poetic identity.

37. November 22, 1955, *Letters Home by Sylvia Plath, Correspondence 1950–1963*, ed. Aurelia Schober Plath (New York: Harper and Row, 1975), p. 198. Subsequent references to this work appear in the text with the abbreviation *LH*.

38. According to Olwyn Hughes, Plath is more self-effacing in her letters to Aurelia than she was in fact.

> In actual fact (much to the Merwins' irritation) Bill Merwin did lend his study to Ted, but it was, in fact Sylvia who used it. She wrote most of the *Bell Jar* there. . . . This is not to belittle Sylvia's concern for Ted's work. She did a great deal for it—typing and sending work out, and so on. But I do think it gives a totally wrong impression of Sylvia, who certainly had a very definite sense of her own "rights," to suggest that she became a subservient wife. In fact, they shared household chores and baby minding fairly equally, except, of course, in such times as just after the birth of a child, etc. It should be pointed out that Ted was at least as keen that she had time for her work as she was for him to have the same advantages. I'm sure if asked about this Sylvia would have been the first to acknowledge it.

This is from a letter to me, August 7, 1981.

39. Interview with Peter Orr.
40. *Winter Trees* (New York: Harper and Row, 1972), pp. 40-42.
41. "Cottage Street, 1953," *The Mind-Reader* (New York: Harcourt Brace Jovanovich, 1965), p. 19.
42. *Silences* (New York: Delacorte Press, 1978), p. 30.
43. *The Anatomy of Criticism* (Princeton: Princeton University Press, 1957), p. 98.
44. *Crossing the Water* (New York: Harper and Row, 1971), pp. 46-47.
45. *The Anxiety of Influence: A Theory of Poetry* (New York: Oxford University Press, 1973), pp. 5, 10, 69.
46. Ibid., pp. 5, 30.
47. *Of Woman Born: Motherhood as Experience and Institution* (New York: W. W. Norton and Co., 1976), pp. 285-86.

Chapter 2

1. Box 6: Correspondence, August 1962-1977. This and all other references to unpublished letters are in Plath MSS II, Lilly Library, Indiana University. Subsequent references to this work appear in the text.
2. "The Absence at the Center: Sylvia Plath and Suicide," *Criticism* 18 (1976):168, 167.
3. Ibid., p. 169.
4. Ibid., p. 149.
5. Ibid., p. 165.
6. *Psychoanalysis and Feminism* (New York: Pantheon Books, 1974), pp. 10-11.
7. 9 April 1935, *Letters of Sigmund Freud, 1873-1939,* ed. Ernest Freud (London: Hogarth Press, 1961), p. 420.
8. Sigmund Freud, "Analysis Terminal and Interminable" (1937), *The Standard Edition of the Complete Psychological Works of Sigmund Freud,* ed. and trans. James Strachey et al. (London: Hogarth Press and Institute of Psycho-Analysis, 1964), vol. 23, p. 235 (hereafter cited as *SE*).
9. *Psychoanalysis and Feminism,* p. 11, n. 4.
10. Sylvia Plath, *Letters Home by Sylvia Plath, Correspondence 1950-1963,* ed. Aurelia Schober Plath (New York: Harper and Row, 1975). As reported by Aurelia in her commentary, p. 123, and again by Plath, in a letter to E., December 28, 1953, p. 130. Subsequent references to this work appear in the text with the abbreviation *LH.*

Ed Cohen's comments on this letter provide an interesting conclusion to the story of their relationship.

> After Sylvia went to McLean we continued to write. She told me that they were not allowing her to communicate with everyone, but that the doctors had decided that this might be good therapy. Her letters, though, were less forthright than they had been in the past, and I was a bit frustrated, because

I simply could not fathom what had made her want to kill herself. Finally, not getting any answers obliquely, I put the question directly.

This, of course, led to the "Dear E." letter which appears in her mother's book. But the crucial point, to me if not to your other readers, is that *the original was never mailed.* For me, this was a betrayal. The whole pleasure of the years of writing had been in the opportunity to express ourselves openly and honestly, at least as we saw it. Now she seemed to be closing the door on that, and my own enthusiasm was severely dampened. The letters became farther and farther apart, and ceased altogether within the year.

From a letter to me, September 18, 1981.

11. Nancy Chodorow, *The Reproduction of Mothering: Psychoanalysis and the Sociology of Gender* (Berkeley: University of California Press, 1978), p. 147. Subsequent references to this work appear in the text.

12. (New York: Harper and Row, 1976), p. xii. Subsequent references to this work appear in the text.

13. *Webster's Third New International Dictionary* (unabridged), ed. Philip Gove (Springfield, Mass.: G. & C. Merriam Co., 1971), p. 66.

14. Sylvia Plath, *The Bell Jar* (New York: Harper and Row, 1971), p. 58.

15. *Webster's Third New International Dictionary*, pp. 66–67.

16. The female child, like the male, develops a contempt for the mother and women because they do not have penises (Chodorow, p. 94), but this does not resolve her ambivalence, for the obvious reason that, unlike the male child, she must simultaneously identify with the mother and feminine aims: "They [i.e., female children] turn to their father, who has a penis and might provide them with this much desired appendage. They give up a previously active sexuality for passive sexuality in relation to him. Finally, they change from wanting a penis from their father to wanting a child from him, through an unconscious symbolic equation of penis and child." The contempt for the mother turns inward into a self-contempt that shapes a woman's heterosexual orientation toward men (Chodorow, p. 182).

    See also Ruth Mack Brunswick, "The Preoedipal Phase of the Libido Development" (1940), in *The Psychoanalytic Reader: An Anthology of Essential Papers With Critical Introductions,* ed. Robert Fliess (New York: International Universities Press, 1969), p. 246: "The little girl, incapable of such contempt because of her own identical nature, frees herself from the mother with a degree of hostility far greater than any comparable hostility in the boy."

17. Marjorie G. Perloff, "On the Road to *Ariel*: The 'Transitional' Poetry of Sylvia Plath," in *Sylvia Plath: The Woman and the Work,* ed. Edward Butscher (New York: Dodd, Mead and Co., 1977). Perloff uses R. D. Laing's discussion of schizophrenia in *The Divided Self* to describe the tension in "Parliament Hill Fields" "between the desire to 'blend into the scenery' . . . and the opposite urge to maintain one's autonomy as a person" (p. 128).

18. "Early psychoanalytic findings about the special importance of the preoedipal mother-daughter relationship describe the first stage of a general process in

which separation and individuation remain particularly female developmental issues. . . . There is a tendency in women toward boundary confusion and a lack of sense of separateness from the world. . . . As long as women mother, we can expect that a girl's preoedipal period will be longer than that of a boy and that women, more than men, will be more open to and preoccupied with those very relational issues that go into mothering—feelings of primary identification, ego and body-ego boundary issues and primary love not under the sway of the reality principle. A girl does not simply identify with her mother, or want to be like her mother. Rather, mother and daughter maintain elements of their primary relationship which means they will feel alike in fundamental ways" (Chodorow, p. 110).

19. Chodorow, p. 140. What this means is that many women never resolve their Oedipal conflicts. Their emotional lives give them less freedom than men to engage in what Dinnerstein calls civilization building, and they are more likely than men to maintain elements of an essentially infantile bond to their mothers long into adulthood: "Most . . . daughters . . . have received enough support from their mothers to emerge from the stage of complete symbiosis in early infancy. But for the vast majority of mothers and daughters, this emergence remains only partial. At some level mothers and daughters tend to remain emotionally bound up with each other in what might be called a semi-symbiotic relationship, in which neither ever quite sees herself or the other as a separate person" (Chodorow, p. 109).

20. Most girls do not "resolve" their Oedipus complex by a simple rejection of "their mother and women in favor of their father and men" (Chodorow, p. 140). While most boys repress and renounce their incestuous wishes for the mother, identify with the father, and therefore dissolve the rivalry of the Oedipal triangle, most girls "remain in a bisexual triangle throughout childhood and into puberty" (Chodorow, p. 140).

21. "Introduction," *A Closer Look at Ariel: A Memory of Sylvia Plath* (New York: Popular Library, 1973), p. 30. Subsequent references to this work appear in the text.

22. Quoted in Lois Ames, "Notes Toward a Biography," in *The Art of Sylvia Plath*, ed. Charles Newman (Bloomington: Indiana University Press, 1970), p. 159.

23. Ibid.

24. Quoted from Philip McCurdy in Edward Butscher, *Sylvia Plath: Method and Madness* (New York: Seabury Press, 1976), p. 32.

25. Ibid., p. 152.

26. Quoted from May Targett in Butscher, *Method and Madness*, p. 47.

27. In *The Feminine Mystique* (New York: Dell Publishing Co., 1963), Betty Friedan uses Stevenson's address as evidence of the cultural ambivalence toward women in the 1950s: "Modern woman's participation in politics is through her role as wife and mother, said the spokesman of democratic liberalism: 'Women, especially educated women, have a unique opportunity to influence us, man and boy' " (p. 53).

28. *The Savage God: A Study of Suicide* (New York: Random House, 1970), pp. 6–8.

29. Quoted from an anonymous student during an interview with Robert Gorham Davis, in Butscher, *Method and Madness*, p. 69.
30. Quoted in Butscher, *Method and Madness*, p. 170.
31. Ibid., p. 173.
32. " 'To the Most Wonderful Mummy . . . a Girl Ever Had'," rev. of *Letters Home*, by Sylvia Plath, ed. Aurelia Plath, *MS.*, December 1975, p. 45.
33. Steiner describes Plath's disapproval and year-long feud with the "beatnik" rebel "Brownie" in their dormitory: "She lay in wait, like a hungry cat, hoping to catch Brownie in the violation of some house rule" and when she discovers Brownie with some smuggled rum in her room, threatens to report her (*A Closer Look*, pp. 106–7).
34. Quoted in Butscher, *Method and Madness*, p. 104.
35. *The Colossus and Other Poems* (New York: Alfred A. Knopf and Random House, 1957), p. 58. Subsequent references to poems from this work appear in the text with the abbreviation *TC*.
36. *LH*, p. 10: "As soon as I was certain I was pregnant, I began reading books related to the rearing of children. I was totally imbued with the desire to be a good wife and mother."
37. Sylvia Plath, *Johnny Panic and the Bible of Dreams: Short Stories, Prose, and Diary Excerpts*, ed. Ted Hughes (New York: Harper and Row, 1979), p. 8. Subsequent references to this work appear in the text with the abbreviation *Johnny Panic*.
38. Quoted in Butscher, *Method and Madness*, p. 164.
39. In a letter to me, September 18, 1981, Ed Cohen goes on to describe this second meeting with Plath.

> It's hard for me to exactly finger what was wrong this time, except to say that it was not real, at least in my perception of that word. The Abels quote in your manuscript probably covers it as well as I can. I recall a conversation we had at that time in which she described herself as a "hedonist." That might have led to quite a discussion, except for the unfortunate fact that I didn't know what the word meant and wasn't about to ask. When I looked it up later, my reaction was "no way." During this interval, the four of us went to hear jazz somewhere in Boston, and Syl and her friend were quite ecstatic about the evening. Chicago has *Jazz*, and this uncritical acceptance of this bloodless, derivative, and unimaginative performance as the real thing somehow disturbed me. This seems oh so picky in the telling of it, but it was crucial at the moment because it was the first revelation I had that Syl was quite a bit less than she had made herself out to be. (Or I had made her out to be?)
>
> There was one other crucial insight that came out of that meeting. (Insight? Conclusion-jumping is more like it, because I have no idea whether I was right or wrong.) Although there was again very little physical contact, it seemed to me that Syl was not, and probably never would be, a truly sexual being. Then, as now, that was a very important thing to me in a woman, and

that judgment, right or wrong, sealed in my own mind any fantasies I might have had about Syl and I being a pair in real life.

40. Marcia Brown, Plath's best friend at Smith, describes Norton to Butscher as "so sweet and so good, sort of sentimental, and I thought he was a drip, really, really square, very little sense of humor as I recall, sweetly bland," but also as "terribly sincere, terribly interested in other people, very, very thoughtful." As Butscher summarizes her comments, "His academic record and general air of certainty instilled in her [i.e., Plath] an 'enormous respect', and Marcia felt Sylvia remained 'in awe of him' for quite some time" (*Method and Madness*, p. 48).

41. "Her breasts, troubled, still seek forwardly / a kind release and compassion" (Box 2, MSS II; January 21, 1953). "If you looked into the lust of my (quote) soul, i would be seen to ache for a celebration by a coming to you naked and taking you quite sexually and lovingly and completely" (Box 3, MSS II; March 3, 1953).

42. See the discussion on pp. 80–81 of Plath's letter to E. after her breakdown.

43. Plath, *The Bell Jar*, p. 46.

44. Butscher, *Method and Madness*, p. 156.

45. See n. 10.

46. Quoted in Butscher, *Method and Madness*, p. 165.

47. Sylvia Plath, *Crossing the Water* (New York: Harper and Row, 1971), p. 16. Subsequent references to this work appear in the text with the abbreviation *CTW*.

48. Butscher, *Method and Madness*, p. 162.

49. Sylvia Plath, *Ariel* (New York: Harper and Row, 1961), p. 11. Subsequent references to this work appear in the text.

50. *Chapters in a Mythology: The Poetry of Sylvia Plath* (New York: Harper and Row, 1976), pp. 253–54, n. 10.

51. Ibid., p. 254, n. 10.

52. Ibid., p. 252, n. 7.

53. Ibid., p. 126.

54. Ibid., p. 127.

55. Ibid., p. 254, n. 10.

56. Quoted from an interview with Peter Orr for the BBC in M. L. Rosenthal, "Sylvia Plath and Confessional Poetry," in *The Art of Sylvia Plath*, ed. Charles Newman (Bloomington: Indiana University Press, 1970), p. 70.

57. Olwyn Hughes confirms this view of Plath's descriptions of Ted Hughes: "I think you're extremely right to stress the exaggerated nature of her descriptions of him. This seems to me to be an acute point and one that needed making. A nostalgia in her here perhaps for the popular idea of Dylan Thomas?" From a letter to me, August 7, 1981.

58. "Recollections of Sylvia Plath," in *Sylvia Plath: The Woman and the Work*, ed. Edward Butscher (New York: Dodd, Mead, and Co., 1977), pp. 54–55.

59. *The Ego and the Id* (1923), trans. Joan Riviere, ed. James Strachey (New York: W. W. Norton and Co., 1960), p. 22.

60. "Medusa's Head" (1922), in *Sexuality and the Psychology of Love*, ed. Philip Rieff (New York: Collier Books, 1963), p. 212.

61. Ibid., p.213.
62. Ibid., p. 212.
63. "When We Dead Awaken. Writing as Re Vision," *On Lies, Secrets, and Silence* (New York: W. W. Norton and Co., 1979), p. 43.
64. Ibid., p. 44.

Chapter 3

1. In his review of the novel for *The New Statesman* (65 [January 25, 1963]:128), Robert Taubman describes *The Bell Jar* as "the first feminine novel in a Salinger mood." Edward Butscher, in *Sylvia Plath: Method and Madness* (New York: Seabury Press, 1976), p. 358, reiterates this analogy. The blurb on the paperback edition of *The Bell Jar* (New York: Bantam Books, 1971) is from Robert Scholes's review in the *New York Times Book Review* and it reads:

   > *The Bell Jar* is a novel about the events of Sylvia Plath's twentieth year; about how she tried to die, and how they stuck her together with glue. It is a fine novel, as bitter and remorseless as her last poems—the kind of book Salinger's Franny might have written about herself ten years later, if she had spent those ten years in Hell.

2. From Aurelia Plath's letter to Harper and Row, published in Lois Ames's "Sylvia Plath: A Biographical Note" in the appendix to *The Bell Jar*, p. 214.
3. Letter to Warren of October 25, 1962, *Letters Home by Sylvia Plath, Correspondence 1950–1963*, ed. Aurelia Schober Plath (New York: Harper and Row, 1975), p. 476.
4. Ames, "Biographical Note," p. 213.
5. In Aurelia Plath's letter to Harper and Row (Ames, "Biographical Note" pp. 214–15), shortly before *The Bell Jar*'s publication in the United States, she claims that her daughter "was frightened, when at the time of publication the book was widely read and showed signs of becoming a success" in England. To the contrary, Plath was eager for its success and was depressed by *The Bell Jar*'s niggardly reviews. For Peter Davison's claim that she was turned down for American publication, see Butscher, *Method and Madness*, p. 310.
6. Ames, "Biographical Note," p. 215.
7. *Sylvia Plath: Her Life and Work* (New York: Harper and Row, 1973), pp. 88–89.
8. *The Bell Jar* (New York: Bantam Books, 1971), p. 2. All further references to the novel appear in the text.
9. Butscher claims to have discovered the exact time, date, and circumstances of Plath's loss of virginity. Shortly after her return to Wellesley from McLean's, she seduced Philip McCurdy, an old high school friend, two years her junior. He describes the experience to Butscher as "incestuous," since he had previously been a "younger brother" and confidant to her. Their date is described in *Method and Madness*, pp. 125–26.
10. Butscher, *Method and Madness*, p. 117.

11. Compare "Lady Lazarus," where the relationship between the woman and her Nazi oppressor is that of creator-creature: "I am your opus, / I am your valuable" (*Ariel* [New York: Harper and Row, 1961], p. 8). And in "The Applicant," the wife is a robot constructed to serve the husband: "It works, there is nothing wrong with it" (*Ariel*, pp. 4–5).

12. (1937), *The Standard Edition of the Complete Psychological Works of Sigmund Freud*, trans. and ed. James Strachey et al. (London: Hogarth Press and Institute of Psycho-Analysis, 1964), vol. 23, pp. 211–53.

13. "Feminism and Literary Study: A Reply to Annette Kolodny," *Critical Inquiry* 2 (Summer 1976):814.

14. (1917), *General Psychological Theory*, ed. Philip Rieff (New York: Collier Books, 1963), pp. 165–67.

15. In " 'Gone, Very Gone Youth': Sylvia Plath at Cambridge, 1955–57," in *Sylvia Plath: The Woman and the Work,* ed. Edward Butscher [New York: Dodd, Mead and Co., 1977], p. 66), Jane Kopp recalls a conversation with Plath showing that she was haunted by this criticism of her work.

> Sylvia went on at great length about how a professor at Smith had once charged her with being "factitious." "*Factitious, factitious,*" she said. "When he said that, I had no idea what it meant. I went home and looked it up, and I was devastated. Factitious. At first I thought it meant I was obsessed with facts." She told this story humorously, but she drew it out to a strange length. I did not really comprehend what it meant to her, but when I later heard her mention the same incident two or three other times, I realized that it went very deep.

16. "Mourning and Melancholia," p. 168.

17. Ibid., p. 169.

18. *Hudson Review* 13 (Autumn, 1960):414–15. Plath's insistence on the "poverty" of her father's grave and Esther Greenwood's rationale for her suicide—that it will save her mother and brother from financial straits—is also in accord with Freud's description of the melancholiac: "Among these . . . ills that the patient dreads or asseverates the thought of poverty alone has a favoured position" ("Mourning and Melancholia," p. 169). Also compare Plath's unwarranted financial worries during the final months of her life (chapter 2).

19. "Electra on Azalea Path," *Hudson Review* 13 (Autumn, 1960):414–15.

20. Ibid.

21. *Chapters in a Mythology: The Poetry of Sylvia Plath* (New York: Harper and Row, 1976), p. 10.

22. "Female Sexuality" (1931), in *Sexuality and the Psychology of Love*, ed. Philip Rieff (New York: Collier Books, 1963), p. 198.

23. Ibid., pp. 194 and 197.

24. Ibid., pp. 197–98.

25. *Psychoanalysis and Feminism* (New York: Pantheon Books, 1974), p. 96. This is

Mitchell's summary of a more extensive description in Freud's "Female Sexuality."

26. Sigmund Freud, "Some Psychological Consequences of the Anatomical Distinction Between the Sexes" (1925), in *Sexuality and the Psychology of Love*, ed. Philip Rieff (New York: Collier Books, 1963), pp. 188–93.

27. Nancy Chodorow, *The Reproduction of Mothering: Psychoanalysis and the Sociology of Gender* (Berkeley: University of California Press, 1978), pp. 188–99. Chodorow cites a number of studies showing that fathers "encourage feminine heterosexual behavior in their young daughters" and enjoy being seduced, flirted with by their little girls.

28. Kroll, *Chapters in a Mythology*, pp. 112–13.

29. *Ariel*, pp. 13–14.

30. Mitchell, *Psychoanalysis and Feminism*, pp. 404–5.

31. Sylvia Plath, *The Colossus* (New York: Random House, 1957), pp. 73–74.

32. *Ariel*, p. 49.

33. In Freud's discussion of the Oedipal complex in both boys and girls, it is important to note that castration anxiety and penis envy are never reified. That is, the little boy's fear of castration by the father is not the result of actual threats by the father or of seeing other little boys being victimized by the father. Castration anxiety resolves the Oedipal complex by permanently tying the knot of hatred and love, identification and separateness that the little boy feels toward the dominance of both parents as a combined presence over his life. Castration anxiety is a "masculine" solution to individual psychic development. Likewise, penis envy is not, as in its popular representations, envy of an actual penis. It is a "feminine" solution to individual psychic development and involves a different commingling of the ambivalent feelings of the child toward the parents. As Freud's case histories show, and as he frequently stated, masculinity and femininity are not biologically determined. Men may resolve their Oedipal complexes in a feminine way, women in a masculine way. Freud argued for a constitutional bisexuality.

This may seem like quibbling, but it is significant to an understanding of the way in which penis envy is portrayed in *The Bell Jar* and in Plath's poems. Part of Esther's problem is the reification of her feeling of inferiority in the biological fact that Buddy has a penis while she does not. If the analyst does so as well, then he is guilty of the same fallacy of misplaced concreteness and there is no way out of Esther's dilemma except for her to capitulate to a "feminine destiny," because she would be, in fact rather than in fantasy, inferior.

The interpretation of penis envy as an unwilling acknowledgment of a real inferiority is a common reading of Freud. As Juliet Mitchell points out, "without their context such notions certainly become either laughable or ideologically dangerous. In the briefest possible terms, we could say that psychoanalysis is about the material reality of ideas both within, and of, man's history; thus in 'penis-envy' we are talking not about an anatomical organ, but about the ideas of it that people hold and live by within the general culture, the order of human society"

(*Psychoanalysis and Feminism*, p. xvi). Likewise, Esther Greenwood does not suffer because she lacks a penis, but because she believes this lack makes her inferior, and the incident with Buddy is surrounded with cultural traumas that give material reality to the idea.

34. Freud, "Female Sexuality," pp. 201–2.
35. (New York: W. W. Norton and Co., 1976), pp. 218–19.
36. Ibid., p. 219.
37. "When We Dead Awaken: Writing as Re-Vision," *On Lies, Secrets, and Silence* (New York: W. W. Norton and Co., 1979), pp. 38–39.
38. *Of Woman Born*, p. 219n.
39. Letter of October 15, 1954, *Letters Home*, p. 146.
40. Sigmund Freud, "The Uncanny" (1919), in *On Creativity and the Unconscious*, ed. Benjamin Nelson (New York: Harper and Row, 1958), pp. 141–42.
41. Cited in Butscher, *Method and Madness*, p. 146.
42. " 'Gone, Very Gone Youth', " p. 76.
43. "Introduction," *A Closer Look at Ariel: A Memory of Sylvia Plath*, by Nancy Hunter Steiner (New York: Popular Library, 1973), pp. 26–27.
44. "When We Dead Awaken . . . , " p. 36.

Chapter 4

1. *Johnny Panic and the Bible of Dreams: Short Stories, Prose, and Diary Excerpts*, ed. Ted Hughes (New York: Harper and Row, 1979), pp. 64–65.
2. Joyce Carol Oates, "The Death Throes of Romanticism: The Poetry of Sylvia Plath," in *Sylvia Plath: The Woman and the Work*, ed. Edward Butscher (New York: Dodd, Mead and Co., 1977), p. 219.
3. Pamela Smith, "Architectonics: Sylvia Plath's Colossus," in Butscher, *The Woman and the Work*, p. 123.
4. Oates, "The Death Throes of Romanticism," p. 214.
5. Smith, "Architectonics," p. 124. Even though Smith explicitly argues against this view of Plath's development, she concludes by supporting it.
6. "On the Road to *Ariel*: The 'Transitional' Poetry of Sylvia Plath," in Butscher, *The Woman and the Work*, pp. 139, 140.
7. Oates, "The Death Throes of Romanticism," p. 218.
8. Ibid., p. 209.
9. Peter Orr, ed., *The Poet Speaks* (New York: Barnes and Noble, 1966), p. 170.
10. *The Second Sex*, trans. and ed. H. M. Parshley (New York: Vintage Books, 1952), p. 670.
11. Ibid., p. 666.
12. Ibid., p. 671. *Existent* is the term used throughout *The Second Sex* to designate a "self" capable of transcendence.
13. *Ariel* (New York: Harper and Row, 1961), p. 44. Subsequent references to this work appear in the text.

14. *The Second Sex*, p. 665.

15. Ibid., p. 688.

16. This is de Beauvoir's argument throughout *The Second Sex*

17. See Smith, "Architectonics," and also John Frederick Nims, "The Poetry of Sylvia Plath—A Technical Analysis," in *The Art of Sylvia Plath*, ed. Charles Newman (Bloomington: Indiana University Press, 1970), pp. 136–52, for a full discussion of Plath's experiments with sound.

18. *Crossing the Water*, (New York: Harper and Row, 1971), pp. 41–42. Subsequent references to this work appear in the text with the abbreviation *CTW*.

19. "Mad Girl's Love Song," *Mademoiselle* 37, no. 10 (August, 1953):358.

20. "By Candlelight," *Winter Trees* (New York: Harper and Row, 1972), p. 29. Subsequent references to this work appear in the text with the abbreviation *WT*.

21. "The Ghost's Leavetaking," *The Colossus and Other Poems* (New York: Alfred A. Knopf and Random House, 1957), p. 42. Subsequent references to this work appear in the text with the abbreviation *TC*.

22. Loren McIntyre, "Brazil's Wild Frontier," *National Geographic Magazine* 52, no. 5 (1977):692.

23. Ibid.

24. (New York: Bantam Books, 1974), p. 12.

25. *Sylvia Plath: Method and Madness* (New York: Seabury Press, 1976), p. 347.

26. *The Second Sex*, p. 667.

27. *Sylvia Plath: Her Life and Work* (New York: Harper and Row, 1973), pp. 110–11.

28. Quoted from an interview with Peter Orr for the BBC in M. L. Rosenthal, "Sylvia Plath and Confessional Poetry," in *The Art of Sylvia Plath*, ed. Newman, p. 70.

29. From the introductory notes to "New Poems," a reading prepared for the BBC Third Programme but never broadcast, and quoted by A. Alvarez, "Sylvia Plath," in *The Art of Sylvia Plath*, ed. Newman, p. 62.

30. "A Comparison (Essay, 1962)," *Johnny Panic*, ed. Hughes, pp. 62–63.

31. See my discussion of Chodorow in chapter 2.

32. *The Second Sex*, pp. 688–89.

33. *Of Woman Born: Motherhood as Experience and Institution* (New York: W. W. Norton and Co., 1976), p. 34.

34. Ibid., pp. 61–62.

35. "Some Notes on Defining a 'Feminist' Literary Criticism," *Critical Inquiry* 1 (Autumn, 1975):82.

36. "On the Road to *Ariel*," p. 128.

37. *Of Woman Born*, p. 23.

38. Ibid.

39. Rich, *Of Woman Born*, p. 67.

40. *The Mermaid and the Minotaur* (New York: Harper and Row, 1976), p. 217.

41. Ibid.

42. *Webster's Third New International Dictionary* (unabridged), ed. Philip Gove (Springfield, Mass.: G. and C. Merriam Company, 1971), p. 1207.

43. *The Mermaid and the Minotaur*, p. 208.

44. *The Second Sex*, p. 157.
45. Ibid.
46. *The Mermaid and the Minotaur*, pp. 209, 212.
47. *Of Woman Born*, p. 29.
48. Ibid., p. 31.
49. Ibid., p. 23.
50. Ibid., p. 36.
51. *Chapters in a Mythology: The Poetry of Sylvia Plath* (New York: Harper and Row, 1976), p. 132.

Chapter 5

1. "You Could Say She Had a Calling for Death," review of *The Collected Poems*, by Sylvia Plath, ed. Ted Hughes, *New York Times Book Review*, November 22, 1981, p. 30.
2. For two different versions of this view, see Arthur K. Oberg's "Sylvia Plath and the New Decadence," in *Sylvia Plath: The Woman and the Work*, ed. Edward Butscher (New York: Dodd, Mead and Co., 1977), p. 177–85; and Joyce Carol Oates's "The Death Throes of Romanticism: The Poetry of Sylvia Plath," also in Butscher, pp. 206–24.
3. Adrienne Rich, in her poem, "Phantasia for Elvira Shatayev" (*The Dream of a Common Language: Poems 1974–1977* [New York: W. W. Norton and Co., 1978], pp. 4–6), for example, adopts a very different strategy than Plath. Her heroines, Shatayev and the women's mountain climbing team she leads, confront nature in the form of a mountain and in choosing to die together in a storm, they are not defeated by the mountain, but transform nature into their female form and consciousness.

> Every cell's core of heat   pulsed out of us
> into the thin air   of the universe
> the armature of rock beneath these snows
> this mountain air   which has taken   the imprint of our minds
> through changes elemental and minute
> as those we underwent
> to bring each other here

In contrast to Plath, whose lyric energy is directed at a private aesthetic solution—at transforming her own body and creating an inviolable space around it for her creative activity—Rich speaks for women as a heroic community ("If in this sleep I speak / it's with a voice no longer personal") and for a nature, the mountain, that is transformed by her mythmaking into an eternal symbol of their shared love, consciousness, and physical effort.
4. See my discussion of this poem in chapter 1.

5. "Three Women: A Poem for Three Voices," *Winter Trees* (New York: Harper and Row, 1972), p. 55. Subsequent references to this work appear in the text with the abbreviation *WT*.

6. *Crossing the Water* (New York: Harper and Row, 1971), p. 31. Subsequent references to this work appear in the text with the abbreviation *CTW*.

7. *Ariel* (New York: Harper and Row, 1961), p. 73. Subsequent references to this work appear in the text.

8. Ted Hughes, "Notes on the Chronological Order of Sylvia Plath's Poems," in *The Art of Sylvia Plath*, ed. Charles Newman (Bloomington: Indiana University Press, 1970), p. 192.

9. *The Colossus and Other Poems* (New York: Alfred A. Knopf and Random House, 1957), p. 80. Subsequent references to this work appear in the text with the abbreviation *TC*.

10. Hughes, "Notes on the Chronological Order," p. 192.

Works Cited

Aird, Eileen. *Sylvia Plath: Her Life and Work*. New York: Harper and Row, 1973.

Alvarez, Alfred. *The Savage God: A Study of Suicide*. New York: Random House, 1970.

———. "Sylvia Plath." In *The Art of Sylvia Plath*, edited by Charles Newman, pp. 56–68. Bloomington: Indiana University Press, 1970.

Ames, Lois, "Notes Toward a Biography." In *The Art of Sylvia Plath*, edited by Charles Newman, pp. 155–73. Bloomington: Indiana University Press, 1970.

Bloom, Harold. *The Anxiety of Influence: A Theory of Poetry*. New York: Oxford University Press, 1973.

Bloomington. Lilly Library. Indiana University Libraries. Plath MSS II.

Bollas, Christopher, and Schwartz, Murray M., "The Absence at the Center: Sylvia Plath and Suicide." *Criticism* 18:147–72.

Boyers, Robert. "Sylvia Plath: The Trepanned Veteran." *Centennial Review* 13:138–53.

Brunswick, Ruth Mack. "The Preoedipal Phase of the Libido Development" (1940). In *The Psychoanalytic Reader: An Anthology of Essential Papers with Critical Introductions*, edited by Robert Fliess, pp. 231–53. New York: International Universities Press, 1969.

Butscher, Edward. *Sylvia Plath: Method and Madness*. New York: Seabury Press, 1976.

———, ed. *Sylvia Plath: The Woman and the Work*. New York: Dodd, Mead and Co., 1977.

Chodorow, Nancy. *The Reproduction of Mothering: Psychoanalysis and the Sociology of Gender*. Berkeley: University of California Press, 1978.

de Beauvoir, Simone. *The Second Sex*. Translated by H. M. Parshley. New York: Vintage Books, 1952.

Dinnerstein, Dorothy. *The Mermaid and the Minotaur*. New York: Harper and Row, 1976.

Donoghue, Denis. "You Could Say She Had a Calling for Death." Review of Sylvia Plath, *The Collected Poems*. *New York Times Book Review*, November 22, 1981, pp. 30–33.

Freud, Sigmund. "Analysis Terminal and Interminable" (1937). *The Standard Edition of the Complete Psychological Works of Freud*. Translated and edited by James Strachey et al., vol. 23, pp. 211–53. London: Hogarth Press and Institute of Psycho-Analysis, 1964.

———. *The Ego and the Id* (1923). Translated by Joan Riviere and edited by James Strachey. New York: W. W. Norton and Co., 1960.

———. *Letters of Sigmund Freud, 1873–1939*. Edited by Ernest Freud. London: Hogarth Press, 1961.

———. "Medusa's Head" (1922). In *Sexuality and the Psychology of Love*, edited by Philip Rieff, pp. 212–13. New York: Collier Books, 1963.

————. "Mourning and Melancholia" (1917). In *General Psychological Theory*, edited by Philip Rieff, pp. 164–79. New York: Macmillan Co., 1963.

————. "Some Psychological Consequences of the Anatomical Distinction Between the Sexes" (1925). In *Sexuality and the Psychology of Love*, edited by Philip Rieff, pp. 183–93. New York: Collier Books, 1963.

————. *The Standard Edition of the Complete Psychological Works of Sigmund Freud.* Edited and translated by James Strachey et al. London: Hogarth Press and Institute of Psycho-Analysis, 1964.

————. "The Uncanny" (1919). In *On Creativity and the Unconscious*, edited by Benjamin Nelson, pp. 122–61. New York: Harper and Row, 1958.

Friedan, Betty. *The Feminine Mystique.* New York: Dell Publishing Co., 1963.

Frye, Northrop. *The Anatomy of Criticism.* Princeton: Princeton University Press, 1957.

Gilbert, Sandra M. " 'A Fine White Flying Myth': The Life/Work of Sylvia Plath." In *Shakespeare's Sisters: Feminist Essays on Women Poets*, edited by Sandra M. Gilbert and Susan Gubar, pp. 245–60. Bloomington: Indiana University Press, 1979.

Gilbert, Sandra M., and Gubar, Susan. *The Madwoman in the Attic: The Woman Writer and the Nineteenth-Century Literary Imagination.* New Haven and London: Yale University Press, 1979.

Hardwick, Elizabeth. "Sylvia Plath." In *Seduction & Betrayal*, pp. 104–24. New York: Random House, 1970.

Holbrook, David. *Sylvia Plath: Poetry and Existence.* London: Athlone Press, 1976.

Howe, Irving. "The Plath Celebration: A Partial Dissent." In *Sylvia Plath: The Woman and the Work*, edited by Edward Butscher, pp. 225–35. New York: Dodd, Mead and Co., 1977.

Juhasz, Suzanne. *Naked and Fiery Forms: Modern American Poetry by Women, a New Tradition.* New York: Harper and Row, 1976.

Kinzie, Mary. "An Informal Check List of Criticism." In *The Art of Sylvia Plath*, edited by Charles Newman, pp. 283–304. Bloomington: Indiana University Press, 1970.

Kolodny, Annette. "Some Notes on Defining a 'Feminist' Literary Criticism." *Critical Inquiry* 2:75–92.

Kopp, Jane. " 'Gone, Very Gone Youth': Sylvia Plath at Cambridge, 1955–57." In *Sylvia Plath: The Woman and the Work*, edited by Edward Butscher, pp. 61–80. New York: Dodd, Mead and Co., 1977.

Kroll, Judith. *Chapters in a Mythology: The Poetry of Sylvia Plath.* New York: Harper and Row, 1976.

Krook, Dorothea. "Recollections of Sylvia Plath." In *Sylvia Plath: The Woman and the Work*, edited by Edward Butscher, pp. 49–60. New York: Dodd, Mead and Co., 1977.

Lowell, Robert. Foreward to *Ariel*. New York: Harper and Row, 1961.

McIntyre, Loren. "Brazil's Wild Frontier." *National Geographic Magazine* 52:690–98.

Mitchell, Juliet. *Psychoanalysis and Feminism.* New York: Pantheon Books, 1974.

Morgan, William W. "Feminism and Literary Study: A Reply to Annette Kolodny." *Critical Inquiry* 2:807–16.

Newman, Charles, ed. *The Art of Sylvia Plath*. Bloomington: Indiana University Press, 1970.

——. " 'Candor Is the Only Wile.' " In *The Art of Sylvia Plath*, edited by Charles Newman, pp. 21–68. Bloomington: Indiana University Press, 1970.

Nims, John Frederick. "The Poetry of Sylvia Plath—A Technical Analysis." In *The Art of Sylvia Plath*, edited by Charles Newman, pp. 136–52. Bloomington: Indiana University Press, 1970.

Oates, Joyce Carol. "The Death Throes of Romanticism: The Poetry of Sylvia Plath." In *Sylvia Plath: The Woman and the Work*, edited by Edward Butscher, pp. 206–24. New York: Dodd, Mead and Co., 1977.

Oberg, Arthur K. "Sylvia Plath and the New Decadence." In *Sylvia Plath: The Woman and the Work*, edited by Edward Butscher, pp. 177–85. New York: Dodd, Mead and Co., 1977.

Olsen, Tillie. *Silences*. New York: Delacorte Press, 1978.

Orr, Peter, ed. *The Poet Speaks*. New York: Barnes and Noble, 1966.

Perloff, Marjorie. "On the Road to *Ariel*: The 'Transitional' Poetry of Sylvia Plath." In *Sylvia Plath: The Woman and the Work*, edited by Edward Butscher, pp. 125–42. New York: Dodd, Mead and Co., 1977.

Plath, Sylvia. *Ariel*. New York: Harper and Row, 1961.

——. *The Bell Jar*. New York: Harper and Row, 1971.

——. *The Colossus and Other Poems*. New York: Alfred A. Knopf and Random House, 1957.

——. *Crossing the Water*. New York: Harper and Row, 1971.

——. "Electra on Azalea Path." *Hudson Review* 13:414–15.

——. Interview with Peter Orr, October 30, 1962, on *Plath Reads Plath*. Credo 3 (1975).

——. *Johnny Panic and the Bible of Dreams: Short Stories, Prose, and Diary Excerpts*. Edited by Ted Hughes. New York: Harper and Row, 1979.

——. *Letters Home by Sylvia Plath, Correspondence 1950–1963*. Selected and edited with commentary by Aurelia Schober Plath. New York: Harper and Row, 1975.

——. "Mad Girl's Love Song." *Mademoiselle* 37, no. 10:358.

——. Plath MSS II. Bloomington: Lilly Library. Indiana University Libraries.

——. *Winter Trees*. New York: Harper and Row, 1972.

Rich, Adrienne. *Of Woman Born: Motherhood as Experience and Institution*. New York: W. W. Norton and Co., 1976.

——. "Phantasia for Elvira Shatayev." In *The Dream of a Common Language: Poems 1974–1977*, pp. 4–6. New York: W. W. Norton and Co., 1978.

——. "When We Dead Awaken: Writing as Re-Vision." In *On Lies, Secrets, and Silence*, pp. 33–49. New York: W. W. Norton and Co., 1979.

Rosenstein, Harriet. " 'To the Most Wonderful Mummy . . . a Girl Ever Had.' " Review of *Letters Home*. MS. 4, no. 12:45–49.

Rosenthal, M. L. "Sylvia Plath and Confessional Poetry." In *The Art of Sylvia Plath*, edited by Charles Newman, pp. 69–76. Bloomington: Indiana University Press, 1970.

Smith, Pamela. "Architectonics: Sylvia Plath's Colossus." In *Sylvia Plath: The Woman and the Work,* edited by Edward Butscher, pp. 111–24. New York: Dodd, Mead and Co., 1977.

Stade, George. Introduction to *A Closer Look at Ariel: A Memory of Sylvia Plath,* by Nancy Hunter Steiner. New York: Popular Library, 1973.

Steiner, Nancy Hunter. *A Closer Look at Ariel: A Memory of Sylvia Plath.* New York: Popular Library, 1973.

Taubman, Robert. Review of *The Bell Jar. The New Statesman* 65 (January 25, 1963):128–29.

Thomas, Lewis. *The Lives of a Cell.* New York: Bantam Books, 1974.

Wilbur, Richard. "Cottage Street, 1953." In *The Mind-Reader,* p. 19. New York: Harcourt Brace Jovanovich, 1965.

Index